# Bite me

Copyright © 2009
by Pinky Swear Press Inc.

Published in 2011 by Kyle Cathie Limited,
23 Howland Street, London W1T 4AY
general.enquiries@kyle-cathie.com
www.kylecathie.com

ISBN 978-1-85626-976-6

First published in Canada in 2009 by Pinky Swear Press Inc.

10 9 8 7 6 5 4 3 2 1

A CIP catalogue record for this title is available from
the British Library.

www.pinkyswearpress.com
www.bitemecookbook.com

Printed and bound in China by C&C Offset Printing Co., Ltd.

FSC
www.fsc.org
MIX
Paper from
responsible sources
FSC® C008047

# Bite me

By the not-so-sweet, tiny-bit-salty sisters
**Julie Albert & Lisa Gnat**

Published by
**Kyle Cathie Ltd**

# Inscribe me

### To Lisa

Your food's mother-forkin' great.
Love you like a sister.

### To Julie

Nice going, Drama Queen.
Love you more than chocolate.

**'After all the trouble you go to, you get about as much actual "food" out of eating an artichoke as you would from licking 30 or 40 postage stamps.'** – Miss Piggy, entertainer

There's not a single thorny artichoke, scrawny quail or roasted chestnut to be peeled in this book. What you will find in **BITE ME** are 175 dependably delicious recipes created for the urban and suburban, the aspiring and well-seasoned home cook. You won't need an army of sous chefs, a pantry of guava paste or a blowtorch in order to turn a bag of groceries into a satisfying meal. We're all about making you confident in the kitchen and relaxed at the table.

**'Anyone who eats three meals a day should understand why cookbooks outsell sex books three-to-one.'** – LM Boyd, journalist

We love poring over cookbooks, admiring the sublime combinations of celebrity chef Jean-Georges Vongerichten and the unmatched techniques of French chef Daniel Boulud. However, these haute tomes don't offer swift responses to the big question, 'What's for dinner?' With the help of **BITE ME** you can stop gnawing your nails, forget all about mushroom foam and smile when someone asks you, 'What's cooking, good looking?' Let **BITE ME**, a thoroughly tested cookbook, make filling yours and others' plates a piece of cake.

**'Take me! I am the hallucinogenic!'**

– Salvador Dali, artist

**BITE ME** speaks to more than your stomach. For us, the creation of food is intimately tied to the world outside the kitchen – family, art, music, movies and pop culture are constant sources of laughter and inspiration. What's a day without a grandmother-related guffaw or a cooking session without tunes blasting? Boring. And where else can you flip to a famous photo while cleaning a chicken breast? Yes, we hope that **BITE ME** will be your multi-sensory smorgasbord, a feast for your eyes, ears, mouth and nose.

# Julie
## Albert

I ADORE _SUSHI CONVEYOR BELTS_

PET PEEVES _TIGHTS, AIR QUOTES_

GUILTY PLEASURE _SIZE 8½ HEELS_

MUCH-LOVED MEAL _LOMBARDI'S PIZZA, NYC_

BEST FAUX PAS _'WHEN'S THE BABY DUE?'_

FAVOURITE PAGE in 'BITE ME' _111_

_IRVING PENN_ LEAVES ME SPEECHLESS

CHOICE CANDY _LIQUORICE ALLSORTS_

SUPERPOWER WISH _To HAVE BARBARELLA HAIR_

MY FREEBIE _DENIS LEARY_

BEST QUOTE _'NOBODY PUTS BABY IN THE CORNER'_

AWARDS _1st PLACE, GRADE 7 HURDLE RELAY_

SISTER'S BEST SECRET _LISA CAN'T RIDE A BIKE_

CURRENTLY WORKING ON _GROWING UP_

# Lisa
## Gnat

I ADORE _MY MAC CHEF KNIFE_

PET PEEVES _WHISTLING, SNUFFLING_

GUILTY PLEASURE _CHOCOLATE BEFORE 9 AM_

MUCH-LOVED MEAL _FRENCH TOAST DRENCHED IN MAPLE SYRUP_

BEST FAUX PAS _CAUGHT SINGING IN MY CAR_

FAVOURITE PAGE in 'BITE ME' _245_

_ALICE WATERS_ LEAVES ME SPEECHLESS

CHOICE CANDY _3 MUSKETEERS_

SUPERPOWER WISH _TO BE INVISIBLE_

MY FREEBIE _GORDON RAMSAY_

BEST QUOTE _'C IS FOR COOKIE THAT'S GOOD ENOUGH FOR ME'_

AWARDS _BAKERY PRODUCTION CLUB AWARD_

SISTER'S BEST SECRET _JULIE CAN'T WINK_

CURRENTLY WORKING ON _FUDGY MARSHMALLOW CAKE_

TGTBT Salad Rolls **14**
Wild Mushroom Crostini with Mint and Parmesan **15**
Slacker's Stacked Sushi **16**
Mona Lisa's Fontina and Rocket Pizza **18**
Sky-High Potato Skins **20**
Crab Cakes with Creamy Mustard Sauce **21**

# Grab me

## Little Nibbles

Creamy White Bean Spread with Asiago Crackers **22**
Tuna Skewers with Wasabi Dip **24**
Beef Satay with Peanut Sauce **25**
Honey-Baked Coconut Prawns **27**
Piled-High Chicken Tostada Cups **28**
Sweet and Sour Candied Salami **30**
DYN-O-MITE! Asian Meatballs **31**

# TGTBT SALAD ROLLS
## Too Good To Be True Salad Rolls

## INGREDIENTS

### Salad Rolls

175g dried rice noodles

10 round rice paper sheets

10 green curly lettuce leaves

1 carrot, peeled and shredded

2 ripe mangos, stoned, peeled and julienned

1 cucumber, peeled, deseeded and julienned

3 tablespoons plus 1 teaspoon chopped basil

### Thai Dipping Sauce

4 tablespoons soy sauce

3 tablespoons mirin

2 tablespoons rice wine vinegar

1 tablespoon sugar

1 teaspoon sesame oil

1 teaspoon grated fresh ginger

⅛ teaspoon Thai hot chilli sauce

**Julie: RU there?**
Are you there?

**Lisa: S^?**
What's up?

**Julie: UCWAP. Din PT. Need GR8 AP PDQ.**
Up the creek without a paddle.
Dinner party. Need great appetiser pretty darn quick.

**Lisa: RPW. Duh. F&E2RL. TM. PFM.**
Rice paper wrap. Duh. Fast and easy to roll. Trust me.
Pure freakin' magic.

**Julie: N1. ^5. G2GLYS.**
Nice one. High five. Got to go, love you so.

**Lisa: LYLAS. OO.**
Love you like a sister. Over and out.

## METHOD

**1)** For the salad rolls, bring a medium saucepan of water to the boil. Add the rice noodles and cook according to the packet instructions. When tender, drain, rinse with cold water and drain well again. Divide into 10 equal portions and set aside. **2)** Place one rice paper sheet in a shallow bowl of hot water for about 1 minute until just softened. Lay the rice paper sheet on a clean tea towel. Place a lettuce leaf down the centre of the rice sheet, leaving a 2.5cm border at the top and bottom. Place one portion of the rice noodles lengthways on the lettuce leaf followed by 1 tablespoon of shredded carrot, 6 slices of mango, 4 slices of cucumber and 1 teaspoon of chopped basil. Fold up the bottom 2.5cm border of rice paper, placing it over the filling. Fold in the right side, followed by the left side and then the top, forming a tight cylinder. Repeat with the remaining rice paper sheets and filling. **3)** For the dipping sauce, whisk all the sauce ingredients together in a medium bowl. **4)** Serve the salad rolls with the dipping sauce.

Makes: 10 large salad rolls

# WILD MUSHROOM CROSTINI with MINT and PARMESAN

## INGREDIENTS

### Crostini

32 diagonal slices of baguette or Italian bread, cut into 5mm-thick slices

4 tablespoons olive oil

½ teaspoon sea salt

### Mushroom Topping

2 tablespoons olive oil

2 tablespoons finely chopped shallots

2 garlic cloves, finely chopped

330g mushrooms, sliced (a mix of shiitake, chanterelle and button)

60ml dry white wine

30g Parmesan cheese, freshly grated

1 tablespoon chopped mint

½ teaspoon sea salt

¼ teaspoon freshly ground black pepper

32 fresh Parmesan curls, made with a vegetable peeler

It's time to put an end to the rumours. Jerry Garcia was NOT spotted eating oatmeal in my kitchen and do not call me at 2am asking me to 'hook you up'. Yes, I admit, there is magic in these mushrooms, but, c'mon neighbourhood Narc, it's nothing illegal. Just a little garlic and white wine. So, to those of you who love these addictive bites, stop complimenting me on my 'shroom-fests' in public... you're ruining my reputation.

## METHOD

1) Preheat the oven to 200°C/400°F/Gas Mark 6. Place the bread slices on a non-stick baking sheet. Brush the bread on both sides with the oil and sprinkle the salt evenly over the top. Bake for 4 minutes, flip the slices over and continue to bake for a further 3 minutes. Remove from the oven and set aside. 2) For the mushroom topping, in a large frying pan, heat the oil over a medium heat. Add the shallots and garlic and sauté for 1 minute. Stir in the mushrooms and sauté for 5–6 minutes until they soften and begin to brown. 3) Turn the heat to high, add the wine and cook, stirring, for 3–4 minutes until the liquid evaporates. Remove from the heat and stir in the grated Parmesan, mint, salt and pepper. 4) To assemble, top each toast with 1 tablespoon mushroom topping and a Parmesan curl. Serve immediately.

Makes: 32 crostini

## BITE ME BIT

'The Smurfs are little blue people who live in magic mushrooms. Think about it.'

– Author unknown, or was it that dude with the little baggy...forget it.

# SLACKER'S STACKED SUSHI

## INGREDIENTS

### Rice

210g short-grain sushi rice

300ml water

2 tablespoons rice vinegar

### Egg

4 large eggs

2 tablespoons chicken stock

1 tablespoon sugar

1 tablespoon soy sauce

2 teaspoons mirin

2 teaspoons vegetable oil

### Mayonnaise Filling

115g mayonnaise

1 tablespoon wasabi powder

4 sheets nori
(roasted seaweed)

3 teaspoon black sesame seeds

1 large avocado, peeled,
stoned and thinly sliced

½ large cucumber, peeled,
cut into half lengthways,
centre scooped out and
flesh thinly sliced

Whoa, man. You know the Japanese epidemic, 'death by overworking'? I don't want any 'karoshi' on my conscience. Training to be a sushi chef STARTS with 3 years of meditation and rice washing, duuude. So forget it. Take a swig of warm sake and feast on this, our chillax-style sushi – you're going to dig these layers of seasoned rice, sweet egg, creamy avocado and crispy cucumbers.

## METHOD

1) For the rice, place the rice in a colander and rinse thoroughly under cold water until the water runs clear. Drain, then transfer to a 2-litre saucepan with the water. Heat on high until boiling. Reduce the heat to low, stir, cover tightly and simmer gently for 20 minutes without lifting the lid. Remove the pan from the heat and leave to stand for 10 minutes. Place the rice in a medium-sized bowl and gently stir in the rice vinegar. 2) While the rice cooks, in a medium bowl, whisk the eggs, stock, sugar, soy sauce and mirin together. Heat a 25cm frying pan over a low heat, add the oil and, using kitchen paper, spread to cover the side and base. Pour the egg mixture into the pan and cover tightly. Cook for 4–5 minutes until the omelette is somewhat set. Remove the lid and, using a large spatula, flip the omelette and continue to cook for a further 2–3 minutes. Remove from the heat and set aside. 3) For the mayonnaise filling, in a small bowl, whisk the mayonnaise and wasabi powder together. Set aside. 4) Line a 20cm square baking tin with clingfilm, leaving a 15cm overhang on the opposite

**Wasabi Mayonnaise Sauce**

2 tablespoons wasabi powder

2 tablespoons water

175g mayonnaise

2 tablespoons soy sauce

1 tablespoon rice vinegar

sides. Place one nori sheet in the base of the pan. Top with 115g of the cooked rice, spreading evenly. Sprinkle with 1 teaspoon black sesame seeds. Top with 4 tablespoons of the mayonnaise mixture, followed by a single layer of sliced cucumber. Top with another sheet of nori. Spread another 115g cooked rice over the nori sheet. Sprinkle with 1 teaspoon black sesame seeds followed by the remaining 4 tablespoons of the mayonnaise mixture. Lay a single layer of avocado on top and place the cooked egg omelette on top of the avocado. Cover with another nori sheet. Spread the remaining rice evenly over the top and sprinkle with the remaining 1 teaspoon black sesame seeds. Top with the final nori sheet. Cover with clingfilm, weigh down with a few small books and refrigerate for 1 hour. Use the clingfilm overhang to remove the sushi from the baking tin. Trim the edges and cut into 6 generous portions. **5)** For the wasabi mayonnaise sauce, in a small bowl, whisk the wasabi powder and water together to form a smooth paste. Add the mayonnaise, soy sauce and rice vinegar. Whisk to combine and refrigerate, covered, until ready to use. Serve with the sushi.

Serves 6

## BITE ME BIT

'Who's ever written a great work about the immense effort required in order not to create?'

– The Dostoyevsky Wannabe (actor Brecht Andersch) in the 1991 movie **Slacker**

# MONA LISA'S FONTINA and ROCKET PIZZA

## INGREDIENTS

### Dough

225ml warm water
(40.5/105°F–46°C/115°F)

2¼ teaspoons dried active yeast

375g plain flour,
plus extra for dusting

1 tablespoon runny honey

2 teaspoons sea salt

2 tablespoons olive oil,
plus extra for oiling

polenta, for dusting

### Pizza Topping

2 tablespoons olive oil

½ teaspoon sea salt

115g Fontina cheese,
coarsely grated

115g mozzarella cheese,
coarsely grated

1 teaspoon chopped thyme

Why the big fuss over Da Vinci's painting? I mean, my sister is THE Mona Lisa – she's got the brown eyes that follow me everywhere, the corners of her mouth in a slight upturn and a constant air of mystery. But she melts down like the Dali clock when I ask her how much longer until her master-piece – this crispy thin-crust pizza topped with nutty-tasting Fontina and rocket – comes out of the oven.

## METHOD

1) For the dough, brush a large bowl with 1 teaspoon olive oil. Set aside. 2) Pour the warm water into a small bowl. Sprinkle over the yeast and set aside for 5–10 minutes until it dissolves and becomes foamy. 3) Meanwhile, place the flour, honey and salt in a food processor fitted with the steel blade and process to mix. With the machine running, add the yeast mixture and the oil in a steady stream. Process for about 10 seconds until a sticky ball forms. Transfer to a lightly floured surface and knead for about 2 minutes until smooth and elastic. Add more flour if the dough is too sticky, 1 tablespoon at a time. Place the dough in the oiled bowl, cover with clingfilm and leave to rise in a warm place for about 1 hour until almost double in size. 4) Preheat the oven to 240°C/475°F/ Gas Mark 9. Dust 2 pizza tins or baking sheets with polenta. 5) Punch down the dough and divide into 2 equal pieces. On a lightly floured surface, roll out one piece at a time, starting in the centre of the dough and rolling outwards, to form a 30cm round. Transfer to one pizza tin or baking sheet. Repeat with the other half of the pizza dough. 6) Brush 1 tablespoon olive oil on each pizza base and sprinkle each with ¼ teaspoon salt. Divide the cheeses and

## Rocket Topping

200g baby rocket

4 tablespoons olive oil

2 tablespoons freshly squeezed lemon juice

½ teaspoon sea salt

½ teaspoon freshly ground black pepper

thyme between each pizza. **7)** Bake for 10–12 minutes until the edges are golden. Leave to stand for 5 minutes before slicing. Slice each pizza into 8 pieces. **8)** For the rocket topping, in a medium bowl, toss the baby rocket with the olive oil, lemon juice, salt and pepper. Divide between the pizzas, topping each slice with a generous handful. Serve immediately.

Makes: 16 slices

# SKY-HIGH POTATO SKINS

## INGREDIENTS

4 baking potatoes, such as Maris Piper, King Edward or Marfona

2 tablespoons olive oil

55g butter, melted

½ teaspoon sea salt

¼ teaspoon freshly ground black pepper

6 turkey rashers or streaky bacon rashers, cooked until crisp and crumbled

115g Cheddar cheese, coarsely grated

115g Monterey Jack or Gruyère cheese, coarsely grated

125ml soured cream, to serve

I don't bother calling Lisa's house on Sunday. No one ever answers. Her husband is probably preoccupied painting his face Dolphins' orange and teal. Her kids are scurrying to get the TV room ready for hours of hibachi-free tailgating. As for my sister, she has the privilege of preparing the ultimate football fare – crispy potato skins. The perennial champs of couch-potato cuisine, these addictive skins are mounded high with crunchy turkey bacon and gooey melted cheese.

## METHOD

1) Preheat the oven to 220°C/425°F/Gas Mark 7. Line a baking sheet with foil. Scrub the potatoes, pat dry and pierce with a fork several times. Rub each potato with ½ tablespoons oil and place on the prepared baking sheet. Bake for 50–60 minutes or until tender. Remove the potatoes from the oven and leave to cool just enough to handle comfortably. 2) Turn the oven up to 230°C/450°F/Gas Mark 8. 3) Cut each potato in half lengthways and scoop out the cooked potato, leaving a 1cm-thick layer of potato around the sides and bases of the skins. Discard the scooped-out potato or use for mash. 4) Brush the hollowed potato skins (inside and outside) with the melted butter and sprinkle with the salt and pepper. Place the potatoes skin-side up on a baking sheet and return to the oven for 10 minutes. Flip the skins and bake for another 8 minutes. 5) Remove from the oven and sprinkle the skins with the crumbled turkey or bacon rashes and grated cheeses. Return to the oven and bake for 2 minutes or until the cheese is melted. Serve warm, topped with the soured cream.

Makes: 8 potato skins

# CRAB CAKES with CREAMY MUSTARD SAUCE

## INGREDIENTS

### Crab Cakes

non-stick cooking spray

1 large egg, lightly beaten

4–5 slices crustless bread, processed in a food processor until coarse crumbs)

55g mayonnaise

1 tablespoon Dijon mustard

1 teaspoon freshly squeezed lemon juice

1 teaspoon Worcestershire sauce

1 teaspoon chopped thyme

½ teaspoon sea salt

¼ teaspoon freshly ground black pepper

⅛ teaspoon cayenne pepper

450g cooked white crabmeat, flaked

40g polenta

2 tablespoons olive oil

### Creamy Mustard Sauce

2 teaspoons vegetable oil

1 small shallot, finely diced

60ml dry white wine

115g mayonnaise

125ml soured cream

1 tablespoon Dijon mustard

1 tablespoon wholegrain mustard

1 tablespoon runny honey

¼ teaspoon sea salt

Maryland gave us Babe Ruth, Frank Zappa and the golden glory of crab cakes. It might be difficult to compete with the masters of the Chesapeake – Faidleys, G&M, Angelina's, Timbuktu – but our delectable version strikes the perfect balance between seasoning and the stuffing that keeps this sweet delicacy from falling apart while still showcasing the luscious lump meat.

## METHOD

**1)** For the crab cakes, preheat the oven to 190°C/375°F/Gas Mark 5. Line a baking sheet with foil and coat with non-stick cooking spray. **2)** In a medium bowl, combine the egg, breadcrumbs, mayonnaise, mustard, lemon juice, Worcestershire sauce, thyme, salt, pepper and cayenne. Stir to combine the ingredients. Add the crabmeat and mix well. **3)** Using moistened hands, shape the crab mixture into 12 patties 1cm thick. Place the polenta in a shallow dish. Dip the patties in the polenta, turning to coat both sides. Place on the prepared baking sheet and bake for 10 minutes, then flip and bake for another 10 minutes until slightly golden. **4)** Remove from the oven. In a large frying pan, heat the olive oil over a high heat. Add the crab cakes and cook for 1 minute on each side to get a golden crust. Remove and serve with the creamy mustard sauce. **5)** For the creamy mustard sauce, in a small saucepan, heat the vegetable oil over a medium heat. Add the shallots and sauté for about 2 minutes until softened. Add the wine and simmer for about 3 minutes until it is almost evaporated. Set aside to cool. **6)** In a blender, combine the mayonnaise, soured cream, the mustards, honey and salt. Add the shallots and blend until smooth. Serve with the crab cakes.

Makes: 12 starter crab cakes and 280g mustard sauce

# CREAMY WHITE BEAN SPREAD with ASIAGO CRACKERS

## INGREDIENTS

### Asiago Crackers

210g plain flour,
plus extra for dusting

½ teaspoon sea salt

115g cold butter, cut into pieces

225g Asiago cheese, finely grated

125ml soured cream

### White Bean Spread

4 tablespoons olive oil

2 large garlic cloves,
finely chopped

400g canned cannellini beans,
rinsed well and drained

1 tablespoon freshly squeezed
lemon juice

1 tablespoon water

1 teaspoon chopped thyme

½ teaspoon sea salt

¼ teaspoon freshly ground
black pepper

⅛ teaspoon cayenne pepper

Some might have looked upon Jack as a most unsavvy businessman – trading a cow for 5 magic beans? Heck, even his mother sent him to bed with no supper. But I applaud him for his astute vision. I, too, think there's nothing better than miraculous white beans, especially when mashed with garlic and piled atop savoury cheese crackers. Fee-fi-fo-fum, I smell a scrumptious swap to come... my brother for 3 beans?

## METHOD

### ASIAGO CRACKERS

1) In a large bowl, combine the flour and salt. Add the butter and rub in with your fingertips, or pulse in a food processor, until you have coarse crumbs. Toss in the Asiago cheese. Add the soured cream and stir until the dough comes together. Turn onto a lightly floured surface, divide the dough into 2 and roll each half into a 4cm-diameter log. Wrap each log in clingfilm and refrigerate for at least 2 hours before slicing. 2) Preheat the oven to 160°C/325°F/Gas Mark 3. Cover a baking sheet with baking paper. 3) Slice the logs into 3mm-thick slices and place on the prepared baking sheet, leaving some space between each. Bake for 10 minutes, flip the crackers over and bake for another 10 minutes until golden. Remove from oven and leave to cool completely on a wire rack. The crackers can be prepared ahead of time, cooled and stored in an airtight container.

Makes: 50 crackers

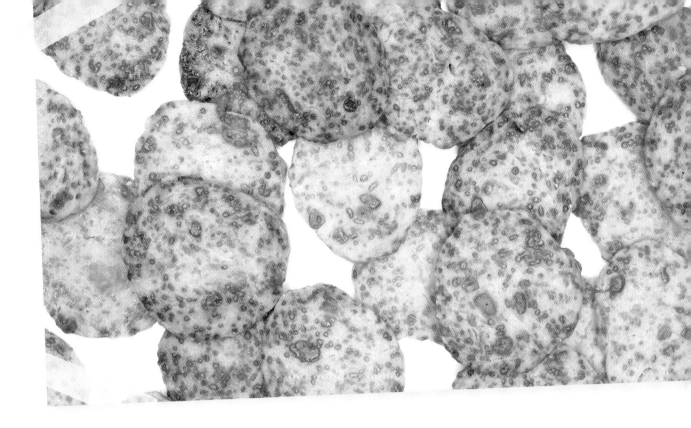

## WHITE BEAN SPREAD

**1)** In a small frying pan, heat the oil over a medium heat. Add the garlic and turn the heat off immediately. Leave the garlic to sit in the oil for 30 seconds and then strain out the garlic pieces, reserving the flavoured oil. Set aside to cool slightly and discard the garlic from the sieve. **2)** In a food processor, combine the beans, reserved garlic-flavoured oil, lemon juice, water, thyme, salt, pepper and cayenne. Process for about 20 seconds until smooth. The dip may be refrigerated, covered, a few hours ahead of serving. Bring to room temperature before serving.

Makes: about 400g

### BITE ME BIT

'He's so cheesy, I can't watch him without crackers.'

– Lelaina Pierce (actress Winona Ryder) in the 1994 movie **Reality Bites**

# TUNA SKEWERS with WASABI DIP

## INGREDIENTS

675g fresh tuna,
cut into 2.5cm cubes

4 tablespoons soy sauce

1 teaspoon freshly ground
black pepper

1½ tablespoons vegetable oil

30 cocktail sticks

30 slices pickled ginger

### Wasabi Dip

3 tablespoons water

2 tablespoons wasabi powder

175g mayonnaise

Canned tuna has its charms. Given the right mood we can even go for some Hot Tuna, especially their 1972 album 'Burgers'. But nothing tinned can top this recipe for fresh tuna, a tasty and exotic way to gussy up this deliciously mild, firm fish. Soak it in savoury soy sauce, sear it to perfection, add a sliver of spicy ginger and dunk it in the piquant mayonnaise and, ta-dah, your guests will think, however mistakenly, that you're the classiest.

## METHOD

1) In a medium bowl, combine the tuna and soy sauce. Cover and marinate for 1 hour at room temperature. 2) For the dip, in a small bowl, combine the water and wasabi powder. Stir to dissolve the powder and add the mayonnaise. Cover and refrigerate until ready to serve. 3) Once finished marinating, drain the tuna and pat dry with kitchen paper. Return to the bowl and toss the tuna with the pepper. 4) In a large frying pan, heat the oil over a medium-high heat. Add the tuna and cook, stirring constantly, for 3–5 minutes until browned on the outside but still pink inside. Remove from the heat. 5) Skewer one piece of tuna and one slice of ginger on each cocktail stick. Serve with the wasabi dip.

Serves 6–8

# BEEF SATAY with PEANUT SAUCE

## INGREDIENTS

550g fillet of beef, cut into 5cm strips

4 tablespoons soy sauce

2 tablespoons soft light brown sugar

1 tablespoon freshly squeezed lime juice

1 small garlic clove, finely chopped

2.5cm piece lemongrass, finely chopped

1 teaspoon ground cumin

¼ teaspoon ground ginger

½ teaspoon sea salt

¼ teaspoon freshly ground black pepper

wooden skewers, soaked in warm water for 20–30 minutes before threading on the meat

### Peanut Dipping Sauce

300ml chicken stock

250g smooth peanut butter

2 tablespoons soft light brown sugar

2 tablespoons freshly squeezed lime juice

2 tablespoons soy sauce

½ teaspoon grated fresh ginger

Whether you're eating yakitori in Japan, shish kebab in Turkey or chuanr in China, there is a universal caveman-thrill from eating meat off a stick. Looking for inspiration we bypassed the North American corn dog and travelled East – aromatic lemongrass and smooth peanut sauce lend our easy beef satay full-bodied flavour.

## METHOD

1) Place the beef strips in a large resealable bag. In a small bowl, stir the soy sauce, sugar, lime juice, garlic, lemongrass, cumin, ginger, salt and pepper together. Pour the marinade over the beef and toss to coat. Seal the bag and refrigerate for 1–2 hours. 2) Preheat a gas barbecue or grill to medium-high. 3) Remove the meat from the refrigerator. Thread the meat onto the presoaked skewers and discard the marinade. 4) Cook for 2–3 minutes per side or until browned and cooked to the desired doneness. 5) For the peanut sauce, in a medium saucepan, whisk the stock, peanut butter, sugar, lime juice, soy sauce and ginger together over a medium-high heat. Cook, whisking, for about 6 minutes until smooth and thickened. Serve with the cooked beef skewers. Leftovers of the sauce can be stored in the refrigerator for up to 1 week.

Serves 8–10

# HONEY-BAKED COCONUT PRAWNS

## INGREDIENTS

### Coconut Prawns

non-stick cooking spray

170g runny honey

90g panko (Japanese) breadcrumbs

90g sweetened flaked coconut or desiccated coconut

½ teaspoon ground cumin

½ teaspoon sea salt

¼ teaspoon freshly ground black pepper

26 large raw prawns, peeled and deveined

### Apricot Dipping Sauce

225g apricot jam

3 tablespoons mild chilli sauce or barbecue sauce

2 teaspoons Dijon mustard

Back in the day, we didn't go to bars for the Tequila shooters or the boys. We went to get our greasy food fix. Despite not doing barstool banquets these days, we still long for the tantalising tastes – we've brought the feast home, but we've left behind the oily glory of the deep fryer and created juicy, coconut-coated, golden-baked prawns dipped in a sweet apricot sauce.

## METHOD

1) Preheat the oven to 220°C/425°F/Gas Mark 7. Line a large baking sheet with foil and coat with non-stick cooking spray. 2) For the prawns, pour the honey into a medium bowl and warm on high in the microwave for 20–25 seconds. 3) On a large plate, combine the panko breadcrumbs, coconut, cumin, salt and pepper. 4) Taking one prawn at a time, dip in the honey and then coat in the coconut mixture. Place on the prepared baking sheet and bake for 14 minutes, gently flipping the prawns halfway through baking. 5) For the sauce, place the jam in a medium microwave-safe bowl. Warm in the microwave for 45 seconds. Add the chilli sauce and mustard and stir to combine. Serve with the coconut prawns.

Serves 4–6

## BITE ME BIT

Save a tree, send a coconut. Affixed with mailing label and correct postage, the US Postal Service will deliver coconut mail.

# PILED-HIGH CHICKEN TOSTADA CUPS

## INGREDIENTS

### Tortilla Cups

non-stick cooking spray

four 20cm tortilla wrappers

2 tablespoons olive oil

1 teaspoon sea salt

### Chicken

4 boneless, skinless chicken breasts

1 small white onion, quartered

2 large garlic cloves, crushed

3 tablespoons coarsely chopped flat-leaf parsley

3 mint leaves

1 dried bay leaf

1 teaspoon sea salt

1.9 litres water

### Bean Mixture

1 tablespoon vegetable oil

500g canned black beans, rinsed and drained

1 teaspoon ground cumin

240g tomato ketchup

2 tablespoons runny honey

2 tablespoons orange juice

2 tablespoons soy sauce

2 tablespoons sherry vinegar

1 tablespoon chipotle chillies in adobo sauce, chopped

Traditionally, tostadas are flat, deep-fried tortillas topped with refried beans, cheese and other accompaniments. Tasty, but try balancing a greasy 'open face' taco in one hand while not spilling your drink from the other...awkward. We won't let your fiesta flop – these tortilla cups mounded with Mexican-spiced chicken and creamy guacamole guarantee the only thing to hit the deck will be your Corona-crocked amigos.

## METHOD

**1)** Preheat the oven to 200°C/400°F/Gas Mark 6. Coat a standard-sized muffin tin with non-stick cooking spray. **2)** Brush both sides of the tortillas with the olive oil and sprinkle with the salt. Cut each tortilla into 8 wedges. Working in batches, mould each tortilla triangle to fit the muffin cups and bake for 7–8 minutes until crisp and golden. Remove from the muffin tin and set aside. **3)** For the chicken, in a large saucepan, combine the chicken breasts, onion, garlic, parsley, mint, bay leaf and salt. Add the water and bring to the boil over a high heat. Reduce the heat and simmer, covered, for 10 minutes. Turn the heat off and leave to stand, covered, for a further 10 minutes. Remove the chicken from stock, leave to cool slightly and then shred the chicken. **4)** For the bean mixture, in a medium saucepan, heat the oil over a high heat. Add the beans and cumin and cook, stirring, for 1 minute. Add the ketchup, honey, orange juice, soy sauce, vinegar and chillies.

### Guacamole

2 large ripe avocados,
stoned and peeled

2 large plum tomatoes,
deseeded and diced

1 tablespoon freshly
squeezed lime juice

1 tablespoon freshly
squeezed lemon juice

½ teaspoon ground cumin

½ teaspoon sea salt

⅛ teaspoon cayenne pepper

Lower the heat to medium and cook for a further 5 minutes until the sauce is syrupy. Add the chicken, stir to coat and then remove from the heat. **5)** For the guacamole, cut the avocados into large chunks and mash in a medium bowl with a fork. Stir in all the remaining ingredients. **6)** To assemble, top each baked tortilla cup with a heaped spoonful of the chicken and bean mixture followed by a dollop of guacamole. Serve immediately.

Makes: 32 tostadas

## BITE ME BIT

'You're not drunk if you can lie
on the floor without holding on.'

— Dean Martin, entertainer

# SWEET and SOUR CANDIED SALAMI

## INGREDIENTS

800g beef salami,
cut into 2.5cm cubes

840g Heinz Chili Sauce, mild
chilli sauce or barbecue sauce

340g apricot jam

juice of 2 lemons

3 tablespoons
Worcestershire sauce

Watch your backs, fussy, flaky puff pastries. Slash your prices, conceited caviar. Salami, once considered déclassé in the haute hors d'oeuvres world, is taking pompous parties by storm. A snap to put together, this salty and spicy beef is baked into a sticky, syrupy scene-stealer. Take that, smug smoked salmon.

## METHOD

**1)** Preheat the oven to 180°C/350°F/Gas Mark 4. **2)** Place the cubed salami in a 33 x 23cm baking dish. **3)** In a medium bowl, whisk all the remaining ingredients together. Pour over the salami. **4)** Bake, uncovered and stirring every 20 minutes, for 1½–2 hours until the sauce is reduced by half and thickened. Serve with cocktail sticks.

Serves 8–10

### BITE ME BIT

'Wait up, girls. I got a salami I gotta hide still.'

– Carl Spackler (actor Bill Murray) in the 1980 movie **Caddyshack**

# DYN-O-MITE! ASIAN MEATBALLS

## INGREDIENTS

### Meatballs

non-stick cooking spray
900g lean beef mince
2 large eggs
55g fresh breadcrumbs
125ml hoisin sauce
1 teaspoon grated fresh ginger

### Asian Sauce

340g apricot jam
125ml hoisin sauce
125ml rice vinegar
½ teaspoon grated fresh ginger
⅛ teaspoon cayenne pepper

The cocktail meatball is one 1970s culinary delight we're thrilled has made a comeback. With a Harvey Wallbanger in one hand and this hoisin one-biter in the other, you get all the sweetness and flavour of the 'Me Decade' without having to shimmy into a spandex halter-neck catsuit.

## METHOD

1) Preheat the oven to 190°C/375°F/Gas Mark 5. Line 2 baking sheets with foil and coat with non-stick cooking spray. 2) Combine all the ingredients for the meatballs in a large bowl. Shape the meat mixture into approximately 60 walnut-sized balls. Place the meatballs on the prepared baking sheets and bake for 24 minutes, turning halfway through the baking time. Remove from oven and leave the meatballs to stand on kitchen paper to drain. 3) Put all the ingredients for the Asian sauce in a large saucepan and bring to the boil over a medium-high heat. Reduce the heat to low and simmer for 5 minutes. Add the cooked meatballs to the sauce, heat through and then serve.

Makes: approximately 60 meatballs

## BITE ME BIT

**Archie:** You are a Meathead.

**Mike:** What did you call me?

**Archie:** Meathead. Dead from the neck up. Meathead.

– From the 1971 US television show 'All in the Family'

Traditional Chicken Soup with Matzo Balls **34**
Bestowed (mushroom) Barley Soup **35**
Roasted Carrot Soup Topped with Candied Pistachios **36**
Restorative Roasted Vegetable Soup **38**
Potato Soup with Spiced Chickpeas **39**
Tomato Soup with Grilled Cheese Croutons **41**
Incroyable French Onion Soup **42**

# Spoon me

## Steamy Soups

Southwestern Chicken Corn Chowder **43**
White Bean Soup with Spinach and Couscous **46**
Nutty Butternut Squash Soup **47**
Minestrone Soup with Pesto Drizzle **49**
Raj's Vegetable Lentil Soup **50**
Moroccan Spiced Chicken Soup **51**
Ian Muggridge's Tuscan Bread Soup **52**

**URGENT, DELIVER WITHOUT DELAY**

# TELEGRAM

January 22, 1907
SICK OF BORSCHT STOP FREEZING MY MATZO BALLS IN
VLADIVOSTOK STOP HOPPING ON SLOW BOAT TO ELLIS ISLAND STOP
HEARD THEY HAVE NICE SOUP ON LOWER EAST SIDE STOP

# TRADITIONAL CHICKEN SOUP with MATZO BALLS

## INGREDIENTS

### Chicken Soup

1.8kg whole chicken, well rinsed

8 chicken wings, split, tips removed

5 large carrots, peeled and cut into 5cm pieces

5 large celery sticks, cut into 5cm pieces

2 parsnips, peeled and sliced

1 large onion, quartered

3 garlic cloves, peeled and left whole

1 large bunch of flat-leaf parsley

1 large bunch of dill

10 black peppercorns

sea salt

### Matzo Balls

4 large eggs, lightly beaten

2 tablespoons vegetable oil

1 teaspoon sea salt

pinch of freshly ground black pepper

150g matzo meal or Matzos pulsed in a food processor until fine crumbs

## METHOD

**1)** For the soup, place the whole chicken and chicken wings in a very large saucepan. Fill with enough cold water to cover the chicken, filling the pan three-quarters full. Bring to the boil over a high heat and skim off the foam that accumulates on the top. Reduce the heat to a simmer and add the vegetables, garlic, herbs, peppercorns and 1 tablespoon salt. Return to the boil, then reduce the heat, cover and simmer gently for 2 hours. Remove the lid and continue to simmer for a further 1 hour. **2)** Strain the soup into another pan through a very fine sieve or a sieve lined with muslin. Shred the meat from the chicken breast and put it in the strained soup or save for another time. Discard the remaining chicken and solids. **3)** Salt the soup to taste. Cool the soup and skim off any fat that has risen to the surface (the easiest way is to refrigerate the soup overnight and then discard the solidified fat from the surface). Serve hot with the shredded chicken, matzo balls and/or cooked egg noodles. **4)** For the matzo balls, in a medium bowl, whisk the eggs, oil, salt and pepper together. Whisk in the matzo meal just until combined. Cover the mixture lightly with clingfilm and refrigerate for 1 hour until slightly firm. **5)** Bring a large saucepan of salted water to the boil. Remove the matzo ball mixture from refrigerator. Gently roll heaped tablespoons of the matzo mixture into balls; too much pressure when rolling the balls will make them too hard. Add to the boiling water, then cover, reduce the heat to low and simmer for 25–30 minutes until doubled in size. Using a slotted spoon, transfer the matzo balls to the prepared soup.

Makes: 20–24 matzo balls; Serves 10–12

# BESTOWED (mushroom) BARLEY SOUP

## INGREDIENTS

20g dried porcini mushrooms

225ml boiling water

2 tablespoons olive oil

2 celery sticks, chopped

2 carrots, peeled and chopped

1 onion, finely chopped

225g assorted mushrooms (shiitake, chestnut, button, portobello), coarsely chopped

1.9 litres beef stock

90g pearl barley, rinsed and drained

½ teaspoon dried thyme

½ teaspoon dried basil

½ teaspoon sea salt

½ teaspoon freshly ground black pepper

2 tablespoons finely chopped flat-leaf parsley

Did your ancestors bring recipes from the old country that 'by accident' omitted the main ingredient? A beloved relative of ours was famous for her meatless meatballs, fruit-free cherry cake and, of course, her impeccable mushroom-less mushroom barley soup. We've done little to improve her genius. We just added an ingredient.

## METHOD

1) Place the dried porcini mushrooms in a small heatproof bowl, cover with the boiling water and leave to stand for 20 minutes or until softened. Drain the mushrooms, rinse well and finely chop. Set aside. 2) Heat the oil in a large saucepan over a medium heat. Add the celery, carrots and onion and cook, stirring frequently, for 5 minutes until tender. Add the fresh mushrooms and cook for another 5 minutes until they begin to brown and release their liquid. Raise the heat to high and add the stock, chopped porcini mushrooms, barley, thyme, basil, salt and pepper. Bring to the boil. Reduce the heat to low, partially cover and simmer for 1 hour until the barley is tender. Stir in the chopped parsley and serve.

Serves 8

### BITE ME BIT

Freud had a fetish for fungi. 'On an expedition for the purpose, he would often leave the children and...then creep silently up to it and suddenly pounce to capture the fungus with his hat as if it were a bird or butterfly,' wrote biographer Ernest Jones. We'll let you interpret the meaning.

# ROASTED CARROT SOUP TOPPED with CANDIED PISTACHIOS

## INGREDIENTS

### Candied Pistachios

3 tablespoons golden syrup

1 tablespoon sugar

¼ teaspoon sea salt

160g shelled pistachio nuts

### Carrot Soup

non-stick cooking spray

900g carrots, peeled and cut into 4cm cubes

2 large parsnips, peeled and cut into 4cm cubes

2 tablespoons olive oil

2 tablespoons runny honey

sea salt

15g butter

115g red onion, chopped

1.9 litres chicken stock

Beep, beep, beep. Our carotene-enhanced bionic eyesight is at labour. We spy nutrient-rich, sweet roasted carrot and golden parsnip soup sprinkled with crunchy candied pistachios. Diners are taking spoons. Inserting them into beta-carotene bowls. They are smiling. Over.

## METHOD

1) For the pistachios, preheat the oven to 160°C/325°F/Gas Mark 3. Line a baking sheet with baking paper. In a small bowl, combine the syrup, sugar, salt and nuts. Spread the nuts on the prepared baking sheet and bake for 15 minutes, stirring every 5 minutes. Remove from the oven, cool completely and then chop into coarse pieces. These can be made up to 2 days ahead and stored in an airtight container. 2) For the soup, preheat the oven to 200°C/400°F/Gas Mark 6. Line a baking sheet with foil and coat with non-stick cooking spray. 3) In a large bowl, toss the carrots, parsnips, oil, honey and ½ teaspoon salt together. Pour onto the prepared baking sheet in a single layer. Bake for 35–40 minutes, stirring once halfway through, until the carrots and parsnips are tender and lightly browned. Remove from the oven and set aside. 4) In a large saucepan, melt the butter over a medium heat. Add the onion and cook for about 3–4 minutes until tender but not browned. Add the carrots, parsnips and stock. Bring to the boil, then reduce heat to low, cover and cook for about 40 minutes until the carrots and parsnips are extremely tender. Remove from the heat and leave to cool slightly. 5) Using a hand-held or freestanding blender, purée the soup until smooth. Season with ¼ teaspoon salt and garnish each serving with 1 tablespoon of the chopped candied pistachios.

Serves 6–8

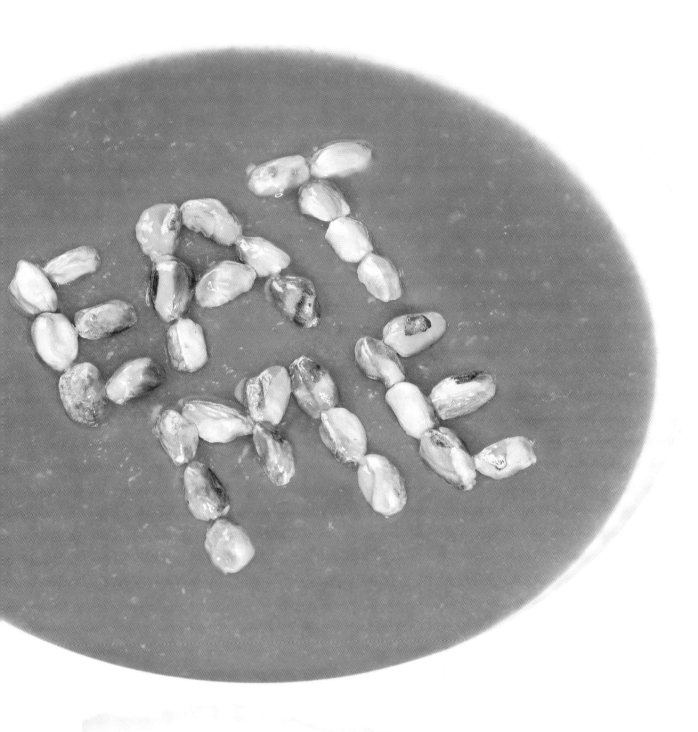

## BITE ME BIT

'A fool bolts a door with a boiled carrot.'

– Proverb

# RESTORATIVE ROASTED VEGETABLE SOUP

## INGREDIENTS

non-stick cooking spray

2 large carrots, peeled and cut into 2.5cm cubes

1 large sweet potato, peeled and cut into 2.5cm cubes

2 courgettes, cut into 2.5cm cubes

1 large red pepper, deseeded and cut into 2.5cm cubes

1 red onion, cut into 2.5cm cubes

75g small mushrooms, peeled and quartered

3 tablespoons olive oil

½ teaspoon sea salt

3 fresh rosemary sprigs

225ml water

1.9 litres chicken stock

3 boneless, skinless chicken breasts, cut into 1cm cubes

225g cooked farfalle pasta

These days everything from souvlaki to astrology is considered good for the soul. Though we love Greek food and stargazing, our souls get fully nourished by this satisfying soup packed with roasted vegetables, succulent chicken and bowtie pasta.

## METHOD

1) Preheat the oven to 190°C/375°F/Gas Mark 5. Line a baking sheet with foil and coat with non-stick cooking spray. 2) In a large bowl, combine the carrots, sweet potato, courgettes, red pepper, onion and mushrooms. Add the oil and salt, tossing well to coat. Spread the vegetables out on the prepared baking sheet and nestle the rosemary sprigs among the vegetables. Bake for 40–45 minutes, stirring occasionally. Discard the rosemary sprigs. 3) In a large saucepan, combine the water, stock and cubed chicken. Bring to the boil over a high heat. Reduce the heat to medium-low and simmer for 10 minutes. Add the roasted vegetables and simmer for a further 10 minutes. Add the cooked pasta and heat through.

Serves 8

## BITE ME BIT

'It takes more than just a good-looking body. You've got to have the heart and soul to go with it.'

– Epictetus, Greek philosopher

# POTATO SOUP with SPICED CHICKPEAS

## INGREDIENTS

### Roasted Chickpeas

non-stick cooking spray

420g canned chickpeas, drained, rinsed and patted dry

1 tablespoon olive oil

1 tablespoon soy sauce

1 teaspoon sesame oil

½ teaspoon chilli powder

### Potato Soup

25g butter

1 small onion, diced

½ teaspoon sea salt

¼ teaspoon freshly ground black pepper

2 large boiling potatoes, such as Yukon Gold or Estima, peeled and diced

250g trimmed courgettes, diced

1 litre chicken stock

2 teaspoons chopped mint leaves

Our Dad often refers to Lisa and me as 'The Twisted Sisters'. We can't disagree. We're two girls who like surprises. Take our silky smooth potato soup. We've added courgettes, which, much like Lisa's personality, lend a mellow and delicate flavour, enhancing the traditional soup. As for myself, I'm more like the spice-roasted chickpeas scattered atop – zippy, biting and salty.

## METHOD

**1)** For the chickpeas, preheat the oven to 200°C/400°F/Gas Mark 6. Line a baking sheet with foil and coat with non-stick cooking spray. Spread the chickpeas on the prepared baking sheet and drizzle with the olive oil. Roast for 30 minutes, shaking the pan once or twice during baking. Remove from the oven. **2)** In a small bowl, stir the soy sauce, sesame oil and chilli powder together. Toss with the chickpeas and set aside. **3)** For the soup, in a large saucepan, melt the butter over a medium-low heat. Add the onion, salt and pepper and cook, covered and stirring occasionally, for 4–5 minutes until the onion begins to soften but not brown. Add the potatoes and cook, uncovered, for 3 minutes. Stir in the courgettes and stock and bring to the boil over a high heat. Cover, reduce the heat to low and simmer for about 20 minutes until the potatoes are tender. **4)** Remove from the heat and purée the soup, using a hand-held or freestanding blender, until smooth. Re-warm the soup if necessary. Taste for additional salt or pepper. Stir in the chopped mint. Garnish each serving with a spoonful of the roasted chickpeas.

Serves 6–8

## BITE ME BIT

'He was so twisted he could eat soup with a corkscrew.'

– Myra Langtry (actress Annette Bening) in the 1990 movie **The Grifters**

# TOMATO SOUP with GRILLED CHEESE CROUTONS

## INGREDIENTS

### Tomato Soup

non-stick cooking spray

4 x 400g canned chopped tomatoes

4 tablespoons olive oil

sea salt and freshly ground black pepper

2 tablespoons olive oil

1 small onion, diced

2 carrots, peeled and diced

2 celery sticks, diced

1 large garlic clove, finely chopped

2 tablespoons plain flour

700ml chicken stock

1 dried bay leaf

2 teaspoons sugar

25g butter

2 tablespoons chopped basil

### Grilled Cheese Croutons

4 slices white bread

25g butter

2 slices Cheddar cheese

If Andy Warhol had tasted our deeply flavoured roasted tomato soup, we're confident he would have chosen it over the bland canned variety. We can picture the canvas…bowl after bowl of velvety, steaming tomato purée topped with crispy mini grilled cheese croutons…a comfort-food masterpiece that'll be remembered long past 15 minutes.

## METHOD

**1)** Preheat the oven to 220°C/425°F/Gas Mark 7. Cover a baking sheet with foil and coat with non-stick cooking spray. Strain the tomatoes, reserving their juices in a medium bowl. Spread the strained tomatoes on the prepared baking sheet, drizzle with 2 tablespoons olive oil and season with ¼ teaspoon salt and ⅛ teaspoon pepper. Roast in oven for 15 minutes. **2)** While the tomatoes are roasting, in a large saucepan, heat the remaining 2 tablespoons oil over a medium-low heat. Add the onion, carrots, celery and garlic and cook for about 8 minutes until softened. Add the flour and stir to coat. Over a high heat, add the roasted tomatoes, reserved tomato juices, stock, bay leaf, sugar and ¼ teaspoon each of salt and pepper. Bring to the boil, then reduce to a gentle simmer, cover and continue to simmer for 30 minutes. **3)** Remove from the heat, discard the bay leaf and purée the soup, using a hand-held or freestanding blender, until smooth. Stir in the butter and chopped basil. **4)** For the croutons, spread the butter on both sides of the bread slices. Heat a frying pan over a medium heat and add 2 slices. Top each with a slice of cheese and place the remaining bread slices on the cheese. Cook for 2 minutes until the underside is golden brown, flip and cook for 1–2 minutes more. Remove from the pan and leave to cool for a few minutes. Cut into 2.5cm squares and sprinkle a small handful on each bowl of soup.

# INCROYABLE FRENCH ONION SOUP

## INGREDIENTS

2 tablespoons olive oil

25g butter

6 white onions, halved and thinly sliced

2 teaspoons plain flour

1 teaspoon sugar

½ teaspoon sea salt, plus ¼ teaspoon if desired

½ teaspoon freshly ground black pepper

2 thyme sprigs

2 dried bay leaves

75ml port

225ml dry red wine

1.1 litres beef stock

225ml chicken stock

### Topping

6–8 baguette slices, cut crossways 1cm thick, lightly toasted on both sides (180°C/350°F/Gas Mark 4 oven for 5 minutes per side)

225g Gruyère cheese, thinly sliced (easily done with a cheese slicer)

2 tablespoons freshly grated Parmesan cheese

Bonjour! Je suis Laurence, la meilleure amie française de Julie. Lorsqu'elle m'a demandé de goûter à sa soupe à l'oignon française, sans rire, je me suis inquiétée. Elle n'a tellement rien à voir avec la France et le fait qu'elle porte un béret ne veut pas dire qu'elle soit capable de réussir cet emblème gastronomique national. En fait, je n'avais pas à m'inquiéter. Sa soupe était aussi authentique que celles que l'on peut déguster dans les environs de la Tour Eiffel. Le bouillon était riche, le Gruyère absolument savoureux et les oignons caramélisés à la perfection. Bien joué, mon amie anglophone, bien joué! (transl. This onion soup is great.)

## METHOD

**1)** For the onion soup, in a large cast-iron saucepan or casserole, heat the oil and butter over a high heat. Add the onions and cook over a high heat for 5 minutes, stirring occasionally. Reduce the heat to medium-low and cook for 40–45 minutes, stirring often, until the onions are tender and caramelised. **2)** Stir in the flour, sugar, ½ teaspoon salt, pepper, thyme and bay leaves and cook for 1 minute. Increase the heat to high, add the port and red wine and bring to the boil. Boil for 2 minutes. Add the beef and chicken stock and return to the boil. Reduce the heat to low. Cook, covered, for 15 minutes, then remove the lid and continue cooking for 30–35 minutes. Remove and discard the thyme sprigs and bay leaves. Adjust the seasoning with an additional ¼ teaspoon salt if desired. **3)** Preheat the grill. **4)** Set 6 flameproof soup bowls on a baking sheet. Fill each bowl with the hot soup. Top with a toasted baguette slice, then cover the toasts with the Gruyère slices and sprinkle with the Parmesan. Grill for 2–3 minutes until the cheese is golden and bubbly.

Serves 6 (large bowls) or 8 (smaller bowls)

# SOUTHWESTERN CHICKEN CORN CHOWDER

## INGREDIENTS

15g butter

1 small onion, chopped

1 large red pepper, deseeded and chopped

2 x 400g cans chopped tomatoes, drained

2–3 mild green chillies, deseeded (for less heat) and finely chopped

750g canned cream-style corn

300g frozen sweetcorn, defrosted

475ml chicken stock

¼ teaspoon sea salt

¼ teaspoon freshly ground black pepper

3 boneless, skinless chicken breasts, cooked and shredded

225ml milk

85g Monterey Jack, Gruyère or Cheddar cheese, coarsely grated

crumbled tortilla chips, to serve

New England and Manhattan have hogged the spotlight long enough. There's a new chowder in town – say goodbye to clams and crackers and ¡hola! to corn and tortillas. The taste of this creamy, flavour-packed chowder comes from the combo of sweet yellow sweetcorn and nacho toppings. For an added Southwestern kick, drizzle on some hot sauce and you'll be warmed from your nose down to your toes.

## METHOD

**1)** In a large saucepan, melt the butter over a medium-high heat. Add the onion and red pepper and cook for about 5 minutes until softened. Add the tomatoes and chopped chillies, mixing well.

**2)** Stir in the cream-style corn, sweetcorn, stock, salt, pepper, shredded chicken and milk. Increase the heat to high and bring to the boil, then reduce the heat to low and simmer for 25 minutes.

**3)** Stir in the cheese, mixing until melted. Top each portion with crumbled tortilla chips to serve.

Serves 6

### BITE ME BIT

'Corn chowder. That's an interesting choice. You do know that cellulite is one of the main ingredients in corn chowder.'

– Nigel (actor Stanley Tucci) in the 2006 movie **The Devil Wears Prada**

# Whoopsie

Recipes for Disaster

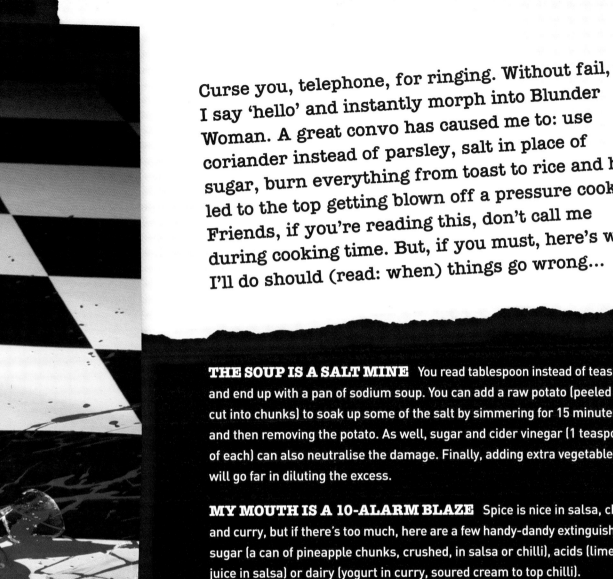

Curse you, telephone, for ringing. Without fail, I say 'hello' and instantly morph into Blunder Woman. A great convo has caused me to: use coriander instead of parsley, salt in place of sugar, burn everything from toast to rice and has led to the top getting blown off a pressure cooker. Friends, if you're reading this, don't call me during cooking time. But, if you must, here's what I'll do should (read: when) things go wrong...

**THE SOUP IS A SALT MINE** You read tablespoon instead of teaspoon and end up with a pan of sodium soup. You can add a raw potato (peeled and cut into chunks) to soak up some of the salt by simmering for 15 minutes and then removing the potato. As well, sugar and cider vinegar (1 teaspoon of each) can also neutralise the damage. Finally, adding extra vegetables will go far in diluting the excess.

**MY MOUTH IS A 10-ALARM BLAZE** Spice is nice in salsa, chilli and curry, but if there's too much, here are a few handy-dandy extinguishers: sugar (a can of pineapple chunks, crushed, in salsa or chilli), acids (lime juice in salsa) or dairy (yogurt in curry, soured cream to top chilli).

**THE VEGETABLES ARE OVERCOOKED** If only there was Viagra for limp vegetables. But until that invention comes around – and we hope Bob Dole will be plugging it – we will have to put them in the food processor and purée. Some suggestions include broccoli or cauliflower with Cheddar and fresh herbs, carrots with cream and salt or sweet potatoes with maple syrup and a touch of cinnamon.

**THE COOKIES ARE BAKING UNEVENLY** Remove the slightly brown cookies to a wire rack. Return the under-baked cookies to the oven; make sure the tray is placed in the centre of the oven to allow the heat to circulate. Rotating your baking sheet from front to back halfway through baking is another option if your cookies are browning unevenly. As well, reduce the risk of burned bottoms by baking your cookies on light-coloured baking sheets with a dull finish.

# WHITE BEAN SOUP with SPINACH and COUSCOUS

## INGREDIENTS

2 teaspoons olive oil

2 leeks, rinsed well, white portions chopped and green discarded

2 large garlic cloves, finely chopped

2 teaspoons ground cumin

1.9 litres chicken stock

780g canned cannellini beans, rinsed and drained

2 dried bay leaves

80g wholemeal couscous

60g fresh spinach leaves

sea salt and freshly ground black pepper

Bean soups can be like exercise bikes. They're healthy, convenient and make you feel virtuous. But sometimes you want to feel like you're going places, having new experiences. This exotic spin on a Tuscan tradition relies on leeks, the mild cousin of the onion, for their subtle flavour, creamy beans for their rich texture and couscous with its nutty taste that makes every trip to the bowl delightful and surprising.

## METHOD

1) Heat the oil in a large saucepan over a medium-high heat. Add the leeks and garlic and sauté for 2 minutes or until tender. 2) Stir in the cumin. Add the stock, beans and bay leaves. Bring to the boil over a high heat. 3) Add the couscous, then reduce the heat to low, cover and simmer for 5 minutes. 4) Remove the bay leaves and discard. Stir in the spinach and cook for about 30 seconds, until wilted. Season to taste with salt and pepper.

Serves 6

## BITE ME BIT

'He couldn't ad-lib a fart after a baked bean dinner.'

— Johnny Carson, TV talk show host and comedian

# NUTTY BUTTERNUT SQUASH SOUP

## INGREDIENTS

2 teaspoons vegetable oil

1 small onion, diced

1 large garlic clove, finely chopped

1 tablespoon mild curry powder

2 teaspoons ground cumin

1 teaspoon sea salt

1.4 litres chicken stock

420g peeled, deseeded and chopped butternut squash

90g peeled and coarsely grated carrots

240g cooked basmati or Thai jasmine rice

115g frozen green peas, defrosted

6 tablespoons smooth peanut butter

This unusual combination could be billed as a gastronomic prizefight, peanut butter in one corner, butternut squash in the other. But the heavyweights come together amazingly on the palate, the smooth peanut butter lending a luscious tinge to the full-flavoured squash.

## METHOD

1) In a large saucepan, heat the oil over a medium-low heat. Add the onion and garlic and cook for 4–5 minutes, stirring occasionally, until softened. Add the curry powder, cumin and ½ teaspoon salt. Cook for 1 minute, stirring constantly. 2) Add the stock, butternut squash and carrots. Bring to the boil over a high heat. Reduce the heat to low, cover and simmer for 20 minutes until the squash has softened. 3) Stir in the rice, peas, peanut butter and remaining ½ teaspoon salt. Cook, uncovered, for 3 minutes until the ingredients are blended.

Serves 6

## BITE ME BIT

'C'mon, he's insane. Look. Right now he's probably dancing around in his grandma's panties, yeah, rubbing himself in peanut butter.'

– Detective Dave Mills (actor Brad Pitt) in the 1995 movie **Se7en**

# MINESTRONE SOUP with PESTO DRIZZLE

## INGREDIENTS

### Minestrone Soup

3 tablespoons olive oil

2 large garlic cloves, chopped

1 onion, chopped

5 celery sticks, chopped

5 carrots, peeled and chopped

1.2 litres chicken stock

2 x 400g cans chopped tomatoes

480g pasta tomato sauce

125ml dry red wine

60g fresh baby spinach

375g canned red kidney beans, rinsed and drained

2 large courgettes, chopped

2 tablespoons chopped basil

1 tablespoon chopped oregano

1 tablespoon sugar

½ teaspoon sea salt

¼ teaspoon freshly ground black pepper

115g cooked conchiglie pasta

### Pesto Drizzle

25g loosely packed fresh basil leaves

1 small garlic clove

30g pine nuts

30g Parmesan cheese, freshly grated

½ teaspoon sea salt

4 tablespoons olive oil

As typically Italian as Fiat and Benetton, this rich-tasting soup transports us to Firenze. No, not Florence, Italy, but the strip mall ristorante that ignited our childhood love for all things Italian, especially frescoes of naked and boozing burly men and voluptuous women. Titillating for sure, but nothing grabbed our attention more than Mary's minestrone. As soon as she'd set down the steaming, vegetable-packed rich broth, focus turned to the full-bodied soup. Now, though Mary and her minestrone are gone, we've got her legendary soup recreated to perfection…only thing missing is the bacchanalian mural.

## METHOD

1) In a large saucepan, heat the oil over a medium-low heat and sauté the garlic and onion for 4–5 minutes. Add the celery and carrots and sauté for a further 5 minutes. 2) Add the stock, chopped tomatoes with their juice and tomato sauce. Bring to the boil over a high heat. Turn to low and add the wine, spinach, beans, courgettes, herbs, sugar, salt and pepper. Simmer, uncovered, for 30 minutes. 3) Add the cooked pasta and simmer for 2–3 minutes to combine the flavours. 4) For the pesto sauce, place the basil leaves and garlic in a food processor and process until the leaves are finely chopped. Add the pine nuts and process until finely chopped. Add the Parmesan and salt and process until combined. With the machine running, add the oil in a slow, steady stream until it is incorporated. If you're not using the pesto sauce immediately, store it, covered, in the refrigerator to prevent it from turning brown. 5) Drizzle 1 teaspoon of the pesto sauce over each bowl of soup.

Serves 8–10

# RAJ'S VEGETABLE LENTIL SOUP

## INGREDIENTS

2 tablespoons olive oil

1 large celery stick, chopped

1 large carrot, peeled and chopped

1 parsnip, peeled and chopped

1 small shallot, diced

1 large garlic clove, finely chopped

1 teaspoon grated fresh ginger

1½ teaspoons curry powder

½ teaspoon ground cumin

⅛ teaspoon dried chilli flakes

1.2 litres chicken stock

175g green lentils

½ teaspoon sea salt

¼ teaspoon freshly ground black pepper

125ml soured cream

2 tablespoons chopped mint

I've been Punk'd, Bollywood style. After teaching me all I ever wanted to know about cricket and Shah Rukh Khan films, my friend Raj moved on to Indian cuisine. I felt honoured to get this spiced, vegetable-packed lentil soup recipe 'straight from grandmother's Calcutta kitchen'. Turns out, his grandmother learned it from her Mahjong partner in Fort Lauderdale.

## METHOD

**1)** In a large saucepan, heat the oil over a medium heat. Add the celery, carrot, parsnip, shallot, garlic and ginger and cook, stirring, for about 5 minutes until softened. Add the curry powder, cumin and chilli flakes and cook, stirring constantly, for about 1 minute until the spices are fragrant. **2)** Add the stock, lentils, salt and pepper. Bring to the boil over a high heat, then reduce the heat to low and simmer, covered, for about 25 minutes until the lentils are tender. **3)** Remove 475ml of the soup and purée using a hand-held or freestanding blender. Return the smooth purée to the remaining soup in the pan. Stir well, adjusting the salt and pepper to taste. **4)** Ladle the soup into bowls and top each serving with a spoonful of soured cream and a sprinkle of chopped mint.

Serves 6

## BITE ME BIT

'These can never be true friends: hope, dice, a prostitute, a robber, a cheat, a goldsmith, a monkey, a doctor, a distiller.'

– Indian proverb

# MOROCCAN SPICED CHICKEN SOUP

## INGREDIENTS

25g butter

1 onion, chopped

2 large celery sticks, chopped

2 large carrots, peeled and chopped

1 teaspoon ground cinnamon

1 teaspoon ground turmeric

1 teaspoon ground cumin

½ teaspoon sea salt

¼ teaspoon freshly ground black pepper

800g passata

840g canned chickpeas, rinsed and drained

1.6 litres chicken stock

175g green lentils

125g dried angel hair pasta, broken into 2.5cm pieces

2 boneless, skinless chicken breasts, cooked and shredded

3 tablespoons chopped flat-leaf parsley

I'm pretty literal. When The Clash tells me to 'Rock The Casbah', who am I to refuse this invitation? I called on the conductor (aka Lisa) to compose a big hit – a thick, hearty and full-bodied soup that would deliver all the allure and rich spices of Morocco. Packed with chickpeas, lentils, pasta and North African flavours, this fragrant soup will take you right to the narrow alleyways and bustling bazaars. Gotta go – London's Calling.

## METHOD

**1)** In a large saucepan, melt the butter over a medium-low heat. Add the onion, celery and carrots and cook for about 8–10 minutes until softened. Add the cinnamon, turmeric, cumin, salt and pepper and cook, stirring, for 2 minutes. **2)** Stir in the passata, chickpeas, stock and lentils. Bring to the boil, then reduce the heat to low and simmer, uncovered, for about 30–35 minutes until the lentils are tender. **3)** Add the pasta and cook for 5 minutes or until softened. Stir in the shredded chicken and chopped parsley and heat through before serving.

Serves 6

# IAN MUGGRIDGE'S TUSCAN BREAD SOUP

## INGREDIENTS

1 French bread (about 225g, preferably day-old), cut into 4cm cubes

4 tablespoons olive oil

½ teaspoon sea salt

1 white onion, chopped

2 garlic cloves, finely chopped

1.7kg plum tomatoes cut into wedges (reserve 6 wedges for garnish)

2 large red peppers, deseeded and chopped

225ml dry white wine

1.4 litres chicken broth

2 dried bay leaves

¼ teaspoon freshly ground black pepper

### Poached Eggs

475ml water

60ml distilled white vinegar

6 large eggs

10g basil leaves, sliced

115g Parmesan cheese, freshly shaved with a vegetable peeler

We confess – we fancy this man we call 'Mugsy'. He's a great bloke, superb food stylist and chef extra-ordinaire. Though he doesn't have a Tuscan bone in his body (Brit to the core), he has generously shared his smashing soup of rustic bread, hearty tomato stock and garlic, finished with a fab poached egg on top. Cheerio, Chap.

## METHOD

1) Preheat the oven to 150°C/300°F/Gas Mark 2. In a large bowl, combine the bread cubes with 2 tablespoons olive oil and ¼ teaspoon salt. Toss to coat and spread out on a baking sheet. Bake for 30–40 minutes until the cubes are crisp all the way through. Remove from the oven and set aside. 2) In a large saucepan, heat the remaining 2 tablespoons oil over a medium heat. Add the onion and sauté for about 4 minutes until softened. Add the garlic and cook, stirring, for about 1 minute until fragrant. Add the tomato wedges and sauté for about 3 minutes until they start to break down. Stir in the red peppers and wine and cook over a medium heat for 15 minutes. Add the stock and bay leaves. Bring to the boil, then reduce the heat to a gentle simmer and cook for a further 15 minutes. Remove from the heat and strain through a fine-mesh sieve, discarding the solids. Return the soup to the pan, season with the remaining ¼ teaspoon salt and the pepper and keep hot. 3) In a small saucepan, heat the water and vinegar over a low heat. When simmering, gently crack 2 eggs at a time into the water and poach for 2–3 minutes. Remove and plunge into a bowl filled with iced water; the yolks should be runny. 4) To serve, ladle the soup into bowls. Add the toasted bread cubes, reserved tomato wedges, basil and a poached egg to each bowl. Finish with the shaved Parmesan. Serve immediately.

Serves 6

# unDress me

## Eye-Popping Salads

# STRAWBERRY SALAD with SUGARED ALMONDS

## INGREDIENTS

### Sugared Almonds

4 tablespoons sugar

2 teaspoons water

85g flaked almonds

non-stick cooking spray

### Poppy Seed Dressing

4 tablespoons sugar

55g mayonnaise

2 tablespoons milk

1 tablespoon white wine vinegar

2 teaspoons poppy seeds

200g cos lettuce, torn into bite-sized pieces

140g sliced strawberries

80g dried cranberries

Some people believe strawberries are an aphrodisiac, others that almonds bring good fortune. So get lucky with our 'perfect bite' – a fork crammed with crisp lettuce, scarlet strawberries and sugared almonds, all coated in a sweet-and-sour poppy seed dressing.

## METHOD

1) For the almonds, in a medium saucepan, combine the sugar and water. Cook over a medium heat until the sugar dissolves. Add the flaked almonds and stir to coat. Continue to cook and stir until the sugar and almonds turn golden. Remove from the heat and place the almonds on a piece of foil that has been coated with non-stick cooking spray. 2) For the dressing, in a small bowl, whisk the sugar, mayonnaise, milk, vinegar and poppy seeds together. 3) In a large bowl, combine the lettuce, strawberries, cranberries and sugared almonds. Toss with the dressing and serve.

Serves 6

### BITE ME BIT

A recent US survey found that strawberry-lovers are happy, fun-loving and smart people; strawberry-haters are weird, dull and picky. Did we mention that we love strawberries?

# MIXED GREENS with SQUASH, PECANS and PEARS

## INGREDIENTS

### Spicy Pecans

non-stick cooking spray

120g pecan nuts, coarsely chopped

1 tablespoon olive oil

¼ teaspoon ground cumin

¼ teaspoon ground cinnamon

¼ teaspoon chilli powder

⅛ teaspoon cayenne pepper (optional)

### Sweet Squash

420g peeled, deseeded and cubed butternut squash

2 tablespoons olive oil

2 tablespoons maple syrup

¾ teaspoon sea salt

### Vinaigrette

3 tablespoons balsamic vinegar

1 tablespoon Dijon mustard

1 tablespoon soft light brown sugar

¼ teaspoon sea salt

4 tablespoons olive oil

### Salad

180g loosely packed mixed salad leaves

2 large pears, cored and thinly sliced

80g dried cranberries

## METHOD

1) Preheat the oven to 230°C/450°F/Gas Mark 8. Line a baking sheet with foil and coat with non-stick cooking spray. 2) For the pecans, in a small bowl, toss the pecans with the oil, cumin, cinnamon, chilli powder and cayenne, if using. Spread the pecans out on the prepared baking sheet. Bake for 5 minutes or until lightly toasted. Set aside to cool. 3) For the squash, line a baking sheet with foil and coat with non-stick cooking spray. In a medium bowl, toss the cubed squash with the oil, maple syrup and salt. Spread on the prepared baking sheet and roast for 20 minutes, stir and continue to cook for a further 5–10 minutes until the squash is tender and lightly browned. Set aside to cool. 4) For the dressing, in a small bowl, whisk the vinegar, mustard, sugar and salt together. Continue to whisk, slowly adding the oil until combined. 5) In a large serving bowl, gently toss the salad leaves with 2 tablespoons of the dressing to lightly coat. Add the pecans, squash, pears and dried cranberries. Drizzle the salad with the remaining dressing.

Serves 6–8

**116  SEDUCED BY THE SALAD**

It was a dark and stormy night. The Duke's eyes were locked on her cascading hair and heaving bosom. He knew the scandal could ruin him, but he couldn't look away. The innocent country girl set down his salad, her tapered fingers brushing his arm, igniting his forbidden desire. She remained at his side as he picked up his fork and took a mouthful of the sweet roasted squash, spicy pecans and juicy pears. He took another bite as she ripped off her bodice. He took another bite as she beckoned him. He took another bite as she got her clothes back on and ran off sobbing. His heart swelled for the salad, and the salad alone.

# MANGO and CRANBERRY SALAD with HONEY MUSTARD DRESSING

## INGREDIENTS

### Sugared Pecans

non-sticking cooking spray

1 large egg white

480g pecan halves

200g sugar

1 teaspoon ground cinnamon

¾ teaspoon sea salt.

### Honey Mustard Dressing

85g runny honey

60g wholegrain mustard

60g honey mustard

4 tablespoons rice vinegar

4 tablespoons rapeseed oil

2 tablespoons orange juice

¼ teaspoon sea salt

### Salad

250g cos lettuce, torn into bite-sized pieces

2 mangoes, stoned, peeled and diced

40g dried cranberries

How is this sweet and savoury salad like a little black dress? Indispensable, versatile and timeless, it too will be a dramatic statement at brunch or an elegant complement to a dinner party. Though both the greens and the frock are easily dressed up, only one will look good with chicken and goat cheese on it.

## METHOD

1) For the pecans, preheat the oven to 120°C/250°F/Gas Mark ½. Coat a baking sheet with non-stick cooking spray. In a large bowl, whisk the egg white with 1 tablespoon water until bubbles form. In a medium bowl, mix the sugar, cinnamon and salt together. Add the pecans to the egg white mixture, mixing to coat. Add the sugar mixture and toss the pecans until they are coated. Spread on the prepared baking sheet and bake for 1 hour, stirring every 20 minutes. 2) For the dressing, in a medium bowl, whisk the honey, mustards, vinegar, oil, orange juice and salt together. 3) In a large bowl, place the lettuce, mango and cranberries. Add half the sugared pecans (save the rest for a sweet snack) and salad dressing and toss well to combine.

Serves 6

# TLT (The Larry T) SALAD

## INGREDIENTS

### Croutons

non-stick cooking spray

8 slices French baguette,
cut into 1cm cubes

1 tablespoon olive oil

30g Parmesan cheese,
freshly grated

1 teaspoon sea salt

### Creamy Basil Dressing

55g mayonnaise

3 tablespoons finely
chopped basil

3 tablespoons white wine vinegar

### Salad

250g cos lettuce, torn
into bite-sized pieces

450g cherry tomatoes, halved

8 turkey rashers or streaky
bacon rashers, cooked until crisp
and crumbled

1 avocado, stoned, peeled
and diced

Our Dad has taught us a lot about eating – in Larry-Land, meatloaf is an appetiser and there's always room for a hot dog. So, in his honour we've named this dish after him. He might be surprised (read: aghast) that we chose a bowl of greens, but, since this He-man-sized salad is a deconstructed BLT coated in creamy basil dressing, we're confident we'll have his blessing.

## METHOD

1) For the croutons, preheat the oven to 180°C/350°F/Gas Mark 4. Coat a baking sheet with non-stick cooking spray. In a large bowl, toss the bread cubes with the oil. Add the Parmesan and salt and toss well. Spread the bread cubes on the prepared baking sheet and bake for 15 minutes, stirring frequently. 2) For the dressing, in a small bowl, whisk the mayonnaise, basil and vinegar together. 3) In a large bowl, combine the lettuce, tomatoes, turkey or bacon rashers, avocado and croutons. Add the dressing and toss to coat.

Serves 6

## BITE ME BIT

'After a good dinner one can forgive anybody, even one's own relatives.'

– Oscar Wilde, playwright

# COBB SALAD featuring TINSELTOWN (aka Thousand Island) DRESSING

## INGREDIENTS

### Dressing

225g mayonnaise

4 tablespoons tomato ketchup

2 tablespoons white vinegar

1 tablespoon sugar

2 teaspoons sweet green relish

¼ teaspoon sea salt

¼ teaspoon freshly ground black pepper

### Cobb Salad

200g cos lettuce, torn into bite-sized pieces

6 turkey rashers or streaky bacon rashers, cooked until crisp and crumbled

5 boneless, skinless chicken breasts, cooked and diced

3 large eggs, hard-boiled and finely chopped

3 large tomatoes, deseeded and diced

2 avocados, stoned, peeled and diced

90g blue cheese, crumbled

## METHOD

1) For the dressing, in a medium bowl, whisk the mayonnaise, ketchup, vinegar, sugar, relish, salt and pepper together. Set aside until ready to use (this recipe makes extra dressing for you to keep in the refrigerator for up to 1 week). 2) In a large bowl, combine the lettuce, turkey or bacon rashers, chicken, egg, tomatoes, avocado and blue cheese. Gently toss with the desired amount of dressing.

Serves 6

```
1937, Hollywood
BROWN DERBY - MIDNIGHT:
BOB COBB stands in his empty restaurant kitchen.
Hungry. Alone. Chefless. He opens the fridge and pulls
out handfuls of produce, eggs, chicken, bacon and
cheese. Chops them up and tosses them together.
Takes a large forkful, chews and swallows.

    BOB (voice-over) Hey, this is a good salad.
    Wonder what I should call it?

CUT TO

2009, Toronto
ALBERT KITCHEN - 5:55pm:
JULIE ALBERT stands in the empty kitchen. Alone.
Chefless. Five minutes until the hungry horde descends.
She opens the fridge and pulls out handfuls of produce,
eggs, chicken, turkey bacon and cheese. She chops
them up and tosses them together.

    JULIE (in a loud voice) Dinner's ready.

    JULIE (whispering to the camera)
    I love you, Bob Cobb.
```

# CREAMY CAESAR CARDINI SALAD

## INGREDIENTS

200g cos lettuce torn into bite-sized pieces

60g croutons

60g Parmesan cheese, freshly grated

**Creamy Caesar Dressing**

55g mayonnaise

4 tablespoons buttermilk

½ small garlic clove, finely chopped

2 teaspoons freshly squeezed lemon juice

½ teaspoon Dijon mustard

¼ teaspoon Worcestershire sauce

¼ teaspoon sea salt

¼ teaspoon freshly ground black pepper

4 tablespoons olive oil

85g Parmesan cheese, freshly grated

A message to all friends, Romans and countrymen: Stop stealing our thunder. You can have your Coliseum, keep your ravioli, but you can't take credit for the all-powerful Caesar. It was Mexican restaurateur Caesar Cardini who, in 1924, tossed together crisp cos lettuce and creamy dressing. All hail Cardini.

Sincerely, Concerned Citizens of the Tijuana Salad Society

PS. We'd also be open to crediting these two sisters for their version, an inspired, perfectly blended creamy dressing with crunchy croutons and premium Parmesan.

## METHOD

1) Place the lettuce and croutons in a large bowl. 2) For the dressing, in a medium bowl, whisk the mayonnaise, buttermilk, garlic, lemon juice, mustard, Worcestershire, salt and pepper together until combined. Gradually add the oil, continuing to whisk until incorporated. Fold in the Parmesan. Spoon the dressing over the lettuce and croutons, tossing to coat. Sprinkle with the remaining 60g grated Parmesan.

Serves 6

## BITE ME BIT

'Why should Caesar get to stomp around like a giant, while the rest of us try not to get smushed under his big feet? What's so great about Caesar? Hm? Brutus is just as cute as Caesar. Brutus is just as smart as Caesar. People totally like Brutus just as much as they like Caesar.'

– Gretchen (actress Lacey Chabert) in the 2004 movie **Mean Girls**

# FIESTA BOWL SALAD

## INGREDIENTS

1 head iceberg lettuce, chopped

4 tomatoes, deseeded and diced

1 avocado, stoned, peeled and diced

1 roasted chicken, breast meat shredded

85g Cheddar cheese, coarsely grated

**Salsa Dressing**

125ml soured cream

115g salsa

55g mayonnaise

2 mild green chillies, or to taste, deseeded (for less heat) and finely chopped

freshly squeezed juice of 1 lime

1 tablespoon sugar

½ teaspoon ground cumin

¼ teaspoon chilli powder

crumbled tortilla chips, for sprinkling

Lisa knows when to draw the line. Though she refused to name her twin girls Peyton and Eli, she continues to elate her husband with the best gridiron grub. Citrus-glazed wings for the Orange Bowl, creamy fudge for the Sugar Bowl and, whenever it's the Fiesta Bowl, she turns out this amazing Southwestern salad of chunky avocado, roasted chicken and a hearty dose of cheese and tortilla chips tossed in a spicy salsa dressing. Darling brother-in-law, you're in charge of the Rose Bowl.

## METHOD

1) Place the lettuce, tomatoes, avocado, chicken and Cheddar in a large bowl. 2) For the dressing, in a medium bowl, whisk the soured cream, salsa, mayonnaise, chillies, lime juice, sugar, cumin and chilli powder together. 3) Add the dressing to the salad bowl, tossing well to coat. Sprinkle with crumbled tortilla chips.

Serves 4

## BITE ME BIT

'The house does not rest upon the ground, but upon a woman.'

– Mexican proverb

# SWEET CHUTNEY CHICKEN SALAD

## INGREDIENTS

5 boneless, skinless chicken breasts

1 Granny Smith apple, cored and diced

1 mango, stoned, peeled and diced

160g seedless red grapes, halved

120g celery, chopped

40g raisins

35g salted cashews

### Chutney Dressing

115g mayonnaise

4 tablespoons soured cream

3 tablespoons mango chutney

2 tablespoons freshly squeezed lime juice

1 teaspoon finely grated lime zest

1 teaspoon mild curry powder

1 teaspoon runny honey

¼ teaspoon sea salt

Taking its cues from the sweet side of Indian cuisine, this healthy and refreshing chicken salad mingles sugary mango, juicy grapes and plump raisins with tart lime and crunchy apples. A winning, timeless and trouble-free marriage of East-West flavours.

## METHOD

1) Place the chicken in a medium saucepan, cover with cold water and bring to the boil over a high heat. Reduce the heat, cover and simmer for 13 minutes or until chicken is no longer pink inside. If you have the time, allow the chicken to cool in the water, but if not, remove the cooked chicken and chop into bite-sized pieces. 2) In a large bowl, combine the chicken, apple, mango, grapes, celery, raisins and cashews. 3) For the dressing, in a medium bowl, whisk the mayonnaise, soured cream, chutney, lime juice, lime zest, curry powder, honey and salt together. Pour over the chicken salad and toss well.

Serves 6

### BITE ME BIT

'All you have to do is hold the chicken, bring me the toast, give me a check for the chicken salad sandwich and you haven't broken any rules.'

– Bobby Dupea (actor Jack Nicholson) in the 1970 movie **Five Easy Pieces**

# SOY-GLAZED CHICKEN SALAD with MAGICAL MANDARINS

## INGREDIENTS

### Soy-Glazed Chicken

non-stick cooking spray

6 boneless, skinless chicken breasts, cubed

2 tablespoons cornflour

1 tablespoon vegetable oil

150g soft light brown sugar

175ml soy sauce

125ml water

85g runny honey

2 tablespoons cornflour

1 teaspoon grated fresh ginger

### Dressing

115g mayonnaise

4 tablespoons rice vinegar

2 tablespoons sugar

1 tablespoon sesame oil

1 tablespoon soy sauceer

### Salad

1 head iceberg lettuce, shredded

2 carrots, peeled and grated

300g cooked medium egg noodles

340g canned mandarin orange segments, drained

190g canned sliced water chestnuts, rinsed, drained and halved

2 tablespoons sesame seeds, toasted

If we need to go to our 'happy place', Lisa and I know exactly what to do. We crack open a few cans of syrupy mandarin slices. Sweet, cold and juicy, they transport us back to the cozy living room of our beloved grandparents in the Big Apple, to dreamy childhood visits and hours spent slurping from little glass bowls. Now, thanks to this mandarin-topped, Asian-dressed salad of crispy lettuce, grated carrots, water chestnuts and succulent soy-glazed chicken, we can easily slip into that bygone New York state of mind.

## METHOD

1) Preheat the oven to 220°/425°F/Gas Mark 7. Coat a 28 x 18cm baking dish with non-stick cooking spray. 2) For the chicken, in a medium bowl, toss the cubed chicken with the cornflour. 3) In a large frying pan, heat the vegetable oil over a medium heat. Add the chicken and cook, stirring, for about 5 minutes until lightly browned but not cooked through. Transfer the chicken to the baking dish. 4) For the sauce, in a small bowl, whisk the sugar, soy sauce, water, honey, cornflour and ginger together. Pour over the chicken. Bake, uncovered, for 18–20 minutes, stirring once halfway through baking. Remove from the oven and leave to cool to room temperature. 5) For the salad dressing, in a medium bowl, whisk the mayonnaise, rice vinegar, sugar, sesame oil and soy sauce together. Cover and chill until ready to use. 6) For the salad, spread the shredded lettuce on a large platter. Add the carrots, noodles, mandarins and water chestnuts and sprinkle with the sesame seeds. Place the soy chicken in the centre and drizzle the entire salad with the dressing.

Serves 6–8

**BITE ME BIT**

'I'm the coleslaw king of the world.'

– Rob Geller (actor David Arquette) in
the 1999 movie **Never Been Kissed**

# APPEL KOOLSLA (transl. APPLE COLESLAW)

## INGREDIENTS

### Spiced Pecans

180g pecan halves

2 tablespoons soft light brown sugar

1 tablespoon melted butter

1 teaspoon Worcestershire sauce

¼ teaspoon sea salt

⅛ teaspoon garlic powder

### Dressing

2 tablespoons rice vinegar

1 tablespoon apple cider vinegar

1 teaspoon Dijon mustard

1 teaspoon sugar

¼ teaspoon sea salt

4 tablespoons olive oil

2 Granny Smith apples, peeled, cored and cubed

1 tablespoon freshly squeezed lemon juice

270g Chinese cabbage, thinly sliced

270g red cabbage, thinly sliced

160g dried cherries or dried cranberries

1 mango, stoned, peeled and cut into 1cm cubes

I tip my hat to the Dutch. Love their cheese, tulips and the way they make the uninviting word 'COLE-slaw' sound appetising. Pleasant to the ear and pleasing to the palate, this salad isn't your traditional limp, fluorescent mush – it's a sweet, tart and crunchy combo of apples, mango and spiced pecans tossed in a tangy vinaigrette. I'd say 'smakelijk eten' but 'bon appétit' sounds better.

## METHOD

**1)** Preheat the oven to 180°C/350°F/Gas Mark 4. **2)** For the pecans, in a large bowl, combine the pecan nuts, sugar, butter, Worcestershire sauce, salt and garlic powder. Mix well. Spread the mixture on a baking sheet and bake for 12–15 minutes, stirring every 5 minutes, until lightly toasted. Set aside and leave to cool completely. **3)** For the dressing, in a small bowl, whisk the rice vinegar, cider vinegar, mustard, sugar and salt together. Gradually whisk in the oil. **4)** In a large bowl, toss the apples with the lemon juice. Add the cabbage, mango and dried fruit to the apples. Mix with the dressing, cover and and chill for 30 minutes before serving to allow the flavours to blend. Add the spiced pecans just before serving.

Serves 6–8

# CHINESE CHICKEN SALAD with CRUNCHY NOODLES

## INGREDIENTS

### Peanut Butter Chicken

non-stick cooking spray

6 boneless, skinless chicken breasts, cubed

65g smooth peanut butter

4 tablespoons soy sauce

1 tablespoon runny honey

1 tablespoon sesame oil

½ teaspoon grated fresh ginger

### Hoisin Peanut Dressing

6 tablespoons hoisin sauce

4 tablespoons rice vinegar

4 tablespoons soft brown sugar

65g smooth peanut butter

1 tablespoon sesame oil

1 teaspoon grated fresh ginger

### Crunchy Noodles

85g dried ramen noodles, crushed

85g flaked almonds

15g butter, melted

200g mangetout, trimmed and cut on the diagonal

180g peeled and grated carrots

225g sweetcorn kernels

650g iceberg lettuce, shredded

Chinese chicken salad wasn't the glorious creation of a steamed-out Shanghai kitchen – it came from big box, suburban restaurant chains that keep you waiting hours to eat their gooey food. That doesn't mean we don't like them, but let's just say this, our homemade healthful rendition – a towering salad topped with peanuty chicken, crunchy baked noodles and golden almonds tossed in a sweet hoisin dressing – beats a trip to the mall any day.

## METHOD

1) For the chicken, preheat the oven to 180°C/350°F/Gas Mark 4. Coat a 28 x 23cm baking dish with non-stick cooking spray. Place the chicken in the baking dish. 2) In a small bowl, whisk the peanut butter, soy sauce, honey, oil and ginger together. Pour over the chicken and bake for 25 minutes or until cooked through. Remove from the oven and cool to room temperature before adding to the salad. 3) For the dressing, in a medium bowl, whisk the hoisin, rice vinegar, sugar, peanut butter, sesame oil and ginger together. Set aside. 4) For the crunchy noodles, preheat the oven to 180°C/350°F/Gas Mark 4 and line a baking sheet with foil. In a small bowl, toss the ramen noodles, flaked almonds and melted butter until evenly coated. Spread the mixture on the prepared baking sheet and bake for 8 minutes or until toasted. Remove from the oven and cool. 5) Fill a medium saucepan with water and bring to the boil over a high heat. Add the mangetout, turn off the heat and cover for 3 minutes. Drain the mangetout and rinse under cold water to prevent further cooking. Drain and set aside. 6) On a large platter, top the lettuce with the mangetout, carrots and sweetcorn. Pile the chicken in the centre. Scatter the noodle mixture on top, drizzle with the dressing and serve.

Serves 8

# BROCCOLI, GRAPE and CRANBERRY SALAD

## INGREDIENTS

2 large heads broccoli, chopped into small florets

240g seedless red or green grapes, halved

120g celery, chopped

160g dried cranberries

30g salted sunflower seeds

### Dressing

150g mayonnaise

125ml soured cream

5 tablespoons sugar

2 tablespoons white wine vinegar

'Raw? Broccoli? Salad?' my husband asked as I set down his plate. 'I might not be an ex-Prez, but if George Bush doesn't have to eat broccoli, neither do I.' He was skeptical and I couldn't really blame the guy – he's not a vegetable lover and, to his ears, this sounded like spa food. But, one bite of this creamy, crispy, sweet, sour and salty broccoli salad was all it took to make him a believer.

## METHOD

1) In a large bowl, combine the uncooked broccoli, grapes, celery, cranberries and sunflower seeds. Set aside. 2) For the dressing, in a medium bowl, whisk the mayonnaise, soured cream, sugar and vinegar together. Pour the dressing over the broccoli mixture and mix well. Cover and refrigerate the salad for at least 1 hour before serving.

Serves 6–8

## BITE ME BIT

'Beulah, peel me a grape.'

– Tira (actress Mae West) in the 1933 movie **I'm No Angel**

# PITTA in SALAD!

## INGREDIENTS

non-stick cooking spray

3 large pittas, cut into 2.5cm pieces

1 tablespoon olive oil

½ teaspoon sea salt

1 cucumber, peeled, deseeded and chopped

4 large tomatoes, deseeded and chopped

1 large green pepper, deseeded and chopped

2 tablespoons chopped flat-leaf parsley

2 tablespoons chopped mint

### Dressing

4 tablespoons freshly squeezed lemon juice

75ml olive oil

1 large garlic clove, finely chopped

½ teaspoon sea salt

¼ teaspoon freshly ground black pepper

Oh pitta! Oh pitta! You are so nice.
A lovely pocket of paradise!
Say! Let's add, add, add in some more.
Veggies and herbs will make you soar!
Up! Up! Up! You go.
A refreshing salad for all to love so!
Gather Flummox, Horton and even the Grinch,
This savoury salad to make is a cinch!

## METHOD

**1)** Preheat the oven to 180°C/350°F/Gas Mark 4. Coat a baking sheet with non-stick cooking spray. **2)** In a medium bowl, toss the pitta pieces with the oil and salt. Spread on the prepared baking sheet and bake for 10–15 minutes until crisp. Set aside and leave to cool. **3)** In a large bowl, toss the cucumbers, tomatoes, green pepper, parsley and mint together. **4)** For the dressing, in a small bowl, whisk the lemon juice, oil, garlic, salt and pepper together. **5)** Just before serving, toss the cucumber-tomato mixture with the dressing. Gently add the toasted pitta and leave to stand for 5–10 minutes to allow the flavours to blend. Season with extra salt to taste.

Serves 8

## BITE ME BIT

'Three tomatoes are walking down the street – a papa tomato, a mama tomato and a little baby tomato. Baby tomato starts lagging behind. Papa tomato gets angry, goes over to Baby tomato and squishes him... and says "Ketchup!"'

– Mia Wallace (actress Uma Thurman) in the 1994 movie **Pulp Fiction**

# MEDITERRANEAN POTATO SALAD

## INGREDIENTS

6 red potatoes, skin on, cubed

2 tablespoons white wine vinegar

225ml soured cream

115g mayonnaise

2 tablespoons olive oil

2 tablespoons finely chopped dill

1 tablespoon capers, rinsed and drained

1 teaspoon dried oregano

½ teaspoon sea salt

135g feta cheese, crumbled

90g Kalamata olives, pitted and halved

Lisa: Potato salad. Red or white? Hot or cold? Mayo or vinegar?

Julie: Why? Are you taking a survey?

Lisa: Pay attention. Potato salad. How do you like it?

Julie: Well, duh, with potatoes.

Lisa: Argh. Forget you – I'm doing my own spin with dill, capers, feta and Kalamata olives.

Julie: But will it have spuds?

Lisa: #@$%!

## METHOD

1) In a large saucepan, cover the potatoes with cold water and bring to the boil over a high heat. Cook for about 15 minutes until just tender. Drain the potatoes and place in a large bowl. Sprinkle with the vinegar and leave to cool. 2) In a medium bowl, combine the soured cream, mayonnaise, olive oil, dill, capers, oregano and salt. Stir in the feta cheese. Gently fold the mixture into the potatoes. Cover and chill for at least 2 hours. Add the olives just before serving.

Serves 6

# CHOPPED GREEK SALAD

## INGREDIENTS

4 large tomatoes,
deseeded and chopped

1 cucumber, peeled,
deseeded and chopped

1 large red pepper,
deseeded and chopped

1 large green pepper,
deseeded and chopped

2 tablespoons finely
chopped mint

1 teaspoon dried oregano

3 tablespoons olive oil

2 tablespoons red wine vinegar

¼ teaspoon sea salt

¼ teaspoon freshly
ground black pepper

100g feta cheese, crumbled

45g Kalamata olives, pitted

Here are a few tips I've gleaned from long nights spent doing 'research' in authentic Greek restaurants – a booze-o-ouzo hangover is epic and it's super-fun to yell Opa! for everything from a plate of flaming cheese to a Mouskouri medley. But here's something I learned the hard way: never ask, 'Where's the lettuce?' A few raised eyebrows and tongue-clicks later, I was informed leafy greens are taboo in Greek salad. We left them out, but I sure hope there's no rule against using fresh mint along with the sweet tomatoes, crisp cucumbers, tangy feta and Kalamata olives...

## METHOD

1) In a large bowl, combine the tomatoes, cucumbers, red and green peppers, mint and oregano. 2) In a small bowl, whisk the oil, vinegar, salt and pepper together. Pour over the salad ingredients and toss to coat. Cover and leave to stand for 30 minutes to allow the flavours to blend. 3) Before serving, stir in the feta and olives.

Serves 4–6

## BITE ME BIT

'There are two kinds of people – Greeks, and everyone else who wish they was Greek.'

– Gus Portokalos (actor Michael Constantine) in the 2002 movie **My Big Fat Greek Wedding**

# JULIE'S TABBOULEH

## INGREDIENTS

700ml water

210g bulgar wheat

240g canned chickpeas,
rinsed and drained

3 tablespoons olive oil

1 teaspoon ground cumin

135g feta cheese, crumbled

3 large tomatoes,
deseeded and diced

1 cucumber, peeled,
deseeded and diced

4 tablespoons oil-packed
sun-dried tomatoes,
drained and finely chopped

2 tablespoons freshly
squeezed lemon juice

2 tablespoons chopped
flat-leaf parsley

2 tablespoons chopped mint

½ teaspoon sea salt

¼ teaspoon freshly
ground black pepper

I'm Julie and this is my tabbouleh. It rhymes with my name coolly. A classic Middle Eastern salad I love truly. Adding sun-dried tomatoes and feta makes it newly. Unruly!

## METHOD

1) In a small saucepan, bring the lightly salted water to the boil. Place the bulgar wheat in a heatproof bowl and cover with the boiling water. Leave to stand at room temperature for 30 minutes. If there is any remaining water, drain the bulgar in a fine-mesh sieve, pushing out the excess liquid. 2) In a large mixing bowl, combine the bulgar, chickpeas, olive oil and cumin. Stir in the feta, tomatoes, cucumber, sun-dried tomatoes, lemon juice, parsley, mint, salt and pepper. Leave to stand for 10 minutes for the flavours to combine. Serve at room temperature.

Serves 6–8

## BITE ME BIT

'Julie, Julie, Julie, do ya love me?
Julie, Julie, Julie, do ya care?
Julie, Julie, are ya thinking of me?
Julie, Julie will ya still be there?'

– 1970 Bobby Sherman song
'Julie, Do Ya Love Me'

# ISRAELI COUSCOUS SALAD with ROASTED VEGETABLES

## INGREDIENTS

### Roasted Vegetables

non-stick cooking spray

280g peeled, deseeded and cubed butternut squash

2 large red peppers, deseeded and diced

2 small courgettes, diced

360g canned chickpeas, rinsed and drained

2 tablespoons olive oil

1 tablespoon balsamic vinegar

1 large garlic clove, finely chopped

1 teaspoon dried oregano

½ teaspoon sea salt

¼ teaspoon freshly ground black pepper

1 fresh rosemary sprig

### Couscous

15g butter

260g Israeli couscous

1 teaspoon finely grated lemon zest

700ml chicken stock

100g feta cheese, crumbled

3 tablespoons chopped mint

2 tablespoons olive oil

2 tablespoons balsamic vinegar

I read the papers every day. I know what's what in the Middle East. But let me tell you this, Jimmy Carter, Shimon Peres and King Abdullah – you want lasting peace in the region? Forget your summits, negotiators, and Nobel Prizes. We know what could bring these feuding Biblical brothers to the table. Couscous. Israeli couscous. Its chewy goodness, nutty taste – combined with the sweetness of its roasted vegetables, fragrant mint, crumbled feta – make this salad a perfect mate for either chicken or fish. Now, when do we fly to Stockholm and collect our award?

## METHOD

1) For the roasted vegetables, preheat the oven to 230°C/450°F/Gas Mark 8. Coat a large baking sheet with non-stick cooking spray. 2) In a large bowl, combine the squash, red peppers, courgettes and drained chickpeas. Toss with the oil, balsamic vinegar, garlic, oregano, salt and pepper. Spread the vegetable mixture on the prepared baking sheet and lay the rosemary sprig in the centre. Roast for 30–35 minutes or until the vegetables are tender and browned, stirring every 10 minutes. Remove the rosemary and set the vegetables aside. 3) For the couscous, in a large saucepan, melt the butter over a medium-high heat. Add the couscous and lemon zest and sauté for 2 minutes. Add the stock and bring to the boil. Reduce the heat to medium-low and cook, uncovered, for 10–12 minutes until the couscous is tender. Strain the excess liquid and set aside. 4) In a large bowl, stir the roasted vegetables, cooked couscous, feta, mint, oil and balsamic vinegar together. Serve at room temperature or cover and refrigerate for 2–8 hours.

Serves 6–8

## INGREDIENTS

non-stick cooking spray

3 courgettes, cubed

2 red peppers, deseeded and cubed

1 yellow pepper, deseeded and cubed

1 aubergine, peeled and cubed

2 tablespoons olive oil

½ teaspoon sea salt

¼ teaspoon freshly ground black pepper

350g dried fusilli pasta

90g semi-soft Asiago cheese, coarsely grated

3 tablespoons olive oil

2 tablespoons white wine vinegar

2 tablespoons finely chopped oregano

2 tablespoons chopped rehydrated sun-dried tomatoes

# SHAZAM! VEGETABLE PASTA SALAD with ASIAGO CHEESE

## METHOD

**1)** Preheat the oven to 220°C/425°F/Gas Mark 7. Line a baking sheet with foil and coat with non-stick cooking spray. **2)** In a medium bowl, toss the courgettes, red peppers, yellow peppers, aubergine, olive oil, salt and pepper together. Transfer to the prepared baking sheet. Roast in the oven for 20–25 minutes, stirring occasionally, until lightly browned. Remove from the oven and leave to cool slightly. **3)** Bring a large saucepan of lightly salted water to the boil. Add the fusilli and cook for about 12 minutes until just tender. Drain and place in a large bowl. Add the roasted vegetables, Asiago cheese, olive oil, vinegar, oregano and sun-dried tomatoes. Toss well to coat. Serve at room temperature or cover and chill.

Serves 6

# CREAMY PESTO PASTA SALAD

## INGREDIENTS

1 tablespoon sea salt

450g dried fusilli pasta

1 tablespoon olive oil

**Basil Pesto**

60g basil leaves

1 large garlic clove, peeled

60g pine nuts

1 teaspoon sea salt

¼ teaspoon freshly ground black pepper

125ml olive oil

115g Parmesan cheese, freshly grated, plus extra to serve (optional)

55g mayonnaise

1 tablespoon freshly squeezed lemon juice

Basil is known as the 'King of Herbs'. But garlic, the so-called 'Stinking Rose', is a lowly clove. Who'd ever think the two would get along so well? My Cuisinart, that's who.

## METHOD

**1)** For the pasta, bring a large saucepan of water to the boil. Add the salt and pasta and cook for about 12 minutes until just tender. Drain well and toss with the oil. Leave to cool to room temperature while preparing the pesto. **2)** For the pesto, wash the basil, discard the stems and dry thoroughly. Set aside.

**3)** Place the garlic, pine nuts, salt and pepper in a food processor. Process for 10 seconds to chop the garlic. Add the basil leaves and pulse 4–5 times to finely chop the basil. Scrape down the side of the bowl. With the machine running, slowly pour in the oil in a steady stream until the mixture is smooth. Add the Parmesan, mayonnaise and lemon juice and process just until incorporated.

**4)** Transfer the pesto to a large serving bowl and toss with the cooled pasta. Serve with additional Parmesan if desired.

Serves 8

## BITE ME BIT

**Eli:** I always wanted to be a Tenenbaum.

**Royal:** Me too, me too.

– from the 2001 movie **The Royal Tenenbaums**

### BITE ME BIT

In Ancient Greece, basil was linked to profanity and insanity. We know a few folks who should lay off the @#$%ing herb.

# CAPRESE ORZO SALAD

## INGREDIENTS

300g cherry tomatoes, halved

200g pearl (bite-sized balls) bocconcini cheese

6 tablespoons olive oil

4 tablespoons chopped fresh basil

1 small garlic clove, finely chopped

1½ teaspoons sea salt

¼ teaspoon freshly ground black pepper

250g dried orzo pasta

We can read our Dad like a book. A bright smile says he won his tennis game. Crossed arms tell us he's starving. Thumb and index finger spread an inch apart, we know he's quizzing the waiter about the firmness of the Caprese salad's tomatoes. We get it – the Italian classic isn't salvageable with mealy, tasteless tomatoes – and that's why this orzo pasta salad hits all the high notes by using year-round juicy and flavourful cherry tomatoes, melt-in-your-mouth bocconcini and slivers of chopped sweet basil. One bite and our Dad started tapping his toe – that's his food-lovers' happy-dance.

## METHOD

1) In a medium bowl, gently stir together the tomatoes, bocconcini, 4 tablespoons olive oil, basil, garlic, salt and pepper. Leave to stand at room temperature for 1 hour to allow the flavours to blend. 2) For the orzo, bring a medium saucepan of water to the boil over a high heat. Add the pasta and cook until just tender. Drain well, place in a large bowl and leave to cool for 20 minutes. 3) Add the remaining 2 tablespoons olive oil and the tomato mixture to the orzo and toss to coat.

Serves 6

# Respect
# me

**Vegetables You'll Still
Love the Next Day**

# CRISPY BAKED COURGETTE CHIPS

## INGREDIENTS

non-stick cooking spray

4 tablespoons milk

85g Parmesan cheese, freshly grated

70g dry breadcrumbs

½ teaspoon sea salt, plus extra for sprinkling

⅛ teaspoon freshly ground black pepper

4 large courgettes, sliced into 5mm thick rounds

Do you always fall for the 'bad boy' greaser? Y'know, the slick bar fly who draws you in and keeps you coming back for more? Don't get duped again – it's time for a healthy relationship with the 'nice guy', the oven chip.

## METHOD

1) Preheat the oven to 220°C/425°F./Gas Mark 7 Line a baking sheet with foil and coat with non-stick cooking spray. 2) For the chips, pour the milk into a small bowl. In a medium bowl, combine the Parmesan, breadcrumbs, salt and pepper. Working with one at a time, dip the courgette rounds in the milk and then coat in the Parmesan mixture. 3) Lay the crusted slices on the prepared baking sheet and bake for 20 minutes. Flip the courgette rounds and continue to bake another 10 minutes. Sprinkle with sea salt and serve.

Serves 4–6

### BITE ME BIT

**Solange:**...Why can't nice guys be more like you?

**James Bond:** Because then they'd be bad.

– from the 2006 movie **Casino Royale**

# CLEVER CARAMELISED CAULIFLOWER

## INGREDIENTS

1 large head cauliflower, about 1.3kg

1 tablespoon sugar

½ teaspoon sea salt

¼ teaspoon freshly ground black pepper

¼ teaspoon ground cinnamon

⅛ teaspoon paprika

⅛ teaspoon ground cumin

⅛ teaspoon cayenne pepper

35g butter, melted

I feel for Mark Twain. At the mention of cauliflower, food writers inevitably blast the literary icon for his slandering the veggie as 'nothing but cabbage with a college education'. Surely he didn't mean to disparage the snowy white heads. When roasted, cauliflower is transformed into an elegant, sweet and tender side dish – a truly brilliant veggie with a PhD in Gastronomy.

## METHOD

1) Preheat the oven to 240°C/475°F/Gas Mark 9. 2) Break the cauliflower apart into large florets and cut off the thicker stems. Place the cauliflower in a single layer in a roasting tin or on a baking sheet. 3) In a small bowl, stir the sugar, salt, pepper, cinnamon, paprika, cumin and cayenne pepper together. 4) Drizzle the melted butter over the cauliflower and sprinkle with the combined spices until evenly coated. Place in the oven and bake for 18–20 minutes, stirring halfway through cooking. Remove from the oven when the cauliflower is tender-crisp and lightly browned around the edges. Serve immediately.

Serves 6–8

# OASTED-RAY EGETABLES-VAY with PECANS and PARMESAN

## INGREDIENTS

900g sweet potatoes, peeled and cubed

450g carrots, peeled and cubed

450g parsnips, peeled and cubed

3 tablespoons olive oil

1 teaspoon sea salt

¼ teaspoon freshly ground black pepper

**Pecan Parmesan Topping**

120g pecan nuts, chopped

40g Parmesan cheese, freshly grated

3 tablespoons finely chopped flat-leaf parsley

1 tablespoon freshly squeezed lemon juice

1 tablespoon finely grated lemon zest

1 tablespoon olive oil

An encoded message for those of you who need to camouflage egetables-vay:

Es-yay. Ese-thay are-way egetables-vay. Ook-lay under-way e-thay uttery-bay ecans-pay and-way ich-ray armesan-pay. Ut-bay on't-day orry-way. O-nay one-way ill-way ever-way ink-thay ese-thay eet-sway oasted-ray egetables-vay are-way actually-way ealthy-hay...ey-thay aste-tay oo-tay ood-gay!

## METHOD

**1)** Preheat the oven to 220°C/425°F/Gas Mark 7. Line a large baking sheet with foil. **2)** In a large bowl, toss the sweet potatoes, carrots and parsnips with the oil. Transfer to the prepared baking sheet and sprinkle with the salt and pepper. Roast the vegetables, stirring often, for 1 hour or until tender. Transfer to a serving plate. **3)** For the topping, in a small bowl, combine the pecans, Parmesan, parsley, lemon juice, lemon zest and oil. Sprinkle over the vegetables before serving.

Serves 6

# SWEET BALSAMIC ROASTED CARROTS

## INGREDIENTS

non-stick cooking spray

900g carrots, peeled and
cut into 5cm sticks
resembling French fries

25g butter

2 tablespoons soft
light brown sugar

1 teaspoon balsamic vinegar

½ teaspoon sea salt

¼ teaspoon freshly ground
black pepper

## METHOD

**1)** Preheat the oven to 230°C/450°F/Gas Mark 8. Line a baking sheet with foil and coat with non-stick cooking spray. **2)** In a small saucepan, melt the butter over a medium heat. Add the sugar and vinegar and heat, stirring to combine, just until the sugar melts. Remove from the heat. **3)** In a medium bowl, toss the cut carrot sticks with the brown sugar glaze, salt and pepper. Spread out on the prepared baking sheet in a single layer.
**4)** Bake for 15–20 minutes until the carrots are starting to brown on the bottom. Stirthe carrots and return to the oven for 5–10 minutes until they are caramelised and tender.

Serves 6

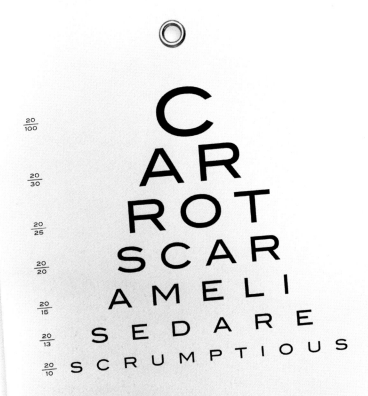

# PRALINE-TOPPED SWEET POTATO CASSEROLE

## INGREDIENTS

non-stick cooking spray

5 sweet potatoes, peeled and quartered

100g soft light brown sugar

1½ teaspoon vanilla extract

2 large egg whites, lightly beaten

125ml evaporated milk

### Streusel Topping

140g plain flour

130g soft light brown sugar

60g chopped pecan nuts, toasted

55g butter, melted

½ teaspoon ground cinnamon

2 teaspoons cinnamon sugar

Eureka! We've discovered the 32nd flavour! A scoop of this irresistible side dish – pillowy mashed sweet potatoes buried under a crunchy streusel topping – and you'll see why it belongs alongside Rocky Road and Mint Chocolate Chip. Enjoy the sweet satisfaction without the ice cream headache, but come Thanksgiving, look for our creation (Pilgrim Praline? Yummy Yam?) in the freezer cabinet.

## METHOD

1) Preheat the oven to 180°C/350°F/Gas Mark 4. Coat a 28 x 18cm baking dish with non-stick cooking spray. 2) Place the sweet potatoes in a large saucepan and cover with cold water. Bring to the boil over a high heat. Reduce the heat and simmer for 15–20 minutes or until very tender. Drain well, place in a large bowl and mash. 3) For the streusel topping, in a small bowl, combine the flour, sugar, pecans, butter and cinnamon. 4) Stir 140g of the streusel topping into the mashed sweet potatoes. Add the sugar, vanilla, egg whites and evaporated milk and stir to combine. Spoon into the prepared baking dish and sprinkle with the remaining topping and cinnamon sugar. Bake, uncovered, for 45 minutes.

Serves 8

## BITE ME BIT

'There's something about the ice cream truck that makes kids lose it. And they can hear that s**t from ten blocks away. They don't hear their mothers calling but they hear that mother-f***ing ice cream truck.'

– Eddie Murphy in the 1983 movie **Delirious**

## BITE ME BIT

'If you don't eat yer meat, you can't have any pudding. How can you have any pudding if you don't eat yer meat?'

– from the Pink Floyd song 'Another Brick in the Wall, Part II'

# ATOMIC #79 (4 letters) CARROT PUDDING with BROWN SUGAR DRIZZLE

## INGREDIENTS

### Carrot Pudding

non-stick cooking spray

115g butter, softened

100g soft light brown sugar

1 large egg

1 tablespoon freshly squeezed orange juice

1 teaspoon vanilla extract

175g plain flour

1 teaspoon baking powder

½ teaspoon bicarbonate of soda

½ teaspoon sea salt

½ teaspoon ground cinnamon

5–6 carrots, coarsely grated

### Brown Sugar Sauce

200g soft light brown sugar

1½ tablespoons cornflour

¼ teaspoon sea salt

225ml water

25g butter

1 teaspoon vanilla extract

New York Times crosswords are my religion and editor Will Shortz is my deity. My day isn't complete without his puzzle, and a meal isn't whole until I've eaten a dessert-like side dish alongside a main course of chicken, meat or fish. Here are a few clues that reminded me that the proof is in the ____(7).

1. It's said that Howard Hughes measured every one he ate. (6)
2. Heroin manufactured illicitly in Mexico. (10)
3. To overwhelm with brilliance. (6)
4. Cannelle, fr. (8)
5. Colour skin turns after a spray-on tan (6)

## METHOD

1) For the carrot pudding, preheat the oven to 180°C/350°F/Gas Mark 4. Coat a 20cm round or square baking dish with non-stick cooking spray. 2) In an electric mixer, cream the butter with the sugar on medium-high speed until light and fluffy. Add the egg, orange juice and vanilla and mix well. 3) In a medium bowl, sift the flour, baking powder, bicarbonate of soda, salt and cinnamon together. Add the flour mixture and grated carrots to the butter-sugar mixture. Mix just until the flour disappears, making sure not to overmix. Transfer to the prepared baking dish. Bake for 32–35 minutes or until golden around the edges. 4) For the brown sugar sauce, in a medium saucepan, whisk the sugar, cornflour and salt together. Whisk in the water and bring to the boil over a high heat. Reduce the heat to medium and cook, whisking constantly, for 4–6 minutes until the sauce is smooth and has thickened slightly. Remove from heat and whisk in the butter and vanilla. Serve drizzled over pieces of the pudding.

Serves 6–8

Dear Auntie Em —

I was following this yellow brick road forever. While Toto nibbled on my shoes, I was ravenous. At first, this dim scarecrow flung a squash at me. I'm like, ding-dong, I can't eat it like that! Kept walking and met up with a tin man who tossed me some melted margarine, told me to oil him and then I could have the leftovers. NO THANKS! Muddled on until we bumped into some fraidy cat who was busy tossing salt over his shoulder. What a wuss! Anyway, dragged them all along until we got to this place called Munchkinland. So welcoming! Lollipop Guild took all the ingredients, poured in some sugar and spice, and cheerfully whipped up a delectable butternut squash casserole topped with crumbled vanilla wafers.

Over the rainbow rocks! Not coming home.

XOXO, Dorothy

## INGREDIENTS

non-stick cooking spray

840g peeled, deseeded and cubed butternut squash

225ml milk

100g sugar

35g butter, melted

2 tablespoons plain flour

1 teaspoon vanilla extract

½ teaspoon ground cinnamon

¼ teaspoon sea salt

2 large eggs, lightly beaten

**Vanilla Biscuit Topping**

460g vanilla-flavoured or plain biscuits, coarsely crushed

150g soft light brown sugar

85g butter, melted

# SWEET SQUASH and VANILLA BISCUIT CASSEROLE, OH MY!

## METHOD

**1)** Preheat the oven to 220°C/425°F/Gas Mark 7. Coat a 33 x 23cm baking dish with non-stick cooking spray. **2)** In a large saucepan, cover the butternut squash with cold water. Bring to the boil over a high heat, reduce the heat to medium and continue to boil for about 15 minutes until tender. Drain well. **3)** Place in a large bowl and mash until smooth. Add the milk, sugar, butter, flour, vanilla, cinnamon, salt and eggs and stir well. Transfer the mixture to the prepared baking dish and bake for 45 minutes. **4)** For the topping, in a medium bowl, combine the crushed biscuits, sugar and butter. Sprinkle over the baked casserole and return to the oven for 5 minutes until lightly browned.

Serves 8

# SOUTHWESTERN SWEET POTATO FRIES

## INGREDIENTS

2 large egg whites

2 tablespoons olive oil

freshly squeezed juice of 1 lime

1 teaspoon sugar

1 teaspoon ground cumin

½ teaspoon chilli powder

½ teaspoon sea salt

¼ teaspoon freshly ground black pepper

900g (about 4) sweet potatoes, peeled and cut lengthways into 1cm thick strips

**Creamy Lemon Dip**

115g mayonnaise

2 teaspoons freshly squeezed lemon juice

1 teaspoon finely grated lemon zest

1 teaspoon chopped thyme

¼ teaspoon sea salt

Welcome Small Fry!

It is with great joy that Lisa and Julie announce the birth of their healthy little fry. Weighing in at a light 2lb, or 900g, she was born perfectly crisp on the outside and creamy on the inside. This Tex-Mex tuber is welcomed with open mouths by proud grandparents, Mr and Mrs M Piper and Dr and Mrs K Edwards.

## METHOD

**1)** Preheat the oven to 220°C/425°F/Gas Mark 7. Line a large baking sheet with baking paper. **2)** In a large bowl, whisk the egg whites until frothy. Whisk in the oil, lime juice, sugar, cumin, chilli powder, salt and pepper. Add the sweet potatoes, tossing to coat. Spread the potatoes in a single layer on the prepared baking sheet and roast them in the oven for 20 minutes or until golden on the bottom. Turn the potatoes over and continue to bake for a further 15 minutes or until golden brown all over. **3)** In a small bowl, whisk all the ingredients for the dip together. Serve with the baked sweet potato fries.

Serves 4

# DOUBLE-STUFFED BAKED POTATOES

## INGREDIENTS

6 large baking potatoes

475ml soured cream

60g Cheddar cheese, coarsely grated

55g butter, softened

½ teaspoon sea salt

¼ teaspoon freshly ground black pepper

30g Parmesan cheese, freshly grated

We challenge any dastardly critic of the poor, maligned tuber to refuse this decadent spud. Baked to perfection, its ivory insides have been scooped out, mashed with butter, cheese and soured cream and baked until golden brown beauties emerge.

## METHOD

1) Preheat the oven to 200°C/400°F/Gas Mark 6. 2) Scrub each potato and pat dry. Use a fork to pierce each potato in several places. Bake the potatoes directly on the oven shelf for 50–60 minutes or until tender and easily pierced with the tip of a knife. 3) Remove from oven and cut the potatoes in half lengthways. Using a small spoon, carefully (don't go too deep or you'll rip the skins) scoop out the flesh from inside the potatoes and place in a medium bowl. 4) Line a baking sheet with foil. Arrange the potato shells on the baking sheet and return to the oven for about 10 minutes until they are slightly crisp. Meanwhile, using a potato masher or fork, mash the potato flesh and stir in the soured cream, Cheddar, butter, salt and pepper. 5) Spoon the potato mixture back into the potato shells, mounding them high, and sprinkle each potato with the Parmesan. Bake for 15 minutes.

Serves 8–10

## BITE ME BIT

In 1987, due to pressure from anti-smoking groups, Mr Potato Head's signature pipe was yanked from his mouth and running shoes were stuck on his feet. In his next incarnation, he'll be carrying a yoga mat.

# STEAKHOME CREAMED SPINACH

## INGREDIENTS

non-stick cooking spray

1.1kg frozen chopped spinach

350g full-fat soft cheese

55g butter, melted

½ teaspoon sea salt

¼ teaspoon freshly ground black pepper

2 tablespoons freshly grated Parmesan cheese

Among the mahogany walls and dirty martinis, something great is happening in swanky steakhouses across the nation...carnivores are eating spinach. A simple side dish that seems healthy next to fried hash browns and marbled rib-eyes, the overly creamy restaurant version is still too flaccid and watery for our taste. Using cream cheese, our easy, silky smooth spinach brings home all the taste of the upscale steakhouse without the £10 side-dish robbery and the velvet banquettes.

## METHOD

**1)** Preheat oven to 180°C/350°F/Gas Mark 4. Coat a 28 x 18cm baking dish with non-stick cooking spray. **2)** Defrost the spinach according to the packet instructions. Drain very well, squeezing to ensure that all the excess liquid is removed. **3)** Place the cream cheese, melted butter, salt, pepper and spinach in a food processor. Process for 10 seconds. Using a rubber spatula, scrape down the side of the bowl and do 3–4 quick pulses to combine. **4)** Transfer to the prepared baking dish, sprinkle the top with the Parmesan and bake, uncovered, for 20 minutes.

Serves 8

## BITE ME BIT

'Did you ever see the customers in health-food stores? They are pale, skinny people who look half dead. In a steakhouse you see robust, ruddy people. They're dying, of course, but they look terrific.'

– Bill Cosby, comedian

# SHOWDOWN CHILlI with CORNBREAD MUFFINS

## INGREDIENTS

### Vegetarian Chilli

1 tablespoon olive oil

1 red onion, chopped

1 tablespoon chilli powder

1 teaspoon dried oregano

1 teaspoon ground cumin

½ teaspoon sea salt

½ teaspoon freshly ground black pepper

2 large red peppers, deseeded and chopped

115g button mushrooms, sliced

1 carrot, peeled and chopped

1 garlic clove, finely chopped

2–3 green chillies, deseeded (for less heat) and finely chopped

2 x 400g cans chopped tomatoes

520g canned black beans, rinsed and drained

420g canned chickpeas, rinsed and drained

375g canned red kidney beans, rinsed and drained

225g mild salsa

225ml vegetable stock

90g couscous

1 tablespoon cocoa powder, sifted

1 teaspoon soft light brown sugar

¼ teaspoon cayenne pepper

150g frozen sweetcorn, defrosted

coarsely grated Cheddar cheese, for topping

11:59am, Main Street

His clickin' spurs announce him before he throws open the saloon doors.

'I'm hungry as a buzzard. Don't want no eggs or mutton. Got that, woman?' he bellows as he fingers his six-shooter.

'First, I ain't your woman and second, I'm standin' right here,' she replies. 'Don't gotta' yell. Think you comin' in here, smellin' of gunpowder, scares me? Now just sit down.'

She slides a bowl of her bean-filled-vegetable-packed chili down the bar. Next, she tosses him a few of her tasty, moist, cornbread muffins.

'I. Said. No. Meat,' he growls after eatin' a big spoonful. At that, he reaches for his holster, but he ain't no match for her quick draw – she points her Colt at him.

'Tastes. Meaty. Just. Vegetables,' she hisses before pulling the trigger. 'Dumber than a bag o' bricks.'

## METHOD

### THE CHILLI

1) In a large saucepan, heat the oil over a medium heat. Add the onion, chilli powder, oregano, cumin, salt and pepper. Cook for about 5 minutes until the onion is tender. Add the red peppers, mushrooms, carrot, garlic and chillies. Cook for a further 5 minutes, stirring occasionally. Stir in the tomatoes and their juice, black beans, chickpeas, kidney beans, salsa, stock, couscous, cocoa powder, sugar and cayenne pepper. 2) Bring to the boil over a high heat. Reduce the heat to low, cover and simmer gently for 40 minutes, stirring occasionally. Stir in the sweetcorn and cook for 5 minutes. Serve in bowls, topped with the cheese.

### Mini Cornbread Muffins

non-stick cooking spray

75g frozen sweetcorn, defrosted

140g plain flour

115g polenta

1 tablespoon baking powder

1 teaspoon sea salt

pinch of cayenne pepper

115g butter, melted

100g sugar

85g runny honey

1 large egg

½ teaspoon vanilla extract

225ml buttermilk

65g roasted red peppers, patted dry and finely diced

## THE MUFFINS

**1)** Preheat the oven to 200°C/400°F/Gas Mark 6. Coat the cups of 2 x 24-cup or 3 x 12-cup mini muffin tins with non-stick cooking spray. **2)** Place the defrosted sweetcorn on a plate. Pat dry and set aside. **3)** In a large bowl, combine the flour, polenta, baking powder, salt and cayenne pepper. **4)** In a small bowl, whisk the melted butter, sugar, honey, egg, vanilla and buttermilk together. **5)** Add butter mixture, roasted red peppers and sweetcorn to the dry ingredients. Stir gently to combine, just until the flour disappears. Spoon the mixture into the prepared muffin cups, filling to the top. Bake for 10 minutes. Leave to cool for 5 minutes before removing from the tins to a wire rack. Serve the muffins alongside the chilli.

Makes: 30–35 mini muffins

## BITE ME BIT

'Chili represents your three stages of matter: solid, liquid and eventually gas.'

— Dan Conner (actor John Goodman) on the television series **Roseanne**

ShucKed

# BOUNTIFUL CORN PUDDING

## INGREDIENTS

non-stick cooking spray

190g polenta 1 litre full-fat milk

½ teaspoon sea salt

75g butter

300g fresh sweetcorn kernels
(from 3–4 corn cobs)

2 teaspoons sugar

½ teaspoon sea salt

⅛ teaspoon cayenne pepper

3 large egg yolks

3 large egg whites

¼ teaspoon cream of tartar

Sing to the tune of 'Three Blind Mice'*

**Fresh-shucked corn, fresh-shucked corn,
I love to say shuck, I love to say shuck**

**It is like saying a few words at once
So naughty yet nice a curser's delight
Did you ever hear such a wonderful sound
As shuck, shuck, shuck, shuck, shuck, shuck**

*for extra fun, sing it in rounds

## METHOD

**1)** Preheat the oven to 190°C/375°F/Gas Mark 5. Coat a 20cm square baking dish with non-stick cooking spray. **2)** Separate the egg yolks into a small bowl and the egg whites into the bowl of an electric mixer. Set both aside. **3)** In a large saucepan, whisk the polenta, milk and salt over a medium heat. Bring the mixture to the boil, whisking constantly, and cook for about 3 minutes until the mixture begins to thicken. Reduce the heat to low and cook, stirring frequently, for 5 minutes until the mixture is very thick. Remove from the heat and transfer to a large bowl. Leave to cool to room temperature (about 20 minutes). **4)** Meanwhile, in a large frying pan, melt the butter over a medium heat. Add the sweetcorn kernels, sugar, salt and cayenne and sauté for 5 minutes. Transfer to a food processor and process for about 10 seconds until the sweetcorn kernels are chopped. **5)** Once the polenta mixture has cooled, stir in the sweetcorn and egg yolks until well combined. **6)** Using an electric mixer with the whisk attachment, beat the egg whites and cream of tartar on high speed until stiff peaks form. Doing half at a time, gently fold the egg whites into the polenta mixture. Spread the mixture into the prepared dish and bake 30–35 minutes until the pudding is puffed and the top is golden. Serve immediately.

Serves 6–8

# MASTERFUL MUSHROOM and FETA BREAD PUDDING

## INGREDIENTS

non-stick cooking spray

3 tablespoons chopped flat-leaf parsley

1 tablespoon chopped oregano

1 teaspoon chopped thyme

1 teaspoon finely grated lemon zest

1 large garlic clove, finely chopped

1 tablespoon olive oil

450g assorted mushrooms (chestnut, shiitake, button, portobello), thinly sliced

120g celery, chopped

½ teaspoon sea salt

¼ teaspoon freshly ground black pepper

260g roasted red peppers, chopped

4 large eggs, lightly beaten

600ml milk

270g feta cheese, crumbled

1½ egg breads (challahs), crusts removed and cut into 2.5cm cubes

Ladies and Gentlemen, the taking of photos inside the museum is strictly prohibited. Please, follow me...here on your left, is a work of true genius. Breathtaking, isn't it? Notice how the brilliant green herbs mingle with the sautéed mushrooms and the ruby red peppers are interwoven throughout. Such style and technique. Admire the genius of contrasting sweet egg bread and tangy feta...the balance...perfection. Now, moving on, let us examine the apples painted by a Frenchman named Cézanne. Not as inspiring, wouldn't you agree?

## METHOD

1) Preheat the oven to 180°C/350°F/Gas Mark 4. Coat a 33 x 23cm baking dish with non-stick cooking spray. 2) In a small bowl, combine the parsley, oregano, thyme, lemon zest and garlic. Set aside. 3) In a large frying pan, heat the oil over a medium heat. Add the mushrooms, celery, salt and pepper. Sauté for about 12 minutes until soft and the liquid has evaporated. Add half the parsley mixture and all the roasted red peppers and cook, stirring over a medium heat, for 2 minutes. Remove from the heat. 4) In a large bowl, combine the remaining parsley mixture, eggs, milk and 200g of the feta, stirring well to combine. Add the mushroom mixture and bread cubes and stir gently. 5) Transfer to the prepared baking dish and sprinkle with the remaining feta. Bake, uncovered, for 40–45 minutes until set and the top is golden.

Serves 8

## BITE ME BIT

'O great creator of being. Grant us one more hour to perform our art and perfect our lives.'

– Jim Morrison, musician

# CHEESY, CHEESY, CHEESY BROCCOLI SOUFFLÉ

## INGREDIENTS

non-stick cooking spray

1 tablespoon freshly grated Parmesan cheese

1 large head broccoli, broken into florets

55g butter

35g plain flour

350ml full-fat milk

1 teaspoon sea salt

½ teaspoon Dijon mustard

115g Cheddar cheese, coarsely grated

6 large egg yolks

6 large egg whites

½ teaspoon cream of tartar

'The Brady Bunch' taught me a lot – pork chops go with apple sauce and freckles can be bleached with lemon juice. But it was Alice tiptoeing as her soufflé baked that really stuck with me. Seems I was duped – loud noises don't level a soufflé, but repeatedly opening the oven does. So leave the door shut and let this airy, savoury soufflé soar. One whiff of the melted cheesy goodness and like Marcia, you too will be saying, 'Oh! My nose!'

## METHOD

1) Preheat the oven to 160°C/325°F/Gas Mark 3. Coat the bottom of a 2-litre soufflé dish with non-stick cooking spray. Sprinkle the Parmesan on the bottom and shake to coat. 2) Bring a large saucepan of water to the boil and add the broccoli. Reduce the heat to low and cook for 2–3 minutes until tender but not mushy. Drain well and chop the florets into smaller pieces. 3) In a medium saucepan, melt the butter over a medium heat. Add the flour and cook, whisking constantly, for 1 minute until smooth. Slowly pour in the milk and continue whisking to prevent lumps from forming. Add the salt and mustard and cook, stirring, for about 2 minutes until the mixture thickens. Remove from the heat and stir in the Cheddar and broccoli. 4) In a small bowl, lightly whisk the egg yolks. Constantly whisking, add a small amount of the cheese mixture. Once combined, add the rest of the yolks to the remaining cheese mixture, whisking briskly to mix. Transfer to a large bowl and leave to cool slightly. 5) Using an electric mixer, beat the egg whites and cream of tartar on high speed until stiff peaks form. Lightly fold half the egg whites into the cheese sauce. Gently fold in the remaining egg whites wihout overmixing. Carefully pour the mixture into the soufflé dish. Bake for 50–55 minutes until puffy and golden brown. Remove from the oven and serve immediately.

Serves 6–8

# PARMESAN-CRUSTED ASPARAGUS

## INGREDIENTS

non-stick cooking spray

170g mayonnaise

2 tablespoons Dijon mustard

2 teaspoons freshly
squeezed lemon juice

1 teaspoon sea salt

90g panko (Japanese)
breadcrumbs

85g Parmesan cheese,
freshly grated

2 large bunches of
asparagus, trimmed

2 tablespoons olive oil

coarse sea salt, for sprinkling

I wouldn't be surprised if one day I was strolling down the supermarket snack aisle and found a box of crispy asparagus tucked in with the Bugles and Cheetos. That's right, asparagus. Coated in a cheesy breadcrumb mixture and baked to a golden crisp, these addictive spears are a family favourite. So put away the party mix – just assemble this ideal company-is-coming side dish in advance and pop it in the oven 15 minutes before dinner.

## METHOD

**1)** Preheat the oven to 230°C/450°F/Gas Mark 8. Coat a large baking sheet with non-stick cooking spray. **2)** In a large bowl, whisk the mayonnaise, mustard, lemon juice and salt together. **3)** On a large plate, combine the panko and Parmesan. **4)** Dip each asparagus spear in turn into the mayonnaise mixture, followed by the panko mixture. Place the asparagus on the baking sheet and drizzle with the oil. **5)** At this point you can place the tray in the refrigerator for a few hours before baking. To cook, bake for 14–16 minutes, turning the asparagus halfway through cooking. Sprinkle with coarse sea salt before serving.

Serves 4

# MINTED SWEET PEA PURÉE

## INGREDIENTS

460g frozen peas

115g full-fat soft cheese

115g butter, at room temperature

2 tablespoons chopped mint

1 teaspoon sea salt

When we take spoon after spoon of this delicious purée, we are reminded of King John II of England. It's reported that the pea-obsessed monarch died after eating seven bowls of the little green legumes. The lesson we carry with us is to stop at six.

## METHOD

**1)** In a medium saucepan, bring salted water to the boil over a high heat. Add the frozen peas, reduce the heat to low and simmer for 5 minutes until tender. Drain well. Transfer the peas to a food processor. Add the cheese, butter, mint and salt. Process for 15–20 seconds until smooth. Remove from the food processor and serve warm.

Serves 6–8

## BITE ME BIT

'I have scarcely closed my eyes all night. Heaven only knows what was in the bed, but I was lying on something hard, so that I am black and blue all over my body. It's horrible!'

– from Hans Christian Andersen's
**The Princess and the Pea**

# BALSAMIC BARBECUED VEGETABLE STACKS

## INGREDIENTS

### Marinade

75ml balsamic vinegar

75ml olive oil

1 small garlic clove, finely chopped

1 teaspoon Dijon mustard

1 teaspoon sea salt

¼ teaspoon freshly ground black pepper

### Vegetables

non-stick cooking spray

2 large red peppers, quartered lengthways and deseeded

2 large yellow peppers, quartered lengthways and deseeded

2 large courgettes, cut into 4mm diagonal slices,12 in total

6 portobello mushrooms (about 7.5cm in diameter), peeled, gills gently scooped out with a small spoon

6 fresh rosemary sprigs (10cm in length), leaves removed from the bottom half

*Julie:* Word association.
*Husband:* Lose-lose?
*Julie:* Grilled.
*Husband:* New York?
*Julie:* Marinated in oil and vinegar.
*Husband:* Veal chop?
*Julie:* Quit it. Edible part of plants.
*Husband:* Vegetables.
*Julie:* Barbeque.
*Husband:* Salami?
*Julie:* Argh. Peppers, zucchini and portobellos.
*Husband:* All yours?
*Julie:* Promise?

## METHOD

**1)** For the marinade, in a large bowl, whisk the vinegar, oil, garlic, mustard, salt and pepper together. Add the peppers and courgette slices, tossing well to coat. Leave to marinate at room temperature for 15 minutes. Add the mushrooms, toss gently and leave to marinate for another 15 minutes. **2)** Lightly coat a gas barbecue rack with non-stick cooking spray and heat to a medium-high heat. Remove the vegetables from the marinade and keep the marinade to brush on the vegetables while cooking. **3)** Working in batches, cook the vegetables on the barbecue until tender and lightly charred, about 8–10 minutes for the peppers and 7 minutes for the mushrooms and courgettes. Brush with the marinade once or twice during cooking. **4)** Remove from the barbecue. When you are almost ready to serve, place the mushrooms upside down on a flat surface. Next, layer with a slice of red pepper, courgette, yellow pepper and another slice of courgette. Poke the rosemary sprig through the middle of each stack with the leaves at the top.

Serves 6

# FALAFEL VEGGIE BURGERS

## INGREDIENTS

non-stick cooking spray

1 tablespoon olive oil

1 small onion, chopped

1 large carrot, peeled and chopped

840g canned chickpeas, rinsed and drained well

250g canned sliced mushrooms, rinsed and drained well

1 tablespoon lime juice

3 tablespoons chopped flat-leaf parsley

1 tablespoon ground cumin

1 tablespoon tahini

½ teaspoon sea salt

¼ teaspoon freshly ground black pepper

5 slices white bread, crusts removed and processed until coarse crumbs

8 pittas

110g iceberg lettuce, shredded

### Creamy Tahini Sauce

115g mayonnaise

125ml soured cream

2 tablespoons lemon juice

1 tablespoon olive oil

1 tablespoon tahini

½ teaspoon sea salt

¼ teaspoon freshly ground black pepper

2 tablespoons finely chopped mint

2 tablespoons finely chopped flat-leaf parsley

Way back when, hauling limestone sure built up an appetite. Yup, falafel is THE original veggie burger, a classic meatless meal traced back to ancient Egyptian times. Don't worry – no heavy lifting required today – grab a McFried falafel, or, better yet, go back to your oasis and bake up your own hearty taste straight off King Tut's table.

## METHOD

**1)** Preheat the oven to 180°C/350°F/Gas Mark 4. Line a baking sheet with foil and coat with non-stick cooking spray. **2)** In a medium frying pan, heat the oil over a medium-low heat. Add the onion and cook for about 6 minutes until softened. Remove from the heat and leave to cool slightly. **3)** In a food processor, combine the cooked onion, carrot, chickpeas, mushrooms, lime juice, parsley, cumin, tahini, salt and pepper. Process until smooth, stopping to scrape down the side of the bowl. Transfer to a large bowl, add the breadcrumbs and mix until all the ingredients are thoroughly combined. **4)** Form 8 burgers from the mixture and place on the prepared baking sheet. Bake for 30 minutes, flipping halfway through. **5)** For the sauce, in a medium bowl, vigorously whisk the mayonnaise, soured cream, lemon juice, oil, tahini, salt and pepper together. Stir in the mint and parsley. **6)** To serve, split the pittas to make pockets. Tuck a veggie burger into each pocket with a few tablespoons of sauce and some shredded lettuce.

Serves 8

### BITE ME BIT

'...and then I would take the other hand with the falafel thing and I'd just put it on your ***** but you'd have to do it really light, just kind of a tease business...'

– Bill O'Reilly, as quoted in a sexual harassment suit filed against him by a Fox News producer in 2004

# Crave me

## Satisfying Pasta, Rice and Grains

# CARAMELISED ONION and GOAT'S CHEESE PASTA

## INGREDIENTS

**Caramelised Onions**

15g butter

1 tablespoon olive oil

2 white onions, halved and thinly sliced

1 teaspoon sugar

½ teaspoon sea salt

4 tablespoons balsamic vinegar

350g dried penne pasta

1 tablespoon olive oil

1 large garlic clove, finely chopped

175ml dry white wine

5 plum tomatoes, deseeded and chopped

120g fresh baby spinach, stems discarded and thinly sliced

2 tablespoons finely diced sun-dried tomatoes in oil

1 tablespoon chopped basil

½ teaspoon sea salt

¼ teaspoon freshly ground black pepper

40g Parmesan cheese, freshly grated

75g soft fresh goat's cheese

Onions are a little like high school gym coaches. They have a reputation for being harsh, but warm them up a little and, boy, can they be sweet. In this case, 20 minutes of heat transforms the pungent bulb into a deep brown, sugary marmalade. Pair it with tangy goat's cheese and you've got a rewarding pasta.

## METHOD

**1)** For the onions, in a large frying pan, melt the butter with the oil over a medium heat. Stir in the onions, sugar and salt. Sauté for 15–20 minutes until the onions are a dark golden brown. Stir in the vinegar and cook for about 1½ minutes until the liquid has evaporated. Remove from the heat and set aside. **2)** Cook the pasta in a large saucepan of boiling salted water until just tender. Drain well and set aside. **3)** In a large frying pan, heat the oil over a medium heat. Add the garlic and sauté for 30 seconds until fragrant. Turn the heat to high, stir in the wine and cook for about 3 minutes to reduce. Lower the heat to medium, add the cooked pasta, caramelised onions, plum tomatoes, spinach, sun-dried tomatoes, basil, salt and pepper and cook for 1–2 minutes.
**4)** Remove from the heat and stir in the Parmesan. Transfer the pasta to a serving platter and crumble over the goat's cheese. Serve immediately.

Serves 6

# LUSTFUL CREAMY CHICKEN FETTUCINE

## INGREDIENTS

### Grilled Chicken

4 boneless, skinless chicken breasts

2 tablespoons olive oil, plus extra for oiling

1 large garlic clove, finely chopped

2 tablespoons freshly squeezed lemon juice

½ teaspoon dried basil

½ teaspoon dried oregano

½ teaspoon sea salt

¼ teaspoon freshly ground black pepper

450g dried fettucine pasta

### Tomato Cream Sauce

2 tablespoons olive oil

1 onion, diced

2 small garlic cloves, finely chopped

525g canned chopped Italian tomatoes with herbs, simmered covered for 20 minutes, then puréed

⅛ teaspoon dried chilli flakes

225ml double cream

115g Parmesan cheese, freshly grated

½ teaspoon sea salt

½ teaspoon freshly ground black pepper

Dear Alfredo –

I don't know quite how to tell you this, but we're done. You bore me. Yes, I used to crave you, but now, you make me weary. My new love can both stand alone and be a big hit around the table… might not be as rich as you, but certainly spicier, smoother, more irresistible and fulfilling.

Arrivederci, Alfie. Xoxo

## METHOD

**1)** Place the chicken breasts in a large resealable plastic bag. Add the oil, garlic, lemon juice, basil, oregano, salt and pepper. Shake to combine, then leave to stand at room temperature for 30 minutes before cooking. **2)** Preheat the grill to medium and lightly oil the rack. Grill the chicken breasts for about 8 minutes on each side or until the chicken is cooked through. Remove from grill and rest for 5 minutes before slicing. Cut into bite-sized pieces and set aside. **3)** Cook the fettucine in a large saucepan of boiling salted water until just tender. Drain well and keep warm. **4)** For the sauce, in a large saucepan, heat the oil over a medium heat. Add the onion and cook, stirring, for about 3 minutes until softened. Add the garlic and cook, stirring, for 30 seconds. Stir in the puréed tomatoes and chilli flakes and continue to cook over a medium heat for 10 minutes. Turn the heat to low, add the cream and cook, stirring, for 2–3 minutes. Remove from the heat and stir in the Parmesan, salt and pepper. **5)** Toss the cooked fettucine and sliced chicken in the sauce and serve immediately.

Serves 8

## BITE ME BIT

'The hottest love has the coldest end.'

— Socrates, philosopher

# MAESTRO'S PASTA alla NORMA

## INGREDIENTS

non-stick cooking spray

1 large aubergine (about 450g), peeled and sliced into 5mm-thick rounds

2 tablespoons olive oil

½ teaspoon sea salt

¼ teaspoon freshly ground black pepper

### Sicilian Sauce

2 tablespoons olive oil

1 small red onion, chopped

2 large garlic cloves, finely chopped

⅛ teaspoon dried chilli flakes

475ml chicken stock

300g plum tomatoes, cored and cut into 2.5cm chunks

1 tablespoon balsamic vinegar

½ teaspoon sea salt

¼ teaspoon freshly ground black pepper

1 tablespoon chopped basil

70g crumbled ricotta salata or soft ricotta

350g dried fusilli or penne pasta

This classic Sicilian sauce has been hitting the right note since 1831, the year it was named for Bellini's opera. Music to your palate, the sweet roasted aubergine is combined with spicy tomato sauce and tangy ricotta salata, giving rise to a full-bodied aria.

## METHOD

1) Preheat the oven to 230°C/450°F/Gas Mark 8. Line a baking sheet with foil and coat with non-stick cooking spray. 2) Place the aubergine slices in a single layer on the prepared baking sheet, drizzle with the oil and season with the salt and pepper. Bake for 10 minutes, turn the slices over and bake for a further 10 minutes until soft and golden. Once cool enough to handle, cut into 2.5cm pieces. Set aside. 3) For the sauce, in a large frying pan, heat the oil over a medium heat. Add the onion and cook, stirring frequently, for about 3 minutes until softened. Add the garlic and chilli flakes and cook, stirring continuously, for 1 minute until the garlic becomes fragrant. Add the stock and bring to the boil over a high heat. Reduce the heat to low and simmer for 3 minutes. Add the tomatoes and continue to simmer on low for 15 minutes until they have softened. Add the aubergine pieces, vinegar, salt and pepper. Stir well to combine. Remove from the heat and add the basil and ricotta salata. 4) For the pasta, bring a large saucepan of lightly salted water to the boil over a high heat. Add the pasta and cook until just tender. Drain well and return to the pan. Toss the hot pasta with the sauce and serve immediately.

Serves 6

# SMOOTH SPINACH and RICOTTA PASTA

## INGREDIENTS

450g dried fusilli pasta

1 tablespoon olive oil

240g baby spinach leaves, stems discarded and cut into 1cm strips

½ teaspoon sea salt

¼ teaspoon freshly ground black pepper

375g ricotta cheese

125ml full-fat milk

125ml single cream

115g Parmesan cheese, freshly grated

2 tablespoons finely sliced basil leaves

True-blue Pastafarians, we ignored all the Carbaphobian warnings and continued to buy bulk-sized boxes. No one was going to scare us away from the luscious white noodles – long and short, hollow and swirled. This is our nirvana, Mon... let's all delight in this creamy dish of tender pasta paired with subtle ricotta cheese, mellow baby spinach and sharp, tangy Parmesan.

## METHOD

1) Bring a large saucepan of lightly salted water to the boil over a high heat. Stir in the pasta and cook until tender. Drain well, reserving 125ml of the pasta cooking water. 2) In a large frying pan, heat the oil over a medium heat. Add the spinach, salt and pepper. Cook for about 1–2 minutes until the spinach just begins to wilt. Stir in the ricotta, milk, cream and the reserved pasta water. Simmer over a low heat for 5 minutes. Add the cooked pasta and Parmesan, stirring until well blended. Garnish with the basil and serve immediately.

Serves 6–8

## BITE ME BIT

'Pattycake, pattycake, Pasta Man. Gimme pasta power as fast as you can.'

– Mario and Luigi in the television show 'The Super Mario Bros. Super Show!'

# PIQUANT PASTA PUTTANESCA

## INGREDIENTS

2 tablespoons olive oil

1 red onion, finely chopped

2 large garlic cloves, finely chopped

90g black olives, pitted and halved

1 tablespoon capers, rinsed and drained

½ teaspoon dried oregano

¼ teaspoon sea salt

⅛ teaspoon dried chilli flakes

2 x 400g cans chopped tomatoes

60ml dry red wine

350g dried fettucine pasta

30g Parmesan cheese, freshly grated

2 tablespoons finely chopped flat-leaf parsley

Quick and easy, spicy and fragrant, robust and satisfying, it's no wonder this Neapolitano dish is also known as 'whore's spaghetti'. Myth has it that prostitutes would use this aromatic sauce to lure men into their bordellos, so, unless you're looking for unexpected visitors, keep your windows closed.

## METHOD

**1)** For the sauce, heat the oil in a medium frying pan over a medium heat. Add the onion and cook 3–4 minutes, stirring occasionally, until softened. Add the garlic and sauté for about 1 minute until fragrant. Add the olives, capers, oregano, salt and chilli flakes and continue to sauté for 2 minutes. Add the tomatoes with their juce and the wine and bring to the boil. Reduce the heat to medium-low and simmer, uncovered, for 10 minutes, stirring occasionally. **2)** For the pasta, bring a large saucepan of lightly salted water to the boil over a high heat. Add the pasta and cook until just tender. Drain well and return to the saucepan. Toss the hot pasta with the puttanesca sauce and Parmesan. Top each serving with some of the chopped parsley.

Serves 6

# SOFT RICOTTA GNOCCHI in TOMATO SAUCE

## INGREDIENTS

### Gnocchi Dough

1kg ricotta cheese

3 large eggs

115g Parmesan cheese, freshly grated

1 teaspoon sea salt

¼ teaspoon freshly ground black pepper

560g plain flour, plus extra for dusting

### Tomato Sauce

2 tablespoons olive oil

1 large carrot, peeled and chopped

1 small red onion, chopped

2 large garlic cloves, finely chopped

4 x 400g cans chopped tomatoes

2 tablespoons tomato purée

⅛ teaspoon dried chilli flakes

2 teaspoons sugar

½ teaspoon sea salt

½ teaspoon freshly ground black pepper

These small dumplings are harder to pronounce – NOK-ee? NYO-ke? NEE-okee? – than to make from scratch. Using basic ingredients such as ricotta, eggs, flour and Parmesan cheese we've created the lightest, most tender-textured gnocchi. Or, is that NYAW-kee?

## METHOD

1) Dust 2 baking sheets with flour. Set aside. 2) For the dough, in a large bowl, using your hands or a wooden spoon, combine the ricotta, eggs, Parmesan, salt and pepper. Add the flour 140g at a time to form a soft dough. Transfer the dough to a lightly floured work surface and knead gently for 2 minutes. 3) Divide the dough into 6 pieces and roll each into a ball. Roll out each ball into 1cm-thick ropes. Cut each rope into 2.5cm slices and gently place on the prepared baking sheets. If not cooking right away, cover and place in refrigerator until ready to use. 4) For the sauce, in a large saucepan, heat the oil over a medium heat. Add the carrot and onion and cook for 3–5 minutes, stirring, until tender. Stir in the garlic and cook for about 1 minute until fragrant. Add the tomatoes and their juice, tomato purée and chilli flakes and bring to the boil over a high heat. Reduce the heat to low and simmer, uncovered, for 15–20 minutes. Remove from the heat and use a hand-held or freestanding blender to process until smooth. Season with the sugar, salt and pepper. 5) To cook the gnocchi, bring a large saucepan of lightly salted water to the boil over a high heat. Drop the dough pieces into the boiling water and cook for about 2–3 minutes until the gnocchi rise to the surface. Remove the gnocchi using a slotted spoon and place in a serving bowl. Top with the tomato sauce and serve.

Serves 8–10; makes approximately 120 gnocchi

# STRIKING THREE-CHEESE POLENTA LASAGNE

## INGREDIENTS

non-stick cooking spray

115g Fontina cheese, grated

250g ricotta cheese

40g Parmesan cheese, freshly grated

1 large egg

2 teaspoons chopped basil

½ teaspoon sea salt

### Polenta

475ml water

350ml full-fat milk

1 teaspoon sea salt

150g polenta

60g Parmesan cheese, freshly grated

1 tablespoon butter

### Tomato Sauce

2 tablespoons olive oil

1 small white onion, chopped

2 small garlic cloves, finely chopped

2 x 400g cans whole Italian plum tomatoes, undrained and crushed by hand

1 teaspoon sugar

1 teaspoon sea salt

¼ teaspoon freshly ground black pepper

1 tablespoon chopped basil

Ready for a curveball? This lasagne is pasta-free. The same basic principle of lasagne construction applies, but, in place of pasta, polenta hugs the cheesy layers of Fontina, ricotta and Parmesan cheese. A unique and most delicious surprise, you won't need steroids to throw this towards the plate.

## METHOD

1) Preheat the oven to 180°C/350°F/Gas Mark 4. Coat a 33 x 23cm baking dish with non-stick cooking spray. Also coat a 20cm square baking dish with non-stick cooking spray. Set both aside. 2) In a medium bowl, stir the Fontina, ricotta, Parmesan, egg, basil and salt together. Set aside. 3) For the polenta, in a large saucepan, bring the water, milk and salt to the boil over a high heat. Slowly whisk in the polenta, reduce the heat to low and simmer, stirring often with a wooden spoon, for 5–7 minutes until the mixture is very thick. Remove from the heat and stir in the Parmesan and butter. Immediately transfer to the rectangular baking dish, spreading evenly to coat the bottom. Leave the polenta to set for 10 minutes. Slice into 12 pieces and then slice each piece lengthways to make 24 narrower pieces. 4) To assemble, lay 8 polenta slices on the bottom of the square baking dish. Top with half the Fontina-ricotta mixture, followed by another 8 polenta slices. Spread the remaining cheese mixture over the polenta and top with the remaining polenta. Bake for 30 minutes or until lightly browned and heated through. Leave to stand for 5 minutes before serving topped with the sauce. 5) While baking the polenta, heat the oil in a saucepan over a medium heat. Add the onion and sauté for about 5 minutes until tender. Add the garlic and cook, stirring, for 30 seconds. Stir in the tomatoes, sugar, salt and pepper. Bring to the boil, then reduce the heat and simmer, uncovered, for 15–20 minutes. Stir in the basil.

Serves 6–8

# FANTASTIC 4 MUSHROOM and CHEESE LASAGNE

## INGREDIENTS

### Mushroom Sauce

non-stick cooking spray

25g dried
porcini mushrooms

225ml hot water

1 tablespoon olive oil

40g shallots, diced

115g button mushrooms, sliced

115g sliced shiitake mushrooms

2 large portobello mushrooms,
stems discarded, gills scraped
with a small spoon, sliced

1 teaspoon dried oregano

135g feta cheese, crumbled

60g rehydrated sun-dried
tomatoes, sliced into thin strips

4 tablespoons plain flour

½ teaspoon sea salt

225ml milk

225ml evaporated milk

### Cheese Filling

625g ricotta cheese

175g mozzarella cheese,
coarsely grated

125ml milk

30g Parmesan cheese,
freshly grated

1 large egg, lightly beaten

¼ teaspoon sea salt

¼ teaspoon freshly
ground black pepper

12 oven-ready lasagne sheets

How do you make vegetarian lasagne meaty? Start with 4 types of savoury and substantial mushrooms, add in intensely robust sun-dried tomatoes and layer mild-to-mature cheese throughout. One bite of this incredibly aromatic lasagne and you'll discover the stretch of the cheese and the might of the mushroom foursome. Look out Dr Doom... this is a powerful quartet.

## METHOD

1) Preheat the oven to 190°C/375°F/Gas Mark 5. Coat a 33 x 23cm baking dish with non-stick cooking spray. 2) For the sauce, place the porcini in a small bowl, cover with the hot water and leave to stand for 20 minutes or until softened. Drain, rinse and pat dry. Chop, discarding any hard stems. 3) In a large frying pan, heat the oil over a medium heat. Add the shallots and sauté for 3 minutes. Add all the mushrooms and oregano. Sauté, stirring frequently, for about 8 minutes until tender. Remove from the heat and stir in the feta and sun-dried tomatoes. Set aside. 4) Place the flour and salt in a saucepan over a medium-high heat. Gradually add the milk and evaporated milk and cook, whisking constantly, for 5 minutes or until thickened. Remove from the heat and stir into the mushroom mixture. 5) For the cheese filling, in a medium bowl, combine the ricotta, 115g of the mozzarella, the milk, Parmesan, egg, salt and pepper. 6) To assemble the lasagne, in the prepared baking dish, spread a thin layer of the mushroom sauce and top it with 4 lasagne sheets. Spread a third of the remaining sauce and top with half the cheese mixture. Top with 4 more lasagne sheets, half the remaining sauce and all the remaining cheese filling. Finish with the remaining lasagne topped with the rest of the sauce. Sprinkle the remaining mozzarella over the top, cover with foil and bake for 30 minutes. Remove the foil and bake for a further 10 minutes.

Serves 8

## BITE ME BIT

Did you know that 'go hang a salami' and 'I'm a lasagne hog', read the same spelled backwards?

# BOLOGNESE-SMOTHERED PARMESAN POLENTA

## INGREDIENTS

### Polenta

1.2 litres water

1 teaspoon sea salt

150g polenta

30g Parmesan cheese, freshly grated

### Bolognese Sauce

450g lean beef mince

4 tablespoons milk

525g mushrooms, chopped (you can use a mixutre of button, shiitake and chestnut)

1 large carrot, peeled and finely chopped

1 small red onion, finely chopped

2 large garlic cloves, finely chopped

1 teaspoon dried basil

1 teaspoon dried oregano

½ teaspoon sea salt

¼ teaspoon freshly ground black pepper

950g tomato pasta sauce

125ml dry red wine

1 piece Parmesan rind, 5–7.5cm inches long

60g Parmesan cheese, freshly grated, to serve

On our insatiable Italian honeymoon my husband ate 18 bowls of pasta Bolognese in 17 days. An impressive feat until you consider that I ate 22 servings of polenta during that same gloriously gluttonous time. I did my new spouse proud. Now, many meals later, our newlywed passions are reunited with a rich and robust Bolognese sauce poured over cheesy polenta. Mangiamo.

## METHOD

### POLENTA

1) Coat a 28 x 18cm baking dish with non-stick cooking spray. In a large saucepan, bring the water and salt to the boil over a high heat. Reduce the heat to low, slowly add the polenta and cook, stirring constantly with a wooden spoon, for about 10 minutes until thick and smooth. 2) Remove from the heat, stir in the Parmesan and spoon into the prepared baking dish. Set aside.

### BOLOGNESE SAUCE

1) For the sauce, in a large frying pan, cook the mince over a medium-high heat, breaking it up as it cooks. Cook for 5 minutes, or until it is no longer pink. Drain in a colander and return to the pan. 2) Add the milk to the pan and cook over a medium heat for 3 minutes until absorbed. Add the mushrooms, carrot, onion, garlic, basil, oregano, salt and pepper. Cook over a medium-low heat for 8 minutes until the onion is softened. 3) Add the tomato sauce, wine and Parmesan rind to the meat mixture. Bring to the boil, then reduce the heat to low and simmer, partially covered, for 30 minutes. Remove from the heat and discard the Parmesan rind. 4) For serving, slice the polenta into 6–8 servings and spoon the Bolognese sauce over each portion. Finish with freshly grated Parmesan cheese.

Serves 6–8

# ENTICING DEEP-DISH MEAT LASAGNE

## INGREDIENTS

### Meat Sauce

non-stick cooking spray

900g lean beef mince

2 x 400g cans chopped tomatoes

240g tomato purée

3 tablespoons soft light brown sugar

1 tablespoon chopped basil

1½ teaspoons sea salt

1 teaspoon dried oregano

### Cheese Filling

2 large eggs, lightly beaten

1kg ricotta cheese

115g Parmesan cheese, freshly grated

1 tablespoon chopped basil

1 teaspoon sea salt

12 oven-ready lasagne sheets

340g mozzarella cheese, coarsely grated

At first, I thought it was my melodious singing, the floral garland atop my flowing hair and the fact that I was only wearing a sheet that was luring construction workers, dogs and letter carriers to my front door. But no, sad to say, it was this lasagne, and, what's worse, it's Lisa's recipe. Guess I can stop my lyre lessons now.

## METHOD

**1)** Preheat the oven to 190°C/375°F/Gas Mark 5. Coat a 33 x 23cm baking dish with non-stick cooking spray. **2)** For the sauce, in a large frying pan, brown the mince over a medium-high heat. Drain and return to the pan, adding the tomatoes with their juice, tomato purée, sugar, basil, salt and oregano. Bring to the boil, then reduce the heat to low and simmer for 30 minutes. **3)** For the cheese filling, in a medium bowl, whisk the eggs, ricotta, 90g of the Parmesan, the basil and salt together. **4)** To assemble, spread one third of the meat sauce in the prepared dish. Top with 4 lasagne sheets, half the ricotta mixture, half the mozzarella and another third of the meat sauce. Top with 4 lasagne sheets, the remaining ricotta and the remaining mozzarella. Place the remaining lasagne on top, cover with the remaining meat sauce and sprinkle with the remaining Parmesan. Bake for 35 minutes.

Serves 8

## BITE ME BIT

'To attract men, I wear a perfume called "New Car Interior".'

— Rita Rudner, comedian

Spending endless hours in the kitchen takes a toll – feet throb, sweat trickles, hair frizzes and sometimes, in the middle of peeling the 30th potato, exhaustion kicks in.

Seeking company and inspiration, I turned on the television. Newscasts were depressing, soap operas distracting and game shows enraging...c'mon dude. Off went the boob tube.

It was then that I figured out how to keep going. Music. The other taste that stirs the soul. Let me share with you the most uplifting mix of cooking music, tunes guaranteed to shake you, wake you and elate you...

# Lip Synch
## Tunes to Cook to

### SONG LIST

**Tired of Being Alone** Al Green
**Mama Told Me Not to Come** Tom Jones
**Can't Take My Eyes Off of You** Lauryn Hill
**Changes** Seu Jorge
**Adventures In Solitude** The New Pornographers
**Big Brother** Stevie Wonder
**Hard Sun** Eddie Vedder
**A Little Less Conversation** Elvis Presley
**Let's Get It On** Marvin Gaye
**Rafters** Moby
**Heaven** Yusuf Islam
**The Lady is a Tramp** Frank Sinatra
**Light My Fire** Erma Franklin
**I Want You Back (Z-trip remix)** Jackson 5
**Sing** Annie Lennox
**I Will** The Beatles

# BOTTOMLESS BOWL CHICKEN LASAGNE

## INGREDIENTS

1 tablespoon olive oil

6 boneless, skinless chicken breasts, cut into 2cm cubes

2 large carrots, peeled and coarsely grated

225g mushrooms, sliced

1 small onion, diced

700ml chicken stock

2 x 400g cans chopped tomatoes

240g tomato pasta sauce

1 teaspoon dried oregano

½ teaspoon dried basil

¼ teaspoon sea salt

⅛ teaspoon freshly ground black pepper

6 oven-ready lasagne sheets, broken

1½ teaspoons cornflour

250g ricotta cheese

60g mozzarella cheese, coarsely grated

30g Parmesan cheese, freshly grated

Lisa sometimes calls me Garfield for my lazy, lasagne-loving ways. When cravings strike, and I don't have the time or patience for layering, this cheese-topped pasta delivers quick-fix happiness in a bowl of tender pasta, succulent chicken and sweet vegetables.

## METHOD

**1)** Heat the oil in a large saucepan over a medium-high heat. Sauté the chicken for 4 minutes until lightly browned. Stir in the carrots, mushrooms and onion and cook for a further 4–5 minutes. **2)** Add the stock, tomatoes with their juice, tomato sauce, oregano, basil, salt and pepper. Bring to the boil over a high heat. Reduce the heat to medium-low and cook, covered, for 5 minutes. Turn the heat to high and return to the boil. Add the lasagne and simmer over a low heat for 20 minutes or until tender. **3)** In a small bowl, combine the cornflour and a ladle of liquid from the pan. Mix to combine, stir into pan and cook until thickened. **4)** Spoon the stew into bowls and top each serving with an equal amount of the ricotta, mozzarella and Parmesan.

Serves 6

# COCONUT LIME STICKY RICE

## INGREDIENTS

90g Thai jasmine rice

350ml canned coconut milk, well shaken

350ml water

1 tablespoon freshly squeezed lime juice

1 teaspoon finely grated lime zest

1 teaspoon sugar

1 teaspoon sea salt

Okay, the song was really irritating, but Harry Nilsson was right. If you put the lime in the coconut, then you do feel better. Less annoying, we hope, our tropical rice dish mixes a plain long grain with creamy coconut milk and tart lime juice, creating a swinging side dish that works great alongside Thai, Indian and Caribbean flavours.

## METHOD

Combine all the ingredients in a medium saucepan. Bring to the boil over a high heat. Cover, reduce the heat to low and simmer for 20 minutes. Remove from the heat and leave to stand, covered, for 5 minutes. Fluff up gently with a fork.

Serves 6

## BITE ME BIT

'I have a wild bunch of coconuts.'

– Benny Hill, comedian

# DRAMATIC RED BEETROOT RISOTTO

## INGREDIENTS

550g beetroot, trimmed, rinsed and peeled

3 tablespoons olive oil

1.2–1.4 litres chicken stock

55g butter

1 red onion, finely chopped

360g Arborio or Carnaroli rice

175ml dry white wine

90g Parmesan cheese, freshly grated

¼ teaspoon sea salt

¼ teaspoon freshly ground black pepper

## METHOD

**1)** Preheat the oven to 230°C/450°F/Gas Mark 8. **2)** Place the whole beetroot on a large piece of foil. Drizzle with 1 tablespoon oil and tightly wrap in the foil. Place the foil packet on a baking sheet and roast for about 45–55 minutes until tender. Remove from the oven and leave to cool. **3)** When the beets are cool enough to handle, cut them into 5mm cubes and set aside to cool completely. **4)** In a medium saucepan, warm the stock over a low heat. Keep at a bare simmer, covered. **5)** In a large saucepan, melt half the butter with the remaining 2 tablespoons oil over a medium-low heat. Add the onion and cook, stirring occasionally, for 8–10 minutes until softened but not browned. Increase the heat to medium-high, stir the rice into the onion and cook, stirring constantly, for 1 minute. Pour in the wine and cook for 1 minute, stirring, until most of the liquid is absorbed. Reduce the heat to low, ladle in 125ml of the hot stock and cook, stirring, until the stock is almost completely absorbed. Add the remaining stock 125ml at a time, stirring constantly until each addition is almost completely absorbed before adding the next. This should take 20 minutes. The risotto is ready when the rice is mostly tender but with a hint of texture to it. Stir in the beetroot, Parmesan, butter, salt and pepper. Remove from heat. Leave to stand for 3–4 minutes before serving.

Serves 8–10

# SPECIAL FRIED RICE

## INGREDIENTS

### Sauce

3 tablespoons soy sauce

2 tablespoons oyster sauce

2 tablespoons tomato ketchup

2 tablespoons soft light brown sugar

1 teaspoon sesame oil

¼ teaspoon grated fresh ginger

dash of hot pepper sauce (optional)

### Vegetable Rice

2 teaspoons vegetable oil

2 large eggs, lightly whisked

1 tablespoon groundnut oil

1 small white onion, diced

1 carrot, peeled and diced

1 red pepper, deseeded and diced

1 small garlic clove, finely chopped

115g frozen peas

640g cooked long-grain white rice, chilled

Fried rice is the yin and yang of Chinese cooking – flexible AND firm. On the one hand you're free to improvise – feel like adding some broccoli or chicken? Go right ahead. On the other hand there is a science to achieving the perfect fried rice, a rule we always adhere to: cold rice. When stir-fried, warm rice will result in a mushy mountain, whereas hardened, day-old grains will remain separated. Must be an ancient Chinese secret, but this one-dish meal is successfully laid back and regimented all at once.

## METHOD

**1)** For the sauce, in a small bowl, whisk the soy sauce, oyster sauce, ketchup, sugar, sesame oil, ginger and hot sauce, if using, together. Set aside. **2)** Over a medium heat, heat the vegetable oil in a deep frying pan or wok. Pour the eggs into the pan and cook, without stirring, for 30 seconds. Break the egg into smaller pieces and cook for a further 1 minute. Transfer to a small plate. **3)** Using the same pan, heat the groundnut oil over a medium-high heat. Add the onion and cook for 1–2 minutes, stirring often, until just softened. Add the carrot and red pepper and continue to cook for 2 minutes. Stir in the garlic and frozen peas and cook for about 1 minute until the garlic is fragrant. Add the cooked rice, reserved egg and soy sauce mixture to the vegetables, stir well to combine and cook for 1 minute to heat through.

Serves 6–8

# SUPER-SAUCY PEANUT BUTTER NOODLES

## INGREDIENTS

### Peanut Sauce

125g smooth peanut butter

125ml hoisin sauce

4 tablespoons freshly squeezed lime juice

2 tablespoons soy sauce

2 tablespoons soft light brown sugar

400g fresh udon noodles

200g cooked peeled prawns, chopped

250g extra-firm tofu, diced

1 red pepper, deseeded and thinly sliced

75g mangetout, trimmed and cut on the diagonal

40g chopped honey-roasted peanuts

3 tablespoons chopped flat-leaf parsley

2 tablespoons sesame seeds, toasted

It's so unfair. Lisa never gets called the saucy sister. Everyone thinks she's the sweet one, but that's just because she doesn't get caught rolling her eyes or crossing her arms. Well, fine, all you gullible ones out there. I'll be the saucy one. That way I get to hoard this addictively sweet and salty peanut-hoisin sauce. So. There.

## METHOD

1) For the sauce, in a small saucepan, whisk the peanut butter, hoisin, lime juice, soy sauce and sugar together. Bring to the boil over a medium heat, stirring often. Remove from the heat and leave to cool. 2) Place the noodles in a large heatproof bowl and cover with boiling water. Leave to stand for 3 minutes and gently loosen the noodles. Drain well. 3) In a large bowl, toss the noodles with the peanut sauce, prawns, tofu, red pepper and mangetout. Garnish with the peanuts, parsley and sesame seeds. Serve at room temperature or chilled.

Serves 6

## BITE ME BIT

'You are a saucy little thing, aren't you?'

– Simon Cowell, judge on 'American Idol'

# TOFU PAD THAI with SWEET CHILI SAUCE

## INGREDIENTS

450g dried wide rice noodles

4 teaspoons vegetable oil

350g extra-firm tofu, cut into 1cm cubes

2 large eggs

3 large egg whites

200g fresh beansprouts

25g finely chopped flat-leaf parsley

100g dry-roasted peanuts, coarsely chopped

lime wedges, to garnish

### Sweet Chili Sauce

300g Heinz chili sauce, mild chilli sauce or barbecue sauce

100g soft light brown sugar

4 tablespoons water

2 tablespoons Thai fish sauce

1 tablespoon freshly squeezed lime juice

2 teaspoons grated fresh ginger

If this cookbook thing doesn't work out, we've always got Bangkok. We'll open a street stall of our own and take the others by storm with our unsurpassed version of their national dish. Sure, our competition will use similar ingredients, but our vibrant Pad Thai will be adored for its spot-on sauce-to-noodle ratio, golden-cooked tofu and still-crispy beansprouts. So delicious, we'll have longer lines than the women offering 'soapies'.

## METHOD

1) Cook the noodles in boiling water for 5 minutes. Drain and rinse under cold water. 2) In a large frying pan, heat 2 teaspoons oil over a medium-high heat. Add the tofu and cook for 5–7 minutes until browned. Remove from the pan. 3) Whisk the whole eggs and egg whites together. In the frying pan, heat the remaining 2 teaspoons oil over a medium-high heat. Add the eggs and cook for 1 minute, stirring constantly. Set aside. 4) For the sauce, in a medium bowl, combine the chilli or barbecue sauce, sugar, water, fish sauce, lime juice and ginger. Add the sauce mixture and drained noodles to the frying pan with the egg mixture in it. Cook for 2 minutes over a medium-high heat. Stir in the tofu, beansprouts and parsley and cook for a further 3–5 minutes. Serve sprinkled with the peanuts and garnished with lime wedges.

Serves 6–8

# Gobble me

## You'll Flip for the Bird

## BITE ME BIT

**Cowardly Lion:** ...What puts the 'ape' in apricot? What have they got that I ain't got?

**Dorothy, Scarecrow & Tinman:** Courage!

– from the 1939 movie **The Wizard of Oz**

# APRICOT AMARETTO CHICKEN

## INGREDIENTS

non-stick cooking spray

6 boneless, skinless chicken breasts

70g plain flour

2 large eggs

90g panko (Japanese) breadcrumbs

2 teaspoons finely grated lemon zest

1 teaspoon sea salt

½ teaspoon freshly ground black pepper

**Apricot Amaretto Sauce**

1 tablespoon cornflour

2 tablespoons water

350ml chicken stock

250g apricot jam

1 tablespoon soy sauce

1 tablespoon amaretto

500g canned apricots, drained and sliced

Warning: If you are a US Marine, turn the page immediately.

**They're certainly a loyal, heroic and fearless bunch, but did you know that many in the Corps consider apricots the enemy? Yes, according to superstition, this velvety-skinned, golden fruit is a jinx – the mere mention of its name, let alone eating one, has the power to unleash a can of whoopass. But our experience with this smooth and sweet fruit has been more delicious than malicious, especially when it's mixed into an amaretto sauce that smothers this crunchy-coated chicken.**

## METHOD

**1)** Preheat the oven to 200°C/400°F/Gas Mark 6. Line a baking sheet with foil and coat with non-stick cooking spray. **2)** Place the chicken breasts between 2 sheets of greaseproof paper and pound to an even thickness, about 1cm thick. **3)** Place the flour in a small bowl. In another bowl, lightly whisk the eggs. In a third bowl, mix the panko crumbs with the lemon zest, salt and pepper. **4)** Dust the chicken with the flour, shaking off any excess. Dip into the egg, then coat in the panko mixture, patting to adhere. Place on the prepared baking sheet. Bake for 20–25 minutes, turning once halfway through. **5)** For the sauce, in a small bowl, mix the cornflour and water together. In a medium saucepan, combine the stock, jam and soy sauce. Bring to the boil over a medium-high heat. Add the cornflour mixture, reduce the heat to medium and cook, stirring continually, for 4–5 minutes or until slightly thickened. Remove from the heat and mix in the amaretto and apricots. **6)** To serve, cut each chicken breast into 3 pieces and pour over the sauce. Serve immediately.

Serves 6

# OVEN-FRIED CHICKEN with BUTTERMILK GRAVY

## INGREDIENTS

### Marinade

350ml buttermilk

2 tablespoons Dijon mustard

1 large garlic clove, finely chopped

1 tablespoon olive oil

1 teaspoon finely grated lemon zest

½ teaspoon sea salt

¼ teaspoon freshly ground black pepper

6 boneless, skinless chicken breasts

non-stick cooking spray

175g corn flakes, coarsely crushed

115g Parmesan cheese, freshly grated

### Buttermilk Gravy

25g butter

3 tablespoons plain flour

475ml chicken stock

4 tablespoons buttermilk

¼ teaspoon sea salt

I know. The term 'oven-fried' is a contradiction. But we've found a most satisfying compromise, a happy medium to the traditionally fat-laden chicken. You can still have your down-home meal, creamy mashed potatoes and buttery corn to boot, just forget the fryer. Enjoy your juicy, crackling chicken smothered in creamy buttermilk gravy without punishing your arteries. See? Give-and-Take, Live-and-Bake.

## METHOD

**1)** In a large shallow dish, whisk the buttermilk, mustard, garlic, oil, lemon zest, salt and pepper together. Add the chicken breasts to the marinade, cover and refrigerate for at least 1 hour or preferably overnight. **2)** Preheat the oven to 190°C/375°F/Gas Mark 5. Line a baking sheet with foil and coat with non-stick cooking spray. **3)** In a medium bowl, combine the corn flake crumbs and Parmesan. Remove the chicken from the marinade (discard the marinade) and coat each breast well in the corn flake mixture. Arrange on the prepared baking sheet and bake for 20–25 minutes until cooked through and the coating is golden. **4)** For the gravy, in a medium saucepan, melt the butter over a low heat. Whisk in the flour until well blended. Gradually add the stock, stirring constantly over a medium heat. Bring the mixture to the boil and cook, stirring, for 3–5 minutes or until thickened to a gravy-like consistency. Remove from the heat and stir in the buttermilk and salt. **5)** To serve, slice the cooked chicken breasts in half and pour the gravy over the top.

Serves 6

# MOM'S LEMON CHICKEN

## INGREDIENTS

**Marinade**

175ml freshly squeezed lemon juice

4 tablespoons olive oil

4 tablespoons dry white wine

6 boneless, skinless chicken breasts

non-stick cooking spray

70g plain flour

1 tablespoon finely grated lemon zest

1 teaspoon sea salt

½ teaspoon freshly ground black pepper

4 tablespoons olive oil

50g soft light brown sugar

125ml chicken stock

4 tablespoons freshly squeezed lemon juice

6 lemon slices

1 tablespoon sesame seeds, toasted

I'm like Pavlov's dog. The whir of the electric juicer instantly triggers my salivary glands. Even as I write about it I drool a bit at the thoughts of the great things – fresh OJ, lemon meringue pie, veal piccata – that can come from its sweet hum. However, the best (slurp), um, tastiest (swallow) thing to come from the juicer is our Mom's lemon chicken. Marinated in white wine and lemon juice (gulp), the chicken is topped with brown sugar and lemon slices and then (glug) baked in a citrus stock mixture.

## METHOD

**1)** Combine the lemon juice, oil, wine and chicken breasts in a large glass bowl. Cover and refrigerate at least 4 hours, but preferably overnight. **2)** Preheat the oven to 180°C/350°F/Gas Mark 4. Coat a 33 x 23cm baking dish with non-stick cooking spray. **3)** In a medium bowl, combine the flour, lemon zest, salt and pepper. Remove the chicken from marinade (discard the marinade) and lightly coat in the flour mixture, shaking off the excess. **4)** In a large frying, heat half the oil over a medium heat. Add half the chicken breasts and cook for about 3 minutes on each side until browned. Transfer the browned chicken to the prepared baking dish, then repeat with the remaining oil and chicken, adding to the baking dish in a single layer. **5)** Sprinkle the sugar over the chicken breasts. Pour the stock and lemon juice around the chicken. Top each breast with a lemon slice and bake for 20 minutes. Sprinkle with the toasted sesame seeds before serving.

Serves 6

### BITE ME BIT

'I believe if life gives you lemons, make lemonade...then find someone that life gave vodka to and have a party.'

– Ron White, comedian

# GREENHOUSE HERB CHICKEN

## INGREDIENTS

2 large egg whites

140g dry breadcrumbs

½ teaspoon dried oregano

½ teaspoon dried basil

½ teaspoon sea salt

¼ teaspoon freshly ground black pepper

6 boneless, skinless chicken breasts

3 tablespoons olive oil

### Herb Sauce

1 tablespoon olive oil

25g spring onions, finely sliced

1 tablespoon dried oregano

1 large garlic clove, finely chopped

1 tablespoon dried thyme

2 tablespoons finely chopped flat-leaf parsley

125ml balsamic vinegar

700ml chicken stock

4 tablespoons tomato purée

We recycle. We walk more than drive. But, we're willing to deforest Mother Nature's herb garden for the sake of this aromatic chicken. Don't start picketing us – this earthy, savoury sauce of oregano, thyme and parsley is our favourite renewable resource.

## METHOD

**1)** Place the egg whites in a small dish and lightly beat. On a large plate, combine the breadcrumbs, oregano, basil, salt and pepper. **2)** Dip each chicken breast in the egg whites, then coat in the breadcrumb mixture, patting well to adhere. **3)** In a large frying pan, heat the oil over a medium-high heat. Add the chicken breasts and cook for about 2 minutes on each side or until golden. Remove from the pan and set aside. **4)** For the sauce, after wiping the frying pan clean, heat the oil over a medium heat. Add the spring onions, oregano, garlic, thyme and parsley. Sauté for 1 minute, stirring constantly. Add the vinegar and cook for 2 minutes. Add the stock and tomato purée and bring to the boil. Reduce the heat to low and simmer, uncovered, for 2 minutes. Return the chicken breasts to the pan and simmer, covered, for a further 20 minutes.

Serves 6

## BITE ME BIT

'Opie, you haven't finished your milk. We can't put it back in the cow, you know.'

– Aunt Bee (actress Frances Bavier) in the television series 'The Andy Griffith Show'

# BODACIOUS HERB and GOAT'S CHEESE CHICKEN BREASTS

## INGREDIENTS

non-stick cooking spray

6 boneless, skinless chicken breasts

6 slices white bread, crusts removed

25g butter, melted

225g mayonnaise

2 tablespoons Dijon mustard

1 tablespoon freshly squeezed lemon juice

¼ teaspoon sea salt

### Creamy Filling

225g cream cheese, softened

55g goat's cheese, softened

3 basil leaves, finely chopped

1 teaspoon finely chopped thyme

1 teaspoon freshly squeezed lemon juice

¼ teaspoon sea salt

¼ teaspoon freshly ground black pepper

Move over, Jenna Jameson. These perfectly plump, beautifully formed, creamy-filled mounds are the new stars of food porn. Thanks to a crispy exterior of homemade breadcrumbs and a rich interior of herbs and cheese, these tantalising, outrageously juicy and flavourful chicken breasts are nothing short of, well, we'll let you guess.

## METHOD

1) Preheat the oven to 220°C/425°F/Gas Mark 7. Coat a 33 x 23cm baking dish with non-stick cooking spray. 2) In a small bowl, mash all the ingredients for the filling together until combined. Divide the mixture into 6 equal portions and form into the shape of a small tube. Set aside. 3) Place the chicken between 2 sheets of greaseproof paper and pound to an even 5mm thickness. Pat the chicken dry, lay the smooth side of the chicken breast down and place a portion of the cheese mixture at the wider end of each piece. Roll the chicken up, starting at the end where the filling was placed. Transfer to the prepared baking dish, seam-side down. Set aside. 4) For the breadcrumb coating, in a food processor, pulse the bread until fine crumbs form. In a small dish, combine the breadcrumbs with the melted butter, tossing with a fork. 5) In a small bowl, whisk the mayonnaise, mustard, lemon juice and salt together. Brush each rolled chicken breast with the mayonnaise mixture and press the breadcrumbs on to coat. Bake for 30–33 minutes until golden. Slice on the diagonal to serve.

Serves 6

# BALSAMIC CHICKEN with SWEET PEPPERS

## INGREDIENTS

non-stick cooking spray

35g plain flour

2 large egg whites

35g dry breadcrumbs

30g Parmesan cheese, freshly grated

2 tablespoons olive oil

6 boneless, skinless chicken breasts

55g toasted flaked almonds

### Balsamic Sauce

2 teaspoons olive oil

2 large red peppers, deseeded and sliced into strips

2 large green peppers, deseeded and sliced into strips

80g raisins

125ml balsamic vinegar

3 tablespoons sugar

½ teaspoon seasalt

¼ teaspoon freshly ground black pepper

I made a really expensive blunder – peppers were sliced, plump raisins measured out and chicken sautéed to a golden crisp. But, oops, no cheap balsamic vinegar. Luckily, I discovered a small bottle of the dark beauty tucked away in the pantry and proceeded to use the entire amount to create the fragrant, syrupy sauce.

Here are the lessons I learned:

1. Always check for all ingredients before starting, 2. Reduced balsamic vinegar has the same rich taste whether it was cheap or expensive in the first place, 3. Licking all the plates clean does not bring with it absolution of guilt.

## METHOD

1) Preheat the oven to 190°C/375°F/Gas Mark 5. Line a baking sheet with foil and coat with non-stick cooking spray. 2) Place the flour in a shallow dish. Put the egg whites in a separate bowl and lightly beat. Combine the breadcrumbs and Parmesan in a third dish. Dust the chicken with the flour, shaking off any excess. Dip in the egg whites and then coat in the breadcrumb mixture. 3) In a large frying pan, heat the oil over a high heat. Sauté the chicken for 2 minutes on each side or until golden brown. Place the chicken on the prepared baking sheet and finish cooking in the oven for 18–20 minutes. 4) For the sauce, in a large frying pan, heat the oil over a medium heat. Add the red and green peppers and sauté for 8 minutes. Add the raisins and cook, stirring, for 1 minute. Add the vinegar, sugar, salt and pepper and cook, mixing to coat the peppers, for 1–2 minutes. 5) To serve, slice the chicken and top with the balsamic sauce and toasted flaked almonds.

Serves 6

## BITE ME BIT

'I could have sexual chemistry with vinegar.'

— Jessica Alba, actress

# CHICKEN PARMESAN, REVAMPED!

## INGREDIENTS

70g plain flour

2 large eggs

60g panko (Japanese) breadcrumbs

175g Parmesan cheese, freshly grated

6 boneless, skinless chicken breasts

3 tablespoons olive oil

475ml chicken stock

240g tomato pasta sauce

55g mozzarella cheese, coarsely grated

She won't organise your junk drawer or suggest a new eye shadow, but Lisa is a makeover maven. She has transformed Chicken Parmesan from a traditionally greasy, leathery mess into a healthful, tender success. Cheesy and moist, this super-quick version (less than 15 minutes) will leave you plenty of time to alphabetise the takeaway menus.

## METHOD

1) Place the flour in a small bowl. In another bowl, lightly beat the eggs. In a third bowl, combine the panko and 115g of the Parmesan. 2) Place the chicken between 2 sheets of greaseproof paper and pound to an even 1cm thickness. Lightly coat the chicken in the flour mixture, shaking off the excess. Dip into the beaten eggs and then transfer to the panko mixture, patting the crumbs on both sides. 3) In a large frying pan, heat the oil over a medium-high heat. Add the chicken and sauté for about 3 minutes on each side until lightly browned. Reduce the heat to low. Add the stock to the pan, spread 3 tablespoons tomato sauce on each chicken breast and sprinkle with the mozzarella and the remaining Parmesan. 4) Cover the pan and simmer for about 6 minutes until the chicken is cooked through.

Serves 6

# PECAN-CRUSTED LIME CHICKEN

## INGREDIENTS

non-stick cooking spray

70g plain flour

½ teaspoon sea salt

¼ teaspoon freshly ground black pepper

6 tablespoons Dijon mustard

55g butter, melted

freshly squeezed juice of 2 limes, finely grated zest of 1 lime

2 large eggs, lightly beaten

240g pecan nuts, chopped

280g dry breadcrumbs

6 boneless, skinless chicken breasts

lime wedges, to serve

This recipe is to cooking what 'Smoke on the Water' is to my kids' learning guitar. No matter your skill level, it'll always turn out good. But the similarities don't end there – both have 4 simple steps and both are confidence boosters that'll have you showing off for company. Now that you've nailed this classic, it's time to move on to some new creations.

## METHOD

Note: Once coated, this chicken should be refrigerated for 2 hours or more. When you are ready to bake it, preheat the oven to 180°C/350°F/Gas Mark 4.

1) Line a baking sheet with foil and coat with non-stick cooking spray. 2) In a medium bowl, combine the flour, salt and pepper. In a large bowl, whisk the mustard, butter, lime juice, lime zest and eggs together. On a large plate, combine the pecans and breadcrumbs. 3) Working with one chicken breast at a time, lightly coat the chicken in the flour (shake off the excess), dip in the mustard mixture and finally coat in the pecan mixture. 4) Place the pecan-crusted chicken on the prepared baking sheet and cover with greaseproof paper. Chill in the refrigerator for 2 hours or more. Bake for 30 minutes and serve with lime wedges.

Serves 6

## BITE ME BIT

'What's the matter, Colonel Sanders? Chicken?'

– President Skroob (actor Mel Brooks) in the 1987 movie **Spaceballs**

# CRUNCHY TORTILLA CHICKEN with AVOCADO DIP

## INGREDIENTS

6 boneless, skinless chicken breasts

350ml soured cream

2 tablespoons soft light brown sugar

2 teaspoons chilli powder

1 teaspoon chopped thyme

1 teaspoon sea salt

½ teaspoon freshly ground black pepper

½ teaspoon garlic powder

non-stick cooking spray

150g panko (Japanese) breadcrumbs

120g tortilla chips, crushed

115g Cheddar cheese, coarsely chopped

40–80g jarred jalapeño peppers, to taste, patted dry and chopped

### Avocado Dip

115g mayonnaise

125ml soured cream

2 ripe avocados, stoned and peeled

2 tablespoons freshly squeezed lime juice

¼ teaspoon ground cumin

¼ teaspoon cayenne pepper

½ teaspoon sea salt

¼ teaspoon freshly ground black pepper

Chicken, here. Word is, my south-of-the-border kin are havin' way more fun...the fiestas, the spices... while all I get is limp breading and a dunk in the deep fryer. What did you say? I get to be el pollo loco too? Tell me more. Marinated in soured cream, chilli powder and brown sugar? Fabuloso. Rolled in crushed tortillas, Cheddar and spicy jalapeños? ¡Caliente! Me...juicy, crunchy tortilla crust and dipped in creamy avocado? ¡Ay, caramba!

## METHOD

1) Place the chicken breasts between 2 sheets of greaseproof paper and pound to even 1cm thickness. 2) In a large bowl, combine the soured cream, sugar, chilli powder, thyme, salt, pepper and garlic powder. Add the chicken and toss to coat, then cover and leave to marinate in the refrigerator for 2 hours. 3) Preheat the oven to 220°C/425°F/Gas Mark 7. Line a baking sheet with foil and coat with non-stick cooking spray. 4) In a large bowl, combine the panko, tortilla crumbs, Cheddar and jalapeños. Remove the chicken from the marinade and coat each piece with the panko mixture, pressing down so that the coating sticks well to each piece. Place on the prepared baking sheet and bake for 20–23 minutes until golden and cooked through. 5) Put all the ingredients for the avocado dip in a food processor and process for about 30 seconds until smooth. Serve alongside the chicken, but if you're not eating it immediately, place the avocado stone in the bowl to keep the dip from turning brown. Cover and refrigerate until ready to use.

Serves 6

# YEE HAW...TEX-MEX CHICKEN TORTILLA CASSEROLE

## INGREDIENTS

non-stick cooking spray

6 boneless, skinless chicken breasts, thinly sliced

freshly squeezed juice of 2 limes

2 teaspoons ground cumin

1 teaspoon chilli powder

½ teaspoon dried oregano

### Rice and Bean Filling

320g cooked white long-grain rice

520g canned black beans, rinsed and drained

2–3 mild green chillies, deseeded (for less heat) and chopped

1 large red pepper, deseeded and diced

1 tablespoon freshly squeezed lime juice

1 teaspoon ground cumin

480g tomato pasta sauce

450g salsa

1 teaspoon ground cumin

1 teaspoon chilli powder

12 (15cm) tortillas

230g Cheddar cheese, coarsely grated

225ml soured cream

This here heap of melted cheese, beans, spices, tortillas and salsa is good for the belly, good for the soul. Now better eat it right quick before the Sheriff comes over the hill, blasts us all to kingdom come and steals our grub.

## METHOD

**1)** Preheat the oven to 190°C/375°F/Gas Mark 5. Coat a 33 x 23cm baking dish with non-stick cooking spray. **2)** In a large bowl, combine the sliced chicken breast, lime juice, cumin, chilli powder and oregano. **3)** Coat a large frying pan with non-stick cooking spray. Over a medium heat, sauté the chicken for about 6–8 minutes until cooked through. Transfer to a medium bowl and stir in the cooked rice, black beans, green chillies, red pepper, lime juice and cumin. Stir well to combine. **4)** In a separate bowl, combine the tomato sauce, salsa, cumin and chilli powder. **5)** To assemble the casserole, spread 240g of the tomato sauce mixture on the bottom of the prepared baking dish. Place 6 tortillas over the sauce, overlapping if necessary. Spoon another 240g of the sauce mixture over the tortillas, followed by half the chicken mixture, half the Cheddar and half the soured cream. Arrange another layer of tortillas, then 240g of the sauce and the remaining chicken, Cheddar and soured cream. Top with the remaining sauce. Cover with foil and bake for 30–35 minutes.

Serves 8

### BITE ME BIT

'One tequila, two tequila, three tequila, floor.'

– George Carlin, comedian

# FEEL-GOOD CHICKEN CURRY

## INGREDIENTS

2 tablespoons mild curry powder

1 teaspoon garam masala

1 teaspoon ground cumin powder

1 teaspoon chilli powder

35g butter

1 onion, diced

2 large garlic cloves, finely chopped

2 teaspoons grated fresh ginger

sea salt

1 tablespoon tomato purée

4 boneless, skinless chicken breasts, thinly sliced

125ml chicken stock

525g canned chopped tomatoes, pulsed 2 times in a food processor

420g canned chickpeas, rinsed and drained

115g frozen green peas

60ml double cream

120g roasted cashew nuts, chopped

225ml natural yogurt

cooked rice, to serve

Some crazy dudes climb straight up mountains to get a natural high. Others jump off the backs of them in search of the same buzz. But we have a much lazier answer: we just grab a bowl of curry. Yes, curry. Studies link curry consumption and the release of endorphins – dig in for your hassle-free Himalayan high.

## METHOD

**1)** In a large frying pan, over a medium-high heat, toast the curry powder, garam masala, cumin and chilli powder for 30–60 seconds until the spices become fragrant. Remove from the pan to a plate and set aside. **2)** In the same pan, melt the butter over a medium heat. Add the onion and cook for 7–8 minutes until tender and golden. Add the garlic, ginger, ½ teaspoon salt, tomato purée and reserved toasted spices, stirring to combine. Increase the heat to high, add the sliced chicken and stir to coat with the spice mixture. Add the stock and tomatoes and bring to the boil. Reduce the heat to a gentle simmer and leave the chicken to cook and the sauce to thicken slightly for about 10 minutes. Add the chickpeas, frozen peas and cream and cook on a medium heat for 3–5 minutes until heated through. **3)** Season to taste with salt. Serve over rice, topped with the chopped roasted cashews and yogurt.

Serves 4–6

# MAGICAL MOROCCAN BARBECUED CHICKEN

## INGREDIENTS

3 tablespoons olive oil, plus extra for oiling

2 teaspoons ground cumin

1 teaspoon dried oregano

½ teaspoon ground ginger

½ teaspoon sea salt

¼ teaspoon freshly ground black pepper

1 large garlic clove, finely chopped

6 boneless, skinless chicken breasts

**Honeyed-Citrus Sauce**

175ml strained orange juice

85g runny honey

1 tablespoon freshly squeezed lemon juice

½ teaspoon ground cinnamon

½ teaspoon sea salt

35g butter

60g toasted flaked almonds

Inspired by the spices of North African cuisine, this barbecued chicken is going to make you want to crack out your beaded bra-sarong-set and gyrate like a Marrakech mama. Now, in between doing figure-of-eights with your hips, put some couscous and barbecued aubergine on the plate to round out this exotic chicken.

## METHOD

**1)** In a large bowl, combine the oil, cumin, oregano, ginger, salt, pepper and garlic. **2)** Place the chicken between 2 sheets of greaseproof paper and pound to an even 5mm thickness. Add to the oil mixture and refrigerate for 10–15 minutes while you heat a gas barbecue to medium-high. Brush the rack with oil. **3)** Arrange the chicken flat on the rack and cook for about 2–3 minutes on each side until firm to the touch. Remove from the rack and keep warm. **4)** In a small saucepan, bring the orange juice, honey, lemon juice, cinnamon and salt to the boil. Reduce the heat and simmer for 8–10 minutes. Remove from the heat and stir in the butter. **5)** Drizzle the sauce over the cooked chicken and top with the toasted flaked almonds.

Serves 6

## BITE ME BIT

'Sticking feathers up your butt does not make you a chicken.'

– from the 1996 Chuck Palahniuk novel **Fight Club**

# LEMON and DILL GRILLED CHICKEN

## INGREDIENTS

### Marinade

2 shallots, cut in half

175ml freshly squeezed lemon juice

3 tablespoons finely grated lemon zest

4 tablespoons Dijon mustard

4 tablespoons olive oil, plus extra for oiling

1 teaspoon dried oregano

1 teaspoon sea salt

1 teaspoon freshly ground black pepper

10 dill sprigs

6 boneless, skinless chicken breasts

freshly squeezed lime juice and lime wedges, to serve

Lisa never minds when her husband springs the 'guess-who's-coming-to-dinner' question on her. She'll just whip up confit, coulis or some other French word that's not in my culinary vocab. Me, on the other hand, I like to have a dependable, delicious and easy 'old faithful' in my repertoire – here it is, a simple yet hugely flavourful grilled chicken that has been marinated in a zesty lemon, dill and Dijon mixture.

## METHOD

**1)** In a large bowl, whisk the shallots, lemon juice and zest, mustard, oil, oregano, salt and pepper together. Pour into a glass 33 x 23cm baking dish. **2)** Place the chicken between 2 sheets of greaseproof paper. Pound to an even 1cm thickness. Add to the marinade and scatter the dill on top. Refrigerate for 2–8 hours, turning once. **3)** Preheat the grill to medium-high and oil the grill rack. Remove the chicken from the marinade. Cook under the grill for 5–6 minutes on each side or until cooked through. Squeeze lime juice over the chicken and serve with lime wedges.

Serves 6

# SMOKIN' BBQ CHICKEN

Ever wonder why there's no Orange Light District? Red, the colour of passion, stokes the appetite. If you're looking for something to ignite your desire and those pay-per-view movies featuring firemen are getting a little stale, this juicy grilled chicken, slathered in a full-bodied, ruby-red BBQ sauce, will satisfy any hunger. Okay, almost any hunger.

## INGREDIENTS

### Marinade

125ml freshly squeezed lemon juice

2 tablespoons vegetable oil

1 teaspoon dried oregano

8 boneless, skinless chicken breasts

### BBQ Sauce

360g tomato ketchup

500g runny honey

1 tablespoon vegetable oil

1 tablespoon soy sauce

1 tablespoon freshly squeezed lemon juice

1 teaspoon Worcestershire sauce

1 teaspoon sugar

½ teaspoon freshly ground black pepper

½ teaspoon paprika

## METHOD

1) In a large glass bowl, combine the lemon juice, oil, oregano and chicken breasts. Cover and leave to marinate in the refrigerator for at least 1 hour. 2) In a large bowl, whisk all the ingredients for the sauce together. Set aside 240g of the sauce in a small bowl for basting and keep the remaining sauce for serving with the cooked chicken. 3) Preheat a gas barbecue to medium heat. Remove the chicken from marinade (discard the marinade) and cook, uncovered, on the rack for 6–8 minutes on each side or until cooked through. In the last few minutes of cooking, brush the chicken with the reserved sauce on both sides.

Serves 8

## BITE ME BIT

'Pornography and cooking shows have created two new spectator sports'

— Mason Cooley, academic

# GRILLED 照り焼き (teriyaki) CHICKEN

## INGREDIENTS

**Teriyaki Sauce**

175ml mirin

225ml soy sauce

60g sugar

2 tablespoons rice vinegar

1 teaspoon sesame oil

1 teaspoon grated fresh ginger

2 tablespoons cornflour

2 tablespoons water

6 boneless, skinless chicken breasts

1 teaspoon olive oil, plus extra for oiling

2 large red peppers, deseeded and cubed

1 large yellow pepper, deseeded and cubed

Our mission is to make your life easier. Why then are we telling you how to make teriyaki sauce from scratch versus buying it? You'll never achieve the lustrous teri (sheen) when you yaki (grill) with preservative-laden bottled versions. Our perfectly balanced, 簡単な (easy) and 楽しい (delicious) sauce is a tasty payoff for 10 minutes' work.

## METHOD

**1)** For the sauce, in a medium saucepan, bring the mirin to the boil over a medium heat. Reduce the heat to low and simmer for 8 minutes. Add the soy sauce, sugar, vinegar, sesame oil and ginger and whisk to combine. **2)** In a small bowl, stir the cornflour and water together. Add to the saucepan, turn the heat to high and cook, whisking, for about 5 minutes until slightly thickened. Remove from the heat and leave to cool. **3)** Place the chicken in a bowl and toss with 125ml of the sauce. Cover and leave to marinate in the refrigerator at least 30 minutes. **4)** Heat the grill to medium-high and oil the grill rack. Remove the chicken from the marinade (discard the marinade) and grill for 6–8 minutes on each side or until cooked through. Leave the chicken to rest for a few minutes before slicing on the diagonal. **5)** In a large frying pan, heat the olive oil over a high heat. Add the peppers and stir-fry for 3 minutes. Add the sliced chicken and 125ml of the teriyaki sauce and heat through. Store the leftover teriyaki sauce in the refrigerator for up to 1 week.

Serves 6

### BITE ME BIT

どうもありがとうミスターロボット (Dōmo arigatō misutō Robotto)
また会う日まで (Mata au hi made)
どうもありがとうミスターロボット (Dōmo arigatō misutā Robotto)
秘密を知りたい (Himitsu wo shiritai)
– from the 1983 Styx song 'Mr Roboto'

# CRUNCHY CHICKEN WINGS with SWEET and SAVORY DIPPING SAUCES

## INGREDIENTS

### Chicken Wings

1.3kg chicken wings, split, tips removed

175ml buttermilk

1 large egg

115g polenta

100g plain flour

1 teaspoon sea salt

1 teaspoon chilli powder

1 teaspoon ground cumin

¼ teaspoon freshly ground black pepper

### Sweet Dipping Sauce

340g apricot jam

4 tablespoons cider vinegar

2 tablespoons soft light brown sugar

1 teaspoon Dijon mustard

¼ teaspoon grated fresh ginger

### Tangy Blue Cheese Dipping Sauce

120g blue cheese, crumbled

125ml buttermilk

125ml soured cream

55g mayonnaise

1 tablespoon white wine vinegar

½ teaspoon sugar

½ teaspoon sear salt

¼ teaspoon freshly ground black pepper

A few Dating 101 tips: less is more, let him pay, don't eat chicken wings, respect his mother. Well, I'm not so sure. My husband said that I sealed the deal at Wing Night, where I rolled my sleeves high and devoured a basketful. I'm still charming him with these polenta-crusted wings baked to a grease-free golden crisp and dunked in a sweet apricot or tangy blue cheese dipping sauce.

## METHOD

1) Place the wings in a glass 33 x 23cm baking dish. In a medium bowl, whisk the buttermilk and egg together. Pour over the wings, cover and leave to marinate in the refrigerator for at least 3 hours and up to 24 hours. 2) Preheat the oven to 200°C/400°F/Gas Mark 6. Line a baking sheet with foil and coat with non-stick cooking spray. 3) In a large bowl, combine the polenta, flour, salt, chilli powder, cumin and pepper. Remove the wings from the marinade (discard the marinade) and, working with a few at a time, coat in the polenta mixture. Place on the prepared baking sheet. 4) Bake for 40–45 minutes, turning once halfway through baking. 5) For the sweet dipping sauce, in a small saucepan, combine the jam, vinegar, sugar, mustard and ginger. Heat over a medium heat until the sugar has dissolved and the ingredients are combined. Leave to cool before serving. 6) For the blue cheese dipping sauce, in a medium bowl, use a fork to mash the blue cheese and buttermilk together until it looks like cottage cheese. Add the soured cream, mayonnaise, vinegar, sugar, salt and pepper and stir well to combine. Serve alongside the sweet dipping sauce with the wings.

Serves 4–6 (or 2 very hungry wing lovers)

# CHICKEN and VEGETABLE NOODLES

A plea to Irish rockers U2. Just once, don't you think you could sing it my way? Try it. 'Where the Sheeps Have Lo Mein'. Catchy and delicious. Our saucy Chinese noodles, with veggies and chicken abounding, are a guaranteed No 1 hit and will curb any craving for the takeaway carton. So, for your next tune, Bono, how do you like 'Someday, buddy, Someday?'

## INGREDIENTS

400g fresh chow mein or other Chinese noodles

225ml chicken stock

75ml soy sauce

3 tablespoons oyster sauce

2 tablespoons hoisin sauce

2 tablespoons mirin

1 tablespoon cornflour

1 tablespoon groundnut oil

210g pak choi, chopped

2 large red peppers, deseeded and chopped

180g celery, chopped

420g roasted chicken breast, shredded or cubed

## METHOD

**1)** Fill a large saucepan with water and bring to the boil. Reduce the heat to low and add the fresh noodles. Stir to loosen the noodles and cook for about 2 minutes. Drain and set aside.
**2)** In a medium bowl, whisk the stock, soy sauce, oyster sauce and hoisin sauce together. In a small bowl, dissolve the cornflour in the mirin. Add the cornflour mixture to the stock mixture, whisking well to combine. Set aside. **3)** In a wok or a large frying pan, heat the oil over a high heat. Add the pak choi, red peppers and celery. Stir-fry for 2–3 minutes until slightly softened. Add the chicken, noodles and stock mixture. Cook, stirring, for 2 minutes until the sauce is thickened.

Serves 6

# CHINESE ORANGE ALMOND CHICKEN

## INGREDIENTS

non-stick cooking spray

6 boneless, skinless chicken breasts

1 large egg

125ml milk

70g plain flour

¼ teaspoon sea salt

120g panko (Japanese) breadcrumbs

230g flaked almonds

25g butter

**Orange Sauce**

4 tablespoons sugar

1 tablespoon plain flour

1 tablespoon cornflour

¼ teaspoon sea salt

175ml orange juice

4 tablespoons water

2 tablespoons freshly sqeezed lemon juice

2 teaspoons butter

1 teaspoon finely grated orange zest

1 teaspoon finely grated lemon zest

Craving Chinese food? Instead of scouring the menu for the No 32 Almond Chicken, save yourself the calories and chemicals and go for our goo-free version. Not only is it easy to make but it's also free of MSG, salt-mine-sodium and the deep-fryer glaze.

## METHOD

**1)** Preheat the oven to 180°C/350°F/Gas Mark 4. Line a baking sheet with foil and coat with non-stick cooking spray. **2)** Place the chicken between 2 sheets of greaseproof paper and pound to an even 1cm thickness. **3)** In a small bowl, whisk the egg, milk, flour and salt together. In a shallow dish, combine the panko and almonds. **4)** Dip the chicken breasts in the egg mixture and then coat in the panko mixture, pressing gently to adhere. **5)** In a large frying pan, melt the butter over a medium heat. Add the coated chicken breasts and cook for 3 minutes on each side or until lightly browned. Remove from the pan and place on the prepared baking sheet. Bake for 20 minutes. **6)** For the sauce, in a medium saucepan, whisk the sugar, flour, cornflour and salt together. Add the orange juice, water and lemon juice and whisk well to combine. Place over a high heat and bring to the boil. Reduce the heat to low and cook, stirring constantly, for 2–3 minutes or until sauce thickens. Remove from heat and add the butter and citrus zests. Stir well to combine. **7)** To serve, diagonally slice each chicken breast into 4 pieces and drizzle with the warm orange sauce.

Serves 6

# ASIAN CHICKEN LETTUCE BUNDLES

## INGREDIENTS

### Sauce

125ml sushi vinegar

125ml soy sauce

3 tablespoons oyster sauce

1 tablespoon sesame oil

2 tablespoons cornflour

### Chicken

3 boneless, skinless chicken breasts

60ml dry white wine

3 tablespoons cornflour

2 large egg whites

½ teaspoon sea salt

1 tablespoon vegetable oil

1 large garlic clove, finely chopped

250g water chestnuts, rinsed and chopped

2 red peppers, deseeded and finely chopped

2 carrots, peeled and julienned

60g dried shiitake mushrooms, rehydrated in boiling water for 20 minutes, rinsed well, patted dry and chopped

### Topping

55g flaked almonds

175g dried ramen noodles, crushed

iceberg lettuce leaves

6 tablespoons hoisin sauce

Chew with your mouth closed. Don't put your feet on the table. That's pretty much the extent of my rules governing dining etiquette. When it comes to eating I like to take my cue from the Indian culture, hands-on. Fiddling with my food since childhood, these moo-shu-like lettuce wraps are another great excuse to hold dinner in the palm of my hand. Now I just have to remember: napkin, not sleeve.

## METHOD

**1)** For the sauce, in a medium bowl, whisk the vinegar, soy sauce, oyster sauce, sesame oil and cornflour together. Set aside.
**2)** For the chicken, in a food processor, pulse the chicken breasts until finely chopped. Place in a medium bowl and set aside. In a small bowl, stir the wine, cornflour, egg whites and salt together. Pour over the chopped chicken, cover and leave to marinate for 10 minutes. **3)** Fill a large saucepan with water and bring to the boil over a high heat. Pour the chicken and marinade into the boiling water and stir constantly to break up the lumps. Cook for 4–5 minutes or until chicken is no longer pink. Drain the chicken mixture into a sieve. Set aside. **4)** In a large frying pan, heat the vegetable oil over a medium-high heat. Add the garlic, water chestnuts, red peppers, carrots and mushrooms and cook, stirring, until softened. Add the chicken mixture and continue cooking for another 3 minutes. Add the reserved sauce to the frying pan, turn the heat to high and cook, stirring, for about 3 minutes until the sauce has thickened. **5)** For the topping, in a small frying pan, brown the almonds and noodles over a medium heat until golden. **6)** To serve, divide the chicken mixture between lettuce leaves, topping each with an equal quantity of the hoisin sauce and a sprinkling of the almonds and noodles.

Serves 4–6

# SWEET 'n' STICKY WINGS

## INGREDIENTS

non-stick cooking spray

1.3kg chicken wings, split, tips removed

340g runny honey

125ml soy sauce

100g soft light brown sugar

60g tomato ketchup

2 tablespoons Heinz chilli sauce, mild chilli sauce or barbecue sauce

½ teaspoon garlic powder

½ teaspoon grated fresh ginger

WINGDING [NOUN]: A NOISY, EXCITING CELEBRATION OR PARTY.

And, if we might amend that definition, it involves intensely gooey, honey-soy chicken wings. They are best shared with those who do not ask where they can find moist towelettes.

## METHOD

**1)** Coat a 33 x 23cm baking dish with non-stick cooking spray. Place the wings in the dish and set aside. **2)** In a small saucepan, combine all the remaining ingredients. Bring to the boil over a medium-high heat. Once boiling, pour the honey mixture over the chicken wings. Leave to cool, cover and marinate in refrigerator for a few hours or overnight. **3)** Preheat the oven to 190°C/375°F/ Gas Mark 5. **4)** Remove the wings from the refrigerator and cover with foil. Bake in the marinade for 55 minutes, stirring occasionally. Remove the foil cover and bake the wings for a further 15 minutes or until the sauce is thickened.

Serves 6

### BITE ME BIT

Competitive eater Joey 'Jaws' Chestnut set a new record at the 2008 Wing Bowl XVI when he ate 241 chicken wings in 30 minutes.

# TURKEY BURGERS with MANGO MAYO

## INGREDIENTS

### Turkey Burgers

80g mango chutney, puréed smooth

4 tablespoons soured cream

30g celery, finely diced

15g panko (Japanese) breadcrumbs

2 teaspoons Dijon mustard

1 teaspoon freshly squeezed lemon juice

½ teaspoon sea salt

450g lean turkey mince

1 tablespoon olive oil, plus extra for oiling

4 hamburger buns

### Mango Mayonnaise

85g diced mango

55g mayonnaise

1 teaspoon freshly squeezed lime juice

1 teaspoon sugar

Before Oprah had anything to say about the subject, turkey burgers elicited as much excitement from carnivores as a Richard Simmons workout. Even more delectable and flexible than its beefy cousin, the turkey burger once again proves what we knew all along – Oprah's always right.

## METHOD

**1)** For the burgers, in a large bowl, mix the chutney, soured cream, celery, panko, mustard, lemon juice and salt together. Add the turkey mince, mix well and shape into 4 patties. Place on a plate, cover and refrigerate for 2 hours to firm up slightly before cooking. **2)** Preheat a gas barbecue to medium-high heat and lightly oil the rack. Brush the burgers with the olive oil, place on the rack and cook for 8–9 minutes on each side until the meat is thoroughly cooked through. The internal temperature of the turkey burgers should be between 71–74°C/160–165°F. **3)** For the mango mayonnaise topping, put all the ingredients in a food processor or blender and process until smooth. To serve, place each turkey burger on a hamburger bun and top with the mango mayonnaise.

Serves 4

### BITE ME BIT

'Allow myself to introduce...myself. I'm Richie Cunningham and this is my wife Oprah.'

– Austin Powers (actor Mike Myers) in the 1997 movie **Austin Powers: International Man of Mystery**

# BANG-ON ROASTED TURKEY BREAST

## INGREDIENTS

2 large garlic cloves, finely chopped

85g runny honey

2 tablespoons olive oil

2 tablespoons Dijon mustard

2 tablespoons soy sauce

1 tablespoon balsamic vinegar

1 tablespoon finely chopped basil

½ teaspoon freshly ground black pepper

1.6kg boneless turkey breast

225ml chicken stock

Sentence starters that make us cringe:

1. 'Anywhoo…'
2. 'But I digress…'
3. 'Do I have a story…'

No, please don't ramble on. For two girls who like to cut to the chase, this quick, oven-roasted turkey breast is ideal. Forget the dark meat and the wings – the breast, beautifully browned, moist and juicy, is both succulent and succinct.

## METHOD

1) For the marinade, in a small bowl, mix the garlic, honey, oil, mustard, soy sauce, vinegar, basil and pepper together. Set aside. 2) Rinse the turkey breast and pat dry. Place in a shallow roasting tin and coat in the marinade. Cover and refrigerate for at least 4 hours, turning occasionally. 3) Preheat the oven to 160°C/325°F/Gas Mark 3. 4) Bring the turkey to room temperature before roasting. Add half the stock to the bottom of the pan and cover the turkey with foil. Roast for 1½ hours, basting with the pan juices once or twice during cooking. Remove the foil and raise the oven temperature to 230°C/450°F/Gas Mark 8. Add the remaining stock to the pan and continue to roast for 20 minutes or until an instant-read thermometer, inserted into the thickest part of the breast, registers 79.5°C /175°F. 5) Remove from the oven and leave the turkey to rest for 10 minutes before carving. In a small saucepan over a high heat, warm any remaining pan juices and serve with slices of the turkey.

Serves 6–8

# LICKITY SPLIT TURKEY, STUFFING and CRANBERRY SAUCE

## INGREDIENTS

### Turkey Marinade

40g dried onion soup mix

680g apricot jam

225ml French salad dressing

1 tablespoon honey mustard

1 tablespoon paprika

1 teaspoon garlic powder

1 teaspoon celery salt

1 teaspoon freshly ground black pepper

7.2–8.2kg whole turkey

1 turkey-sized roasting bag

1 tablespoon plain flour

### Stuffing

2 egg breads (challahs), crusts removed and cut into 2.5cm cubes

non-stick cooking spray

115g butter,

1 white onion, finely chopped

4 large celery sticks, finely chopped

1 tablespoon chopped sage

1 tablespoon chopped thyme

1 litre chicken stock

1 tablespoon soy sauce

People often groan at the thought of eating leftover turkey for a week...we look forward to it. Our turkey, roasted in a roasting bag, not only cooks in half the time of traditional recipes but also has twice the moistness and flavour. The gravy is smooth and rich, the stuffing is sweet and savoury and the cranberry sauce is perfection – finally a feast we can be thankful for year-round.

## METHOD

### TH/E TURKEY

1) Keep only the bottom shelf in the oven. Preheat the oven to 180°C/350°F/Gas Mark 4. 2) In a medium bowl, combine the onion soup mix, jam, French dressing, mustard, paprika, garlic powder, celery salt and pepper. Mix well and set aside. 3) Make sure the turkey cavity is empty. Rinse and pat the turkey dry. Sprinkle the bottom of the roasting bag with the flour and shake around the bag to prevent it from bursting during cooking. Place the roating bag in a large roasting tin with sides at least 5cm high. Place the turkey in the bag and pour the onion soup mixture over the turkey, making sure that the entire turkey is covered with the sauce. Seal the bag with the tie provided. Cut 6 slits, each 1cm long, in the top of the bag to allow the steam to escape. NOTE: You do not turn or baste the turkey during cooking. 4) Roast the turkey in the oven until an instant-read thermometer inserted into the thickest part of the thigh reaches 82°C/180°F and the breast of the turkey at the thickest point reaches an internal temperature of 77°C/170°F. Don't be surprised if the turkey takes under 2 hours, as the bag dramatically speeds up cooking time...go by the thermometer dial, not the time in the oven. 5) When the turkey is done, slit the bag,

4 large eggs

175ml full-fat milk

175ml single cream

2 tablespoons chopped
flat-leaf parsley

1 teaspoon sea salt

½ teaspoon freshly ground
black pepper

160g dried cranberries
or dried cherries

**Sweet Cranberry Sauce**

350g fresh or frozen cranberries

225ml orange juice or
cranberry juice

100g sugar

100g soft light brown sugar

80g dried cherries

lift out the turkey and place it on a large chopping board. Leave the turkey to rest for 20 minutes before carving. **6)** For the gravy, take the sauce that remains in the roasting tin and strain it into a large saucepan. Leave it to stand for a few minutes and then skim off any fat that has come to the surface. Over a high heat, reduce the sauce to the desired consistency. Taste for salt and pepper and pour over the sliced turkey.

Serves 10-12

**THE STUFFING**

**1)** Preheat the oven to 160°C/325°F/Gas Mark 3. Arrange the bread cubes in a single layer on 2 baking sheets. Bake for 30 minutes or until golden, swapping the tray positions and rotating them halfway through baking. Set aside to cool.
**2)** Coat a 33 x 23cm baking dish with non-stick cooking spray. Set aside. **3)** In a large frying pan, melt half the butter over a medium heat. Add the onion and celery and sauté for 10 minutes or until golden. Stir in the sage, thyme, stock and soy sauce and simmer for about 10 minutes or until vegetables are tender. Leave to cool for 5 minutes. **4)** In a large bowl, whisk the eggs, milk, cream, parsley, salt and pepper. Stir in the onion-celery mixture. Add the bread cubes and cranberries and gently toss to coat, ensuring that all the bread is soft and moist. Transfer to the prepared baking dish. Drizzle with the remaining butter, melted, and bake for 45–50 minutes until the top is golden.

Serves 8–10

**SWEET CRANBERRY SAUCE**

**1)** Rinse and drain the cranberries. In a large saucepan, combine the cranberries with all the remaining ingredients. Bring to the boil over a high heat. Reduce the heat to medium and simmer, uncovered, for about 10 minutes until the cranberries pop open and the sauce thickens. Spoon off any foam that has formed and leave to cool to room temperature before serving.

Makes: about 480g

# Catch me

## Hooked on Fish

# HALIBUT, TOMATOES and THYME in WHITE WINE

## INGREDIENTS

### Halibut

2 tablespoons olive oil

6 halibut fillets, about 175g each, skin removed

¼ teaspoon sea salt

¼ teaspoon freshly ground black pepper

### Wine and Tomato Stock

1 tablespoon olive oil

1 large shallot, thinly sliced

1 large garlic clove, finely chopped

60ml dry white wine

2 x 400g cans chopped tomatoes, drained well

475ml chicken stock

450g canned cannellini beans, rinsed and drained

½ teaspoon finely chopped thyme

½ teaspoon sea salt

¼ teaspoon freshly ground black pepper

**TOP 10 REASONS TO MAKE THIS:**

10. To show up Captain High Liner, the bearded dude who breads everything.
9. Nobody will say, 'Mmm...tastes like chicken'.
8. Your mother-in-law is allergic to fish.
7. Thyme is an herb. Now that Simon & Garfunkel song makes even less sense.
6. With a glass of milk, you cover all your food groups.
5. Can drop 'Order Pleuronectiformes' (n. flatfish) into the convo.
4. Less 'experimental' than blowfish.
3. If ever you meet someone fluent in Mennonite Low German, you'll be able to communicate: Halibut = en Seefesch.
2. So easy to make. Like shooting fish in a barrel.
1. You get to eat and drink your dinner at the same time.

## METHOD

1) In a large frying pan, heat the oil over a high heat. Season the fish with the salt and pepper. Add the fish to the pan and cook for 2 minutes on each side until golden. Remove from pan and set aside. 2) For the stock, wipe the pan clean and heat the oil over a medium-low heat. Add the shallots and garlic and cook, stirring continuously, for 1 minute. Add the wine, increase the heat to medium-high and cook for 1 minute. Stir in the drained chopped tomatoes, stock, beans, thyme, salt and pepper. Bring to the boil, then reduce heat to low and simmer for 10 minutes. Add the fish to the pan, cover and simmer for a further 10 minutes or until the fish is cooked through.

Serves 6

# WALNUT-CRUSTED HALIBUT with LEMON WINE SAUCE

## INGREDIENTS

non-stick cooking spray

6 halibut fillets, 175–225g each, skin removed

½ teaspoon sea salt

¼ teaspoon freshly ground black pepper

### Walnut Crust

90g panko (Japanese) breadcrumbs

120g walnuts, chopped

60g Parmesan cheese, freshly grated

25g butter, melted

1 tablespoon horseradish

1 tablespoon Dijon mustard

1 tablespoon chopped flat-leaf parsley

1 tablespoon chopped dill

1 teaspoon finely grated lemon zest

1 tablespoon olive oil

### Lemon Wine Sauce

1 teaspoon olive oil

2 tablespoons finely chopped shallots

225ml dry white wine

2 tablespoons freshly squeezed lemon juice

25g butter

2 tablespoons chopped dill

sea salt and freshly ground black pepper to taste

**PISCES FEBRUARY 19 – MARCH 20**

You've been feeling pretty blah and boring lately. Don't fret because today's your day to dive in. Take the bait and get ready for a thrilling experience – becoming part of the 'in' crowd, happily mingling amongst bold, rich and nutty sorts. Surprisingly, you'll get on especially well with the cheesy, crusty and whiny ones too.

## METHOD

**1)** Preheat the oven to 220°C/425°F/Gas Mark 7. Line a baking sheet with foil and coat with non-stick cooking spray. **2)** Pat the fish dry with kitchen paper and season with the salt and pepper. Place on the prepared baking sheet 1cm apart. **3)** For the crust, in a medium bowl, combine the panko, walnuts and Parmesan. Mix in the melted butter, horseradish, mustard, parsley, dill and lemon zest to form a crumbly mixture. Divide the panko mixture evenly atop the fish and press gently to adhere. Drizzle the oil on top of the fish. Bake for 12–15 minutes until cooked through.

**4)** For the sauce, in a medium saucepan, heat the oil over a medium heat. Add the shallots and cook, stirring, for 2 minutes until slightly softened. Turn the heat to high and add the wine and lemon juice. Boil for about 6–8 minutes until the liquid is reduced. Reduce the heat to low and stir in the butter until melted. Remove from the heat and add the dill. Season to taste with salt and pepper. Serve the sauce over the crusted halibut.

Serves 6

### BITE ME BIT

'Fish, to taste right, must swim three times – in water, in butter and in wine.'

– Polish proverb

# SWEET and SOUR HALIBUT

## INGREDIENTS

### Halibut

non-stick cooking spray

8 halibut fillets, 175–225g each, skin removed

60ml dry white wine

1 teaspoon sea salt

### Sweet and Sour Sauce

240g tomato ketchup

175ml rice vinegar

140g sugar

4 tablespoons soy sauce

60ml dry white wine

1 tablespoon sesame oil

3 large red peppers, deseeded and diced

2 large celery sticks, diced

1 small onion, diced

500g deseeded and diced tomatoes

230g frozen green peas

5 tablespoons water

3 tablespoons cornflour

I love a good bet. You'll eat a spoonful of cinnamon for £10? Count me in. A swig of suicide hot sauce for £15? Money well spent. But here's the one thing I'd never bet against...this halibut. It's the 21, the Royal Flush, baby. Perfectly sweet and sour flavours and guaranteed rave reviews from company make this an ace fish dish.

## METHOD

**1)** Preheat the oven to 230°C/450°F/Gas Mark 8. Line a baking sheet with foil and coat with non-stick cooking spray. **2)** Place the fish on the prepared baking sheet and sprinkle with the wine and salt. Bake for 10–12 minutes or until the fish flakes easily. Set aside. **3)** For the sauce, in a large bowl, whisk the ketchup, vinegar, sugar, soy sauce, wine and sesame oil together. Set aside. **4)** Place the red peppers, celery and onion in a large frying pan over a medium heat. Cover and leave the vegetables to sweat for about 6 minutes until softened. Uncover, add the tomatoes and peas and stir gently to combine. Add the ketchup mixture and cook, uncovered, for 5 minutes. **5)** To thicken the sauce, in a small bowl, dissolve the cornflour in the water. Add to the sauce and cook over a medium heat for 3 minutes or until slightly thickened. Pour the sauce over the fish and serve.

Serves 8

## BITE ME BIT

'I'd be willing to bet you, if I was a betting man, that I have never bet on baseball.'

– Pete Rose, baseball player

# MISO GLAZED COD

## INGREDIENTS

### Miso Marinade

175ml sake

175ml mirin

225g white miso paste

2 tablespoons soy sauce

100g soft light brown sugar

6 cod fillets, about 175g each, (you can also use halibut or sea bass)

non-stick cooking spray

Made famous by celebrity chefs Nobuyuki 'Nobu' Matsuhisa and Wolfgang Puck, the pairing of miso and cod is, well, like peanut butter and jelly...they belong together. Though super-simple to make, remember to plan ahead because the longer the fish marinates, the better.

## METHOD

**1)** For the marinade, combine the sake and mirin in a medium saucepan over a high heat. Boil for 30 seconds. Turn the heat to low, add the miso paste and soy sauce and cook, stirring, until the paste is completely dissolved. Add the sugar, turn the heat back to high and cook, stirring continuously, until the sugar has dissolved. Remove from the heat and leave to cool to room temperature.
**2)** Pat the cod fillets dry with kitchen paper. Place the fish in a large resealable plastic bag, pour in the marinade and seal. Refrigerate for 12–24 hours, turning the bag occasionally.
**3)** Preheat the oven to 230°C/450°F/Gas Mark 8. Line a baking sheet with foil and coat with non-stick cooking spray. **4)** Remove the fish from the marinade, lightly wiping off any excess marinade clinging to the fillets. Place the cod on the prepared baking sheet and bake for 6–7 minutes. Finish cooking the fish under a preheated grill for 2–3 minutes, to get a glaze on top.

Serves 6

## BITE ME BIT

'...Ok, let's go to John Travolta. He wrote down "miso", a type of Italian soup. What was your wager? You wrote down "horny", "miso horny".'

– Alex Trebek (played by actor Will Ferrell) in a 1997 episode of 'Saturday Night Live'

# SURPRISE! COD WRAPPED in RICE PAPER

## INGREDIENTS

1½ teaspoons chopped basil

¾ teaspoon sea salt

½ teaspoon freshly ground black pepper

6 rice paper sheets

6 cod fillets, 175–225g each and 2.5cm thick

2 tablespoons olive oil

### Sauce

1 teaspoon olive oil

2 shallots, finely chopped

1 large garlic clove, finely chopped

6 tablespoons soy sauce

4 tablespoons rice vinegar

1½ teaspoons sugar

⅛ teaspoon dried chilli flakes

I'm a sucker for anything that arrives gift-wrapped. One time Lisa really threw me when she delivered a fine little bundle to my doorstep. At first I thought it was a new iPod, but then she unveiled a perfect parcel of cod wrapped in Vietnamese rice paper. I never could imagine – a present where you get to eat the gift AND the wrapping paper.

## METHOD

1) Preheat the oven to 230°C/450°F/Gas Mark 8. 2) In a small bowl, mix the basil, salt and pepper together. Set aside. 3) Fill a shallow dish with warm water. Carefully submerge one piece of rice paper in the water for 20 seconds, then remove, lay on a clean tea towel and place one cod fillet in the centre of the softened wrapper. Repeat with the remaining 5 rice paper sheets and cod. Divide the basil mixture between the fish fillets. Fold the ends of the rice paper around the cod and enclose securely. Set aside. 4) For the sauce, in a small sauté pan, warm the oil over a low heat. Add the shallots and garlic and sauté until softened. Add the soy sauce, vinegar, sugar and chilli flakes and cook, stirring, for 1 minute. Remove from the heat and set aside. 5) In a large ovenproof frying pan, heat the remaining 2 tablespoons oil over a high heat. Add the cod parcels and sear for 2 minutes on each side. Place the frying pan in the preheated oven for 5 minutes to finish cooking. Spoon the sauce over each piece and serve.

Serves 6

## BITE ME BIT

'Advice is cheap, Ms Molloy. It's the things that come gift-wrapped that count.'

– Horace Vandergelder (actor Walter Matthau) in the 1969 movie **Hello, Dolly!**

# LIP-SMACKING CRISPY COD SANDWICH

## INGREDIENTS

**Polenta-Crusted Cod**

non-stick cooking spray

75g polenta

½ teaspoon sea salt

¼ teaspoon freshly ground black pepper

4 tablespoons milk

6 cod fillets, about 175g each

6 hamburger buns

shredded iceberg lettuce

**Tartar Sauce**

225g mayonnaise

35g pickled dill cucumber, finely chopped

1 tablespoon freshly squeezed lemon juice

2 teaspoons Dijon mustard

pinch of cayenne pepper

Sing to the tune of 'My Bonnie Lies over the Ocean'

Today is the best day of his life,
Today is the day he eats fish,
My hubby will surely be drooling,
When he takes a big bi-ite of this.

Fish fillet, fish fillet,
Oh pile the tartar on high, -igh, -igh,
Fish fillet, fish fillet,
Baked crispy and easy as pie.

## METHOD

**1)** Preheat the oven to 230°C/450°F/Gas Mark 8. Line a baking sheet with foil and coat with non-stick cooking spray. **2)** In a medium bowl, combine the polenta, salt and pepper. Pour the milk into a separate bowl. **3)** Working with one fillet at a time, dip the fish in the milk and then dredge in the polenta mixture, completely coating the fish. Place on the prepared baking sheet and bake for 7 minutes. Flip the fillets and bake for a further 6 minutes until golden. **4)** For the tartar sauce, whisk all the ingredients together in a small bowl. **5)** To serve, put the crusted fish in the hamburger buns and top with the tartar sauce and shredded lettuce.

Serves 6

# CRUNCHY BAKED SEA BASS

## INGREDIENTS

non-sticking cooking spray

30 Ritz crackers, crushed into coarse crumbs

2 tablespoons chopped dill

75g mayonnaise

1 large garlic clove, finely chopped

2 tablespoons freshly squeezed lemon juice

2 teaspoons finely grated lemon zest

4 sea bass fillets, about 225g each, skin removed

¼ teaspoon sea salt

¼ teaspoon freshly ground black pepper

What's caviar without toast points, lobster without melted butter, shrimp without cocktail sauce? Half of a perfect whole. So too is sea bass without a crisp cracker top. A firm and versatile whitefish, sea bass acts as the perfect base for lemon-garlic mayonnaise, refreshing dill and a rich buttery cracker topping.

## METHOD

1) Put your oven shelf in the mid-to-lower part of the oven to ensure that the crumb topping doesn't burn before the fish is cooked through. 2) Preheat the oven to 230°C/450°F/Gas Mark 8. Line a baking sheet with foil and coat with non-stick cooking spray. 3) In a medium bowl, combine the cracker crumbs and 1 tablespoon of the dill. In another medium bowl, mix the remaining dill, mayonnaise, garlic, lemon juice and lemon zest together. 4) Pat the fish dry with kitchen paper and season with the salt and pepper. Place on the prepared baking sheet, spread the mayonnaise mixture over the fish and press the cracker crumbs on top. Bake for 13–15 minutes until the crumbs are golden and the fish is cooked through.

Serves 4

## BITE ME BIT

**Dr Evil:** When I ask for sharks with frickin' laser beams on their heads, I expect sharks with frickin' laser beams on their heads! What do we have?

**Number Two:** Sea Bass

– From the 1997 movie **Austin Powers: International Man of Mystery**

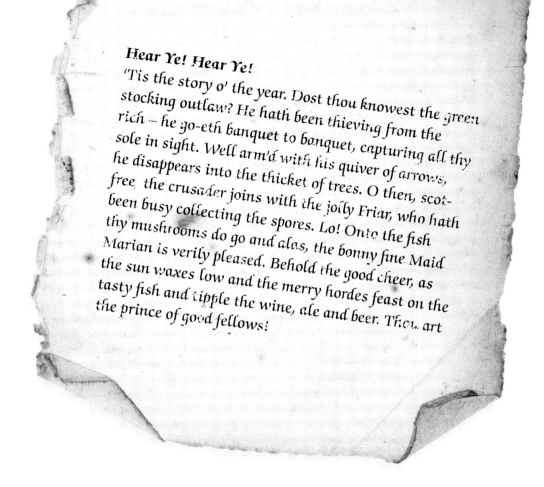

*Hear Ye! Hear Ye!*
*'Tis the story o' the year. Dost thou knowest the green stocking outlaw? He hath been thieving from the rich – he go-eth banquet to banquet, capturing all thy sole in sight. Well arm'd with his quiver of arrows, he disappears into the thicket of trees. O then, scot-free, the crusader joins with the jolly Friar, who hath been busy collecting the spores. Lo! Onto the fish thy mushrooms do go and alas, the bonny fine Maid Marian is verily pleased. Behold the good cheer, as the sun waxes low and the merry hordes feast on the tasty fish and tipple the wine, ale and beer. Thou art the prince of good fellows!*

## INGREDIENTS

non-stick cooking spray

1 tablespoon olive oil

2 shallots, finely chopped

1 large garlic clove, finely chopped

450g mushrooms (button, shiitake and chestnut), chopped

60ml chicken stock

60ml dry white wine

1 tablespoon flat-leaf parsley

2 teaspoons chopped thyme

½ teaspoon sea salt

¼ teaspoon freshly ground black pepper

60g panko (Japanese) breadcrumbs

4 sole fillets, about 175g each and 1cm thick

# MERRYMAKING MUSHROOM-CRUSTED SOLE

## METHOD

**1)** Preheat the oven to 220°C/425°F/Gas Mark 7. Line a baking sheet with foil and coat with non-stick cooking spray. **2)** In a large frying pan, heat the oil over a medium heat. Add the shallots and garlic and cook, stirring, for about 4 minutes until softened. **3)** Add the mushrooms and continue to cook until the liquid released from the mushrooms has evaporated. **4)** Remove from the heat and add the stock, wine, parsley, thyme, salt, pepper and panko. Stir to combine; the mixture should stick together. **5)** Pat the fish dry with kitchen paper and place on the prepared baking sheet. Top the fillets with the mushroom mixture, patting down to cover the whole piece. Bake for 10–12 minutes until the topping becomes slightly crusty.

*Serves 4*

# Pssssst...

## The Best Kitchen Secrets

**SERVING REFRESHMENTS** To make sure that you never experience premature evacuation, remember that a 750ml bottle of wine pours out 4 glasses' worth. As well, you get 16 shots out of a 750ml bottle of spirits and 5 flutes out of a bottle of champagne.

**BUYING FISH** Look in the eyes (should be bright and clear), inspect the skin (taut skin should be blemish-free and gills should be bright red) and take a whiff (there shouldn't be any offensive smell – fresh means virtually no odour).

**TOASTING NUTS** Put the nuts in a small ungreased frying pan and place over a medium heat for 4–6 minutes, stirring often, until golden brown. Alternatively, you can toast them by spreading them in a single layer on an ungreased baking sheet. Bake at 180°C/350°F/Gas Mark 4, stirring or shaking often, for 5–10 minutes. Watch carefully in order not to burn them. Transfer to a plate and leave to cool.

**SOFTENING BROWN SUGAR, MARSHMALLOWS AND CREAM CHEESE** To soften rock-hard brown sugar or marshmallows, place a slice of white bread in the bag or container. As for cream cheese, if you need it at room temperature quickly, put the cream cheese tub in a resealable plastic bag and submerge it in hot water for 5–10 minutes.

**AVOIDING STICKY UTENSILS** If you're worried about cling-ons such as honey, peanut butter or cheese, coat your weighing scales, spoons or cheese grater with non-stick cooking spray.

**MAKING PERFECT CORN** To husk corn cobs, using a damp cloth, brush in a downward motion to remove the corn silks. Bring a large saucepan of water to the boil. Add 1 tablespoon sugar and 125ml milk. Add the corn and return to the boil. Remove the pan from heat, cover and leave to stand for 10–15 minutes.

**HOW TO HARD-BOIL AN EGG** Place the eggs in a saucepan, cover with cold water and add a pinch of salt. Bring to a rapid boil over a high heat. Once the water boils, remove the pan from the heat and cover. Leave the eggs to stand, covered, for 12 minutes. Rinse under cold water and peel.

# SIZZLING TILAPIA with SWEET MANGO SALSA

## INGREDIENTS

### Mango Salsa

2 mangoes, stoned, peeled and diced

1 red pepper, deseeded and diced

2 tablespoons freshly squeezed lime juice

2 tablespoons olive oil

1 teaspoon deseeded and finely chopped green chilli

½ teaspoon sea salt

¼ teaspoon freshly ground black pepper

### Tilapia

4 tilapia fillets, 115–175g each

2 teaspoons chilli powder

2 teaspoons ground cumin

1 teaspoon dried oregano

1 teaspoon sea salt

2 tablespoons olive oil

Lights, Camera...I know it can be hard to get enthusiastic about fish. A reputation as 'healthy' certainly doesn't bring on the glitz and glam. But don't be blinded by the charm of chicken or the magnetism of meat. A mild fish like tilapia, rubbed in spices and sautéed, delivers exciting razzle-dazzle, and, topped with a sweet mango salsa... it's ShowTime!

## METHOD

1) Combine all the ingredients for the mango salsa in a medium bowl. Gently fold together with a rubber spatula, then leave the mixture to stand at room temperature for at least 30 minutes. 2) Pat the fish dry with kitchen paper. In a small bowl, mix the chilli powder, cumin, oregano and salt together. Rub both sides of each piece of tilapia with the spice mixture. 3) In a large frying pan, heat the oil over a medium-high heat. Add half the fish to the pan and sauté for about 3 minutes on each side until lightly browned and cooked through. Transfer the cooked fish to a serving platter. Repeat with the remaining tilapia, using the oil left in the pan. Spoon mango salsa on each piece before serving.

Serves 4

# ASIAN TUNA BURGERS

## INGREDIENTS

### Tuna Burger

675g fresh tuna steaks, finely chopped by hand

1 tablespoon soy sauce

1 tablespoon rice vinegar

1 large garlic clove, finely chopped

2 teaspoons grated fresh ginger

½ teaspoon sea salt

¼ teaspoon freshly ground black pepper

vegetable oil, for oiling

6 hamburger buns

115g shredded iceberg lettuce

3 large tomatoes, sliced

### Wasabi Mayonnaise

6 tablespoons mayonnaise

2 teaspoons soy sauce

2 teaspoons rice vinegar

1 teaspoon wasabi powder (or more if you want it spicier)

**You don't care where the beef is and you don't want to talk turkey? Well, try this – topped with a spicy wasabi mayonnaise, this tuna burger will give you plenty of meat to chew on.**

## METHOD

**1)** Line a baking sheet with baking paper. Set aside. **2)** For the burgers, in a medium bowl, mix the chopped tuna with the soy sauce, vinegar, garlic, ginger, salt and pepper. Using wet hands to prevent sticking, divide the mixture into 6 equal portions, shaping into patties about 2.5cm thick. Place on the prepared baking sheet and refrigerate for 20 minutes before grilling. **3)** Whisk all the ingredients for the sauce together in a small bowl. Cover and refrigerate for at least 15 minutes to allow the flavours to blend. **4)** Coat the rack of a gas barbecue with oil and heat to medium. Grill the tuna burgers for about 3 minutes on each side for medium doneness. Remove from the heat and leave to stand for 5 minutes. Place each burger on a bun and top with the wasabi mayonnaise, shredded lettuce and sliced tomato.

Serves 6

## BITE ME BIT

'What if you mix the mayonnaise in the can with the tuna fish? Or... hold it! Chuck! I got it! Take live tuna fish and feed 'em mayonnaise! Oh this is great. [speaks into tape recorder] Call Starkist!'

– Bill Blazejowski (actor Michael Keaton) in the 1982 movie **Night Shift**

# BARBECUED SWORDFISH with OLIVE RELISH

## INGREDIENTS

4 swordfish steaks,
175–225g each

4 tablespoons olive oil,
plus extra for oiling

freshly squeezed juice
of 1 lemon

1 tablespoon capers, chopped

1 tablespoon chopped
flat-leaf parsley

1 large garlic clove,
finely chopped

1 teaspoon finely grated
lemon zest

½ teaspoon dried oregano

½ teaspoon sea salt

¼ teaspoon freshly ground
black pepper

**Olive Relish**

45g green olives, pitted
and chopped

45g black olives, pitted
and chopped

4 tablespoons olive oil

1 tablespoon red wine vinegar

1 tablespoon chopped basil

1 teaspoon capers, drained
and chopped

⅛ teaspoon freshly ground
black pepper

Open secret. Free gift. Tight slacks. All oxymorons. If you'd add 'meaty fish' to the list, think again. Mild and firm swordfish is both hearty and filling. Why else would it be sold as 'steaks'? Move aside, beef. Straight off the barbecue, topped with an aromatic, bold relish of olives and capers – this swordfish is terribly good.

## METHOD

**1)** For the swordfish, place the steaks in a large resealable plastic bag. In a medium bowl, whisk the oil, lemon juice, capers, parsley, garlic, lemon zest, oregano, salt and pepper together. Pour over fish, seal the bag and place in the refrigerator to marinate for at least 1 hour and up to 12 hours. Turn the bag occasionally so that the marinade covers the fish. **2)** Combine all the ingredients for the olive relish in a small bowl. Cover and refrigerate until ready to use. Allow to come to room temperature before serving with the fish. **3)** Bring the swordfish to room temperature. Preheat a gas barbecue to medium-high and lightly oil the rack. Remove the fish from marinade and pat dry with kitchen paper. Place the fish on the rack and cook for 3–4 minutes on each side or until cooked through and the flesh flakes easily. Top the cooked swordfish with a heaped spoonful of the olive relish.

Serves 4

### BITE ME BIT

'There isn't any symbolism. The sea is the sea. The old man is an old man. The boy is a boy and the fish is a fish.'

– Ernest Hemingway, American author commenting on his 1952 classic **The Old Man and the Sea**

# SWEET CITRUS and SPICED SALMON

## INGREDIENTS

### Marinade

75ml pineapple juice

6 tablespoons freshly squeezed lemon juice

6 salmon fillets, about 175g each, skin removed

non-stick cooking spray

### Topping

100g soft light brown sugar

2 teaspoons freshly grated lemon zest

2 teaspoons chilli powder

1 teaspoon ground cumin

½ teaspoon sea salt

¼ teaspoon ground cinnamon

We are gathered here today to pay our respects to old-style salmon. It has had a long run, having lived in such diverse places as Michelin-rated restaurants and tin cans. Sharp and pungent, dear salmon was the kind of fish that lingered in the home and, even with the help of a mint-chaser, repeatedly roosted on the palate. Well, the funky days are behind us, but salmon lives on, survived by these mild, delicate and beautifully flavoured fillets. We will always keep the Omega-3s in our hearts. And let us say, Amen.

## METHOD

1) In a large resealable plastic bag, combine the pineapple juice, lemon juice and salmon. Seal the bag and refrigerate for 1 hour, turning occasionally. 2) Preheat the oven to 200°C/400°F/Gas Mark 6. Coat a 28 x 18cm baking dish with non-stick cooking spray. 3) Combine all the ingredients for the topping in a small bowl. Remove the salmon from the refrigerator and dispose of the marinade. Place the fillets in the prepared baking dish and rub the brown sugar mixture over salmon. Bake for 12 minutes or until the fish is flaky.

Serves 6

# CHILLED SALMON with LEMON DILL SAUCE

## INGREDIENTS

350ml dry white wine

350ml water

1 lemon, sliced

2 dill sprigs

1 dried bay leaf

½ tablespoons whole black peppercorns

1 teaspoon sea salt

½ teaspoon freshly ground black pepper

6 salmon fillets, about 175g each, skin removed

### Lemon Dill Sauce

225g mayonnaise

60ml buttermilk

1 tablespoon chopped dill

1 tablespoon fresh lemon juice

1 teaspoon wholegrain mustard

½ teaspoon finely grated lemon zest

Say 'Mrs Smith's Fish Sauce Shop' five times fast... I can't do it twice. But rather than taking 10 minutes to untwist your tongue, you could pull together this super-easy poached fish dish. By the time you can utter 'Fisherman Fritz fishes fresh fish, fresh fish does fisherman Fritz fish', the salmon will be perfectly chilled and ready to be smothered in the zesty dill sauce.

## METHOD

1) In a large frying pan, combine the wine, water, lemon slices, dill sprigs, bay leaf and peppercorns. Bring to the boil over a high heat. 2) Season the salmon fillets with the salt and pepper. Once the water has boiled, add the salmon to the frying pan, cover, turn the heat off and leave the fish to poach for 10 minutes or until flaky. Remove the salmon from the liquid and transfer to a plate. Cover and refrigerate for at least 2 hours before serving. 3) Whisk all the ingredients for the sauce together in a medium bowl. Cover and chill. Serve with the poached salmon.

Serves 6

## BITE ME BIT

Cookbook author Bob Blumer has turned urban legend into reality – he developed a foolproof method for poaching salmon in the dishwasher that requires foil, a wash-dry cycle and lemon-scented detergent.

# Meet me

## A Bloody Good Time For Meat Lovers

# ROAST BEEF with HERBED BREADCRUMB CRUST

## INGREDIENTS

non-stick cooking spray

2.25kg boned and rolled beef sirloin

1½ teaspoons sea salt

1 teaspoon freshly ground black pepper

1 tablespoon vegetable oil

6 slices white bread with crusts, pulsed in the food processor into coarse crumbs

2 tablespoons chopped flat-leaf parsley

2 large garlic cloves, finely chopped

1 large shallot, finely chopped

1 teaspoon dried thyme

1 teaspoon dried rosemary

55g butter, melted

75g Dijon mustard

1 tablespoon dry white wine

### Horseradish Sauce

225ml soured cream

4 tablespoons (or to taste) bottled grated horseradish in vinegar

2 tablespoons Dijon mustard

1 teaspoon freshly squeezed lemon juice

½ teaspoon sea salt

⅛ teaspoon cayenne pepper (optional)

In the lore of Greek mythology, or in the lore of Wikipedia, the Delphic oracle was having a chat with Apollo and happened to mention that horseradish is worth its weight in gold. Maybe they had just wolfed down some gefilte fish together. Or maybe they were discussing how much it enhances this classic Sunday dish.

## METHOD

1) Place the oven shelf on the bottom level to prevent the roast beef crust from burning. Preheat the oven to 200°C/400°F/Gas Mark 6. Line a baking sheet with foil. Place a roasting rack on the baking sheet and coat with non-stick cooking spray. 2) Trim the meat of visible fat and then pat dry with kitchen paper. Season with 1 teaspoon of the salt and the pepper, rubbing in on all sides. 3) In a large frying pan, heat the oil over a medium-high heat. Brown the meat for about 3 minutes on each side. Transfer to the prepared roasting rack. Set aside. 4) In a large bowl, combine the breadcrumbs, parsley, garlic, shallot, thyme, rosemary, remaining ½ teaspoon salt and the melted butter. In a small bowl, combine the mustard and wine, then brush over the roast and lightly press with the breadcrumb mixture to adhere. 5) Insert a meat thermometer into the thickest portion of the roast. Roast in the oven for between 1 hour and 20 minutes and 1 hour and 30 minutes for rare meat; the thermometer should read 60°C/140°F. Should the crust start to brown before cooking is finished, tent the roast with foil and continue cooking. 6) Combine the ingredients for the horseradish sauce in a small bowl. Cover and refrigerate until ready to use. 7) After removing roast from oven, leave the meat to rest for 10 minutes, uncovered, before slicing. Serve the sliced beef with the horseradish sauce on the side.

Serves 8–10

# BARBECUED NY STEAKS with RED WINE SAUCE

## INGREDIENTS

**Red Wine Sauce**

15g butter

1 tablespoon olive oil

40g white onion, diced

35g peeled and chopped carrot

30g celery, chopped

1 teaspoon chopped thyme

¾ teaspoon freshly ground black pepper

225ml dry red wine

900ml beef stock

1 tablespoon tomato purée

½ teaspoon sea salt

4 prime porterhouse steaks, 280–350g each and 4cm thick

2 tablespoons olive oil

2 teaspoons sea salt

2 teaspoons freshly ground black pepper

Sing to the tune of 'New York, New York'

Start lightin' the que, the beef is prime
I'm gonna gorge on it – NEW YORKS, NEW YORKS
These classic steaks, are timeless beauties
Right through the juicy core of them –
NEW YORKS, NEW YORKS

I wanna cut my meat with a fork, it's so tender
And perfectly cru-u-u-sted – top o' the grill

These forkfuls of mine, are made divine
When I add rich red wine sauce – to old New Yorks
If my lipids can take it, I'll make steak everyday
It's up to my ticker – NEW YORKS, NEW YORKS

## METHOD

**1)** For the sauce, in a large frying pan, melt the butter with the oil over a medium heat. Add the onion, carrot, celery, thyme and ½ teaspoon pepper. Stir and sauté for 5 minutes until tender but not browned. Add the wine and cook for 5 minutes. Increase heat to medium-high, add the stock and tomato purée and cook, stirring occasionally, for 25 minutes or until reduced to 225ml. Season with the salt and ¼ teaspoon pepper. Set aside until the steaks are prepared. **2)** Remove the steaks from the refrigerator 30 minutes before cooking to bring to room temperature. **3)** Preheat a gas barbecue to high. Just prior to cooking, season the steaks on both sides with the oil and the salt and pepper. Place on the hottest part of the rack to sear the outside and seal in the juices. Turn after 5 minutes and cook for a further 5 minutes for a pink, medium centre. Remove from the heat and leave to rest for 5 minutes before slicing, during which time they will cook a few degrees more. If you're unsure if done, use a meat thermometer: 43.3°C/110°F (rare), 48.9°C/120°F (medium-rare), 51.7°C/125°F (medium), 54.4°C/130°F (medium-well), 60°C/140°F (well-done).

Serves 4–6

## BITE ME BIT

'If we're not supposed to eat animals,
how come they're made out of meat?'

– Tom Snyder, TV talk show host

# BEEF, MUSHROOM and PEPPER SHISH KEBABS

## INGREDIENTS

**Sweet Marinade**

360g tomato ketchup

175ml Manischewitz wine (sweet kosher wine)

6 tablespoons soft light brown sugar

1 teaspoon freshly ground black pepper

4 garlic cloves, peeled and cut in half

675g sirloin steak, cut into 4cm cubes

1 red pepper, deseeded and cut into 4cm pieces

1 yellow pepper, deseeded and cut into 4cm pieces

1 green pepper, deseeded and cut into 4cm pieces

225g button mushrooms, left whole, stems trimmed

Forget tannins, lees and acidity. Try sniffing and swigging Manischewitz wine, our One and Only, the perfect blend of Concord grapes and corn syrup. Yes, corn syrup. Don't stick your noses in the air, you oenophiles out there – consider the magic this superior kosher wine can perform. Chunks of beef, crisp peppers and meaty mushrooms are marinated in a syrupy Manischewitz sauce and barbecued to sweet-crusted, tender perfection.

## METHOD

**1)** In a medium bowl, whisk the ketchup, wine, sugar and pepper together. Pour 300ml of the marinade into a large resealable plastic bag and add the garlic halves, beef cubes, all the peppers and the mushrooms to the marinade. Seal the bag, turn to coat and refrigerate for at least 2 hours and up to 24 hours. Refrigerate the remaining marinade to use for basting at the end of cooking. **2)** Preheat a gas barbecue to medium-high heat. **3)** Remove the meat and vegetables from the plastic bag and discard the marinade. Thread the beef onto metal skewers. Thread the peppers and mushrooms onto separate skewers from the beef to ensure even cooking. **4)** Cook the kebabs for 8–10 minutes, turning one-quarter rotation every 2–3 minutes or until the meat is cooked through and vegetables are tender-crisp. In the final 2 minutes of cooking time, baste all sides of the beef and vegetable kebabs with the reserved marinade. **5)** Remove the beef and vegetables from skewers and toss with extra marinade.

*Serves 6*

# BRAISED BEEF THIN RIBS

## INGREDIENTS

2.7kg beef thin ribs, bone-in, trimmed of excess fat

sea salt and freshly ground black pepper

2 tablespoons rapeseed oil

2 onions, chopped

2 carrots, peeled and chopped

2 celery sticks, chopped

4 large garlic cloves, finely chopped

2 tablespoons tomato purée

2 tablespoons plain flour

700ml dry, full-bodied red wine, such as Zinfandel

700ml chicken stock

240g barbecue sauce

4 tablespoons sugar

2 thyme sprigs

2 (7.5cm long) strips orange zest, pared with a vegetable peeler

2 dried bay leaves

mashed potatoes or polenta, to serve

In Act 5, Scene 5, Line 19, methinks Macbeth is soliloquising about this recipe – yes, tomorrow, and tomorrow, and tomorrow. Or maybe it was Orphan Annie. In either case, it will always be a day away when you finally enjoy these fork-tender thin ribs. What you'll need to do today is wait as the beef slowly cooks until it becomes succulent and falls from the bone. Worth every braising-hour, the ribs are then transferred to the refrigerator overnight, allowing the deep, rich flavours time to intensify.

## METHOD

**1)** Preheat the oven to 230°C/450°F/Gas Mark 8. In a large roasting tin, arrange the trimmed ribs in a single layer. Season them on both sides with 2 teaspoons salt and 2 teaspoons pepper. Roast the ribs for 25 minutes. Turn them over using tongs and roast for another 20–25 minutes until they are nicely browned. Transfer the ribs to a large plate and set aside. **2)** Reduce the oven temperature to 150°C/300°F/Gas Mark 2. **3)** In a large, flameproof casserole dish, heat the oil over a medium-high heat. Add the onions, carrots and celery and sauté, stirring often, for about 10 minutes until tender. Add the garlic and sauté for 1 minute. Stir in the tomato purée and flour and cook for 1 minute. Add all the remaining ingredients along with 1 teaspoon salt and ½ teaspoon pepper. Increase the heat to high, bring to the boil and add the ribs, preferably in a single layer, along with any accumulated juices. Reduce the heat to low and spoon some of the liquid over the ribs. Cover the dish and transfer to the oven. **4)** Braise for 2½ hours, turning the ribs with tongs every 45 minutes and skimming and discarding whatever fat may have risen to the surface. After the cooking time, the meat should be tender and pulling away from the bone. **5)** Remove from the oven and leave the ribs to cool in the liquid for 2 hours. **6)** Using a slotted spoon, transfer the meat that has fallen off the ribs into a storage container, shred the meat and refrigerate overnight. **7)** Strain the braising liquid through a fine-mesh sieve into a jug, pressing gently on the solids to extract the liquid. Cover the liquid and refrigerate overnight. Discard the solids from the sieve. **8)** The next day, remove the excess fat that has solidified at the top of the braising liquid. **9)** In a large, heavy saucepan, bring the defatted liquid to the boil. Lower the heat to medium-low and simmer for 15 minutes to reduce and thicken sauce. Add the shredded meat from the ribs and continue to simmer for 10–15 minutes, stirring occasionally, until heated through. Remove from the heat and add salt and pepper to taste. Serve over mashed potatoes or creamy polenta.

Serves 6

## BITE ME BIT

**Jeffries:** When am I going to see you again?

**Lisa:** Not for a long time...at least not until tomorrow night.

– from the 1954 movie **Rear Window**

# H-CRUSTED BEEF FILLET

## INGREDIENTS

non-stick cooking spray

1.3kg fillet of beef

1 teaspoon sea salt

½ teaspoon freshly ground black pepper

35g Dijon mustard

2 tablespoons wholegrain mustard

3 tablespoons chopped basil

3 tablespoons chopped flat-leaf parsley

2 tablespoons chopped thyme

Lisa asked me, 'What's with the h?' and I told her that I wanted to show my sensitive side. A certain kind of seasoning leaves people mumbling, unsure whether to say, 'Herb', 'erb' or 'cannabis'. So now there's no more tension. Just grab the basil, parsley and thyme because you're going to sculpt a crust on a lean, luscious cut of beef. And don't worry. You won't have to wrap it in – how do you say it? Fy-lo? Fee-lo?

## METHOD

1) Preheat the oven to 200°C/400°F/Gas Mark 6. Line a baking sheet with foil and coat with non-stick cooking spray. 2) Place the beef on the prepared baking sheet and sprinkle with the salt and pepper. Spread the Dijon and wholegrain mustard over the top and sides of the beef. 3) In a small bowl, combine the basil, parsley and thyme and pat evenly over the beef. 4) Bake for 45 minutes for medium-rare, and when a meat thermometer registers 63°C/145°F. Remove from the oven and leave to rest for 10 minutes before slicing.

Serves 8

### BITE ME BIT

'You say "erbs", and we say "herbs", because there's a f***ing 'H' in it!'

— Eddie Izzard, comedian

# BEEF BOURGUIGNON

Crème anglaise. Foie gras. Bouillabaisse. Somehow everything sounds more complicated in French. Even the name of the French chef who helped make beef bourguignon famous, Auguste Escoffier, makes him sound very complicated. But don't be put off by the haute name. This retro classic dish isn't as EMBROUILLÉ as it sounds – it's rustic beef stew made robust with a bottle of full-bodied wine. So, in other words, chillez-vous.

## INGREDIENTS

900g stewing beef, cubed

sea salt and freshly ground black pepper

2 tablespoons vegetable oil

1 large onion, cut into 2.5cm cubes

1 large red onion, cut into 2.5cm cubes

4 carrots, peeled and thickly sliced on the diagonal

2 garlic cloves, finely chopped

1 teaspoon finely chopped rosemary

1 teaspoon finely chopped thyme

½ teaspoon sea salt

½ teaspoon freshly ground black pepper

60ml brandy or cognac

1 bottle full-bodied red wine (cabernet or pinot noir)

475ml beef stock

1 tablespoon tomato purée

1 tablespoon olive oil

675g chestnut mushrooms, wiped clean, stems discarded, left whole if not too large

35g butter, softened

3 tablespoons plain flour

## METHOD

**1)** For a deeply flavoured stew, you'll need to brown the beef. Dry the beef cubes well with kitchen paper and toss with ½ teaspoon salt and ½ teaspoon pepper. In a large flameproof casserole dish, heat the vegetable oil over a medium heat. Add the beef and sauté until it is well browned on all sides but not burned. Add the onions and carrots and cook, stirring, for about 5 mintues until lightly browned. Add the garlic, rosemary, thyme and ½ teaspoon salt and ½ teaspoon pepper and cook, stirring, for another minute.
**2)** Turn the heat to high, add the brandy and cook until only a thin glaze of liquid remains. Add the wine, stock and tomato purée, scraping up all the browned bits that remain. Lower the heat, cover and simmer gently for 2 hours or until the beef is tender.
**3)** When the beef is finished cooking, in a medium frying pan, heat the olive oil over a medium-high heat. Add the mushrooms and cook for 5–6 minutes until well browned. Stir into the beef mixture. **4)** In a small bowl, blend the softened butter and flour into a paste. Add to the beef and simmer over a low heat for about 10 minutes until the liquid becomes slightly thickened. Season to taste with salt and pepper. This stew is even better the following day as the flavours have a chance to blend.

Serves 6–8

# MAGNIFIQUE MEATLOAF with MUSHROOM GRAVY

## INGREDIENTS

### Meatloaf

non-stick cooking spray

2 tablespoons olive oil

1 small white onion, diced

1 large garlic clove, finely chopped

3 slices white bread, crusts removed, pulsed in a food processor until coarse crumbs

2 large eggs

120g tomato ketchup

1 tablespoon soy sauce

2 teaspoons Worcestershire sauce

2 teaspoons Dijon mustard

1 teaspoon sea salt

½ teaspoon freshly ground black pepper

½ teaspoon hot Asian chili sauce

900g lean beef mince

### Mushroom Gravy

2 tablespoons olive oil

900g mixed chestnut and button mushrooms, peeled and sliced

1 small white onion, finely chopped

1 large garlic clove, finely chopped

1 tablespoon tomato purée

25g butter

¼ teaspoon sea salt

¼ teaspoon freshly ground black pepper

2 tablespoons plain flour

60ml dry red wine

475ml beef stock

1 tablespoon soy sauce

So I said to Lisa, embellishing this diner delight is pas de problème. Just give it a French name. La Plaque-Bleue Spéciale. But my blue ribbon-obsessed-sister outdid herself again, creating a tour de force – an elegant, moist, most flavourful meatloaf, topped with the perfect complement, a rich mushroom medley.

## METHOD

**1)** For the meatloaf, preheat the oven to 190°C/375°F/Gas Mark 5. Cover the top of a wire rack with foil and poke small holes all over the foil to ensure drainage while the meatloaf cooks. Coat the foil with non-stick cooking spray and place atop a large baking sheet. **2)** Heat the oil in a small frying pan over a medium heat. Add the onion and sauté for 4–5 minutes until tender. Turn the heat off and add the garlic. Leave to cool slightly. **3)** In a large bowl, mix the breadcrumbs, eggs, ketchup, soy, Worcestershire sauce, mustard, salt, pepper, chilli sauce and onion mixture together. Add the beef mince and gently mix just until combined. Transfer the meat to the foil-covered rack and shape into an oval about 5cm high. Bake for 60–65 minutes or until cooked through. Remove from the oven and leave to rest for 10 minutes before slicing. **4)** For the gravy, in a large frying pan, heat the oil over a medium heat. Add the sliced mushrooms and sauté for 3 minutes. Add the onion, garlic, tomato purée, butter, salt and pepper and continue to cook for 2–3 minutes until the onion is tender. Sprinkle the flour over the mushrooms and toss to coat. Turn the heat to high, add the wine and cook, stirring, until the liquid has evaporated. Add the stock and soy sauce and bring to the boil. Reduce the heat to low and simmer for about 5 minutes until the gravy has thickened. Serve immediately with the meatloaf.

Serves 6–8

# RUSTIC MEATBALLS in MARINARA SAUCE

Rocco's Mama inspires us. She spends endless hours rolling meatballs in her son's restaurant basement, which made us wonder what it would take to persuade our own talented Mom to move from matzo balls to meatballs. Mom…you ok down there?

## INGREDIENTS

### Marinara Sauce

1 white onion, chopped

4 large garlic cloves, finely chopped

3 tablespoons olive oil

6 x 400g cans chopped tomatoes

125ml dry red wine

sea salt

¼ teaspoon dried chilli flakes

¼ teaspoon freshly ground black pepper

3 tablespoons chopped basil

3 tablespoons sugar

### Meatballs

non-stick cooking spray

3 large eggs, lightly beaten

5 slices white bread, crusts removed, pulsed in a food processor until coarse crumbs

115g Parmesan cheese, freshly grated

1 tablespoon chopped flat-leaf parsley

2 large garlic cloves, finely chopped

1 teaspoon dried oregano

1 teaspoon sea salt

½ teaspoon freshly ground black pepper

1.3kg lean beef mince

cooked pasta, to serve

## METHOD

**1)** For the sauce, in a large saucepan, combine the onion, garlic and oil over a medium-low heat and cook, stirring often, for about 8 minutes until the onion is tender. Add the canned tomatoes and their juice, wine, 1 teaspoon salt, chilli flakes and pepper. Bring to the boil over a high heat. Reduce the heat to low and simmer, uncovered, for 30 minutes. Remove from the heat and, using a hand-held or freestanding blender, purée the sauce to the desired consistency. Stir in the basil and sugar. Cover, return to a medium-low heat and cook for 5 minutes. Season to taste with salt. **2)** For the meatballs, preheat the oven to 190°C/375°F/Gas Mark 5. Line 2 baking sheets with foil and coat with non-stick cooking spray. **3)** In a large bowl, combine the eggs, breadcrumbs, Parmesan, parsley, garlic, oregano, salt and pepper. Add the beef mince and mix to combine. **4)** Shape the meat mixture into approximately 50 meatballs and place on the prepared baking sheets. Bake for 20 minutes, turning the meatballs halfway through cooking. Remove from the oven and place the meatballs on kitchen paper to drain off any excess fat. Place the meatballs in the marinara sauce and serve with cooked pasta.

Serves 8–10

# PA-ANA-A-KA-LA (Sunshine) PINEAPPLE MEATBALLS

## INGREDIENTS

### Meatballs

non-stick cooking spray

900g lean beef mince

55g fresh breadcrumbs

175ml milk

2 large eggs, lightly beaten

2 teaspoons sea salt

½ teaspoon freshly ground black pepper

### Sweet and Sour Pineapple Sauce

750g canned pineapple chunks in syrup

420g Heinz chili sauce or barbecue sauce

1 red pepper, deseeded and cubed

125ml soy sauce

125ml cider vinegar

100g soft light brown sugar

40g cornflour

225ml water

Can't you just hear Elvis strumming a uke? See Harry Truman sporting an Aloha shirt? Well, now you can taste some Polynesian paradise in these sweet and sour pineapple meatballs. Rock-a-hula Baby and get rolling on these supremely saucy, tender spheres best piled atop a Mauna-kea (white mountain) of rice.

PS. A special Mahalo Nui Loa to Susan Hall for sharing her recipe.

## METHOD

1) For the meatballs, preheat the oven to 200°C/400°F/ Gas Mark 6. Line a large baking sheet with foil and coat with non-stick cooking spray. 2) In a large bowl, mix the beef mince, breadcrumbs, milk, eggs, salt and pepper together until combined. Add 2 handfuls of very cold water to the bowl and mix until combined. Shape the beef mixture into 2.5cm meatballs. Place in a single layer on the prepared baking sheet and bake for 12–15 minutes. Remove from the oven and drain on kitchen paper. 3) For the pineapple sauce, in a large saucepan, combine the pineapple chunks with their syrup, chilli or barbecue sauce, red pepper, soy sauce, vinegar and sugar. Place the cornflour in a small dish, stir in the water until smooth and add to the saucepan. Bring to the boil over a medium heat and cook, stirring continuously, until the sauce thickens. Gently stir the meatballs into the sauce and cook until heated through.

Serves 8–10

## BITE ME BIT

**Grandpa Gustafson:** I have been to Hawaii.

**Mama Ragetti:** Oh yeah? Which island?

**Grandpa Gustafson:** ComeonIwannalayya.

– from the 1995 movie **Grumpier Old Men**

# HOISIN and GINGER BEEF STIR-FRY

## INGREDIENTS

675g fillet of beef, cut into thin, bite-sized strips

4 tablespoons hoisin sauce

½ teaspoon grated fresh ginger

### Vegetables

2 tablespoons groundnut oil

1 large garlic clove, finely chopped

1 teaspoon grated fresh ginger

85g mushrooms (shiitake, button or portobello), sliced

180g celery, thinly sliced

1 large red pepper, deseeded and sliced into thin strips

150g mangetout, trimmed and cut on the diagonal

### Asian Sauce

125ml beef stock

4 tablespoons teriyaki marinade

4 tablespoons hoisin sauce

1 tablespoon sesame oil

2 tablespoons cornflour

2 tablespoons cold water

1 tablespoon sesame seeds, toasted

1 tablespoon thinly sliced basil leaves

Most stir-fry recipes commit the worst wok offences: rubbery beef, not enough sauce and bland, mushy vegetables. Not ours. Get ready to stir-fry beef fillet until it's sweet and juicy. Get ready to be amazed by saucy, crisp vegetables. But most of all, get ready...do all the slicing and whisking before you even turn on the burner and you'll get a gold medal in the fast and furious sport of stir-frying.

## METHOD

**1)** Place the beef in a medium bowl and add the hoisin sauce and ginger. Cover and leave to marinate for at least 20 minutes.
**2)** For the vegetables, heat the groundnut oil in a large wok over a high heat. Add the garlic, ginger, mushrooms, celery and red pepper and stir-fry for 2 minutes. Add the mangetout and stir-fry for a further 1 minute. Remove the vegetables from the wok and set aside. **3)** For the Asian sauce, in a medium bowl, whisk the stock, teriyaki marinade, hoisin sauce and sesame oil together. In a small dish, blend the cornflour and water until smooth. Add to the stock mixture and whisk to combine. Set aside. **4)** Reheat the wok over a high heat. Add the beef and stir-fry for 3 minutes until browned. Add the sauce and continue to cook for 1 minute, allowing it to thicken slightly. Return the vegetables to the wok and toss to combine. Remove from the heat and sprinkle with the sesame seeds and basil.

Serves 6

# BEEF FAJITAS with SOUTHWESTERN RICE

## INGREDIENTS

900g sirloin steak

8 (20-cm) flour tortillas

125ml soured cream

115g salsa

### Marinade

75ml freshly squeezed lime juice

60ml tequila

3 tablespoons vegetable oil

1 large garlic clove, finely chopped

1 teaspoon chilli powder

1 teaspoon ground cumin

½ teaspoon dried oregano

½ teaspoon freshly ground black pepper

½ teaspoon sea salt

### Vegetables

1 tablespoon vegetable oil

1 large white onion, halved and thinly sliced

1 large red pepper, deseeded and thinly sliced

1 large yellow pepper, deseeded and thinly sliced

½ teaspoon sea salt

Julie: Breaker, breaker. Got your ears on, Dough Girl?

Lisa: Yes, Julie.

Julie: No, not Julie. It's Pencil Head and say 10-4.

Lisa (sigh): Big 10-4, Pencil Head.

Julie: What's your 20?

Lisa: Where else? On the way home from the supermarket.

Julie: Peel your eyeballs for Kojak with a Kodak.

Lisa: What are you talking about?

Julie: Smokey Bear. City Kitty. Johnny Law. Black 'n' Whites.

Lisa: Yah, ok. I mean, copy.

Julie: What's the grub tonight at Home Base?

Lisa: Fajitas. Want some, Pencil Head?

Julie: Roger Dodger. Put the hammer down and let the motor toter. Catch you on the flip-flop, Dough Girl. Eights.

## METHOD

1) Preheat the oven to 160°C/325°F/Gas Mark 3. 2) Trim the visible fat from the steaks and set aside. 3) For the marinade, in a large bowl, whisk the lime juice, tequila, 2 tablespoons vegetable oil, garlic, chilli powder, cumin, oregano and pepper together. Add the steak and turn to coat well. Cover and leave to marinate in the refrigerator for at least 2 hours or overnight. 4) Drain the marinade from the meat and discard. Pat the steaks dry with kitchen paper and season with the salt. Cut the meat across the grain, diagonally, into thin, finger-length strips. In a large frying

### Southwestern Rice

1 tablespoon olive oil

1 small white onion, finely chopped

1 green pepper, deseeded and diced

1 small garlic clove, finely chopped

475ml chicken stock

200g long-grain rice

½ teaspoon ground cumin

½ teaspoon chilli powder

260g canned black beans, rinsed and drained

225g salsa

pan, heat the remaining 1 tablespoon vegetable oil over a high heat. Add the sliced steak and cook, stirring, for 2–3 minutes until the desired doneness. Remove the beef from the pan and set aside. **5)** For the vegetables, heat the vegetable oil in the pan over a high heat. Add the onion and peppers and sauté for about 4 minutes just until they start to soften. Season the mixture with the salt. Add the beef, stir to combine and remove from the heat. **6)** Warm the tortillas by sealing them in a foil packet. Place them in the preheated oven for 10 minutes. Keep wrapped until ready to assemble. **7)** For the rice, in a large saucepan, heat the olive oil over a medium heat. Add the onion, green pepper and garlic and sauté for 3 minutes until the vegetables have softened. Stir in the stock, rice, cumin and chilli powder and bring to the boil. Reduce the heat to low, cover and simmer for 15 minutes or until the water is absorbed and the rice is tender. Remove the lid and stir in the black beans and salsa. **8)** To serve, place a spoonful of rice on the bottom of each warmed tortilla. Top with the meat mixture. Add a spoonful of soured cream and salsa. Fold the 2 sides of the tortilla in and roll up into a cylinder.

Serves 6–8

# SWELL VEAL PICCATA

## INGREDIENTS

2 teaspoons olive oil

1 large shallot, finely chopped

475ml chicken stock

675g (about 6) veal cutlets, 5mm thick

½ teaspoon sea salt

½ teaspoon freshly ground black pepper

70g plain flour

2 tablespoons olive oil

3 tablespoons freshly squeezed lemon juice

2 tablespoons chopped flat-leaf parsley

25g butter

1 tablespoon capers, drained

**Son No 1:** Someone saw you messin' around in the schoolyard with a girl. Wait'll the guys find out...

**Son No 2:** I'm gonna slug you, you rat fink.

**Mother:** Boys, stop the ruckus. I have 5 minutes to get Father's dinner on the table.

**Son No 1:** Don't sweat it, Mom. Just make that super duper saucy veal.

**Mother:** We don't sweat in this house, son. We perspire. I'll wash your mouth out with soap. Boys, to your room.

**Sons:** Aw, gee, Mom.

Father arrives home and immediately sits down and cuts into the zesty, tender veal scaloppini.

**Mother:** Dear, I'm very worried about the Beaver.

**Father:** Why, dear, this isn't beaver. It's veal.

## METHOD

**1)** In a medium saucepan, heat the oil over a medium heat. Add the shallot and cook for 2 minutes or until it begins to soften. Add the stock and bring to the boil over a high heat. Turn the heat down to medium and simmer for 6 minutes or until the liquid is reduced by half. Set aside. **2)** Pat the veal dry with kitchen paper. Sprinkle each piece with the salt and pepper. Place the flour on a flat surface. **3)** Working in 2 batches, heat 1 tablespoon oil in a large frying pan over a high heat. Dredge the first batch of cutlets on one side in the flour, shaking off the excess. Place in the pan, flour-side down. Cook for 1½ minutes, flip and cook for a further minute or until the veal is no longer pink. Transfer to a serving plate. Repeat with the remaining veal cutlets. Add to the serving plate. **4)** Add the stock mixture to the pan. Bring to a simmer over a medium heat and cook for 2 minutes, scraping up the browned bits from the bottom. Remove from the heat and stir in the lemon juice, parsley, butter and capers. Pour over the cutlets and serve.

Serves 4

# VEAL MARSALA

## INGREDIENTS

70g plain flour

½ teaspoon sea salt

¼ teaspoon freshly ground
black pepper

675g veal scaloppini

25g butter

2 tablespoons olive oil

### Marsala Sauce

1 large shallot, finely chopped

225g button mushrooms, sliced

225g shiitake mushrooms, stems
discarded and sliced

225ml dry Marsala

225ml chicken stock

225ml beef stock

25g butter

### NOTES FROM THE SOFA

'During our first session, she told me all about her sweet daughter, Marsala. This made me pause. An interesting name choice. Motivated by love for Marcello Mastroianni? Marcel Marceau? It left me wondering what she might be sublimating. I had to delve deeper into the recesses of her subconscious. It wasn't until our third session that it became abundantly clear I was heading in the very wrong direction as she raved about her tender son, a kid named Vitello.

## METHOD

1) Combine the flour, salt and pepper in a shallow dish. Pat the veal dry with kitchen paper, then dredge both sides of the veal in flour, shaking off the excess. 2) In a large non-stick frying pan, heat half the butter with half the oil over a medium-high heat. Add half the veal and sear for about 1–1½ minutes on each side to just cook through. Remove and place on a serving plate. Repeat with the remaining butter, oil and veal. Remove the veal from the pan and set aside. 3) For the Marsala sauce, add the shallot and mushrooms to the frying pan. Cook over a high heat, stirring continually, for about 3 minutes until the mushrooms begin to soften. Add the Marsala and cook for 3 minutes. Stir in the chicken and beef stocks and bring to the boil. Boil for 7–8 minutes, stirring often. Turn the heat to low and stir in the butter. Return the veal to the pan, turn once or twice to baste it in the sauce and warm through before serving.

Serves 4–6

# BARBECUED VEAL CHOPS

## INGREDIENTS

### Marinade

4 tablespoons olive oil

2 tablespoons red wine vinegar

2 tablespoons freshly squeezed lemon juice

1 tablespoon Dijon mustard

1 tablespoon chopped thyme

1 tablespoon chopped rosemary

1 teaspoon finely grated lemon zest

½ teaspoon sea salt

¼ teaspoon freshly ground black pepper

4 bone-in veal rib chops, 400–450g each and about 4cm thick

1 lemon, cut into 4 wedges

Lisa's been trying out her jokes on me: Did you hear the one about the cow and the lamb? I can't tell you the punch line. I'm too ashamed. But I guess I have to cut her some slack – it's her heifer humour for her butcher. 'He thinks I'm hilarious,' she claims, 'and he calls me honey.'

## METHOD

**1)** In a small bowl, whisk the oil, vinegar, lemon juice, mustard, thyme, rosemary, lemon zest, salt and pepper together. Place the veal chops in a resealable plastic bag and pour in the marinade, turning to coat. Seal the bag and leave to marinate in the refrigerator for 4–6 hours. **2)** Preheat a gas barbecue to medium-high heat. **3)** Remove the chops from the marinade and cook for 6–8 minutes on each side for medium-rare. Quickly sear all the edges and remove from rack. **4)** Cook the lemon wedges on the rack until lightly charred and tender. Serve each veal chop with a lemon wedge.

Serves 4

## BITE ME BIT

'All normal people love meat. If I went to a barbecue and there was no meat, I would say "Yo Goober! Where's the meat?" I'm trying to impress people here, Lisa. You don't win friends with salad.'

– Homer Simpson on the television series 'The Simpsons'

# THE TOTALLY TUBULAR BURGER

## INGREDIENTS

### Burgers

900g lean beef mince

60g barbecue sauce

15g fresh breadcrumbs

1 tablespoon Dijon mustard

1 tablespoon olive oil, plus extra for oiling

1 large egg

1½ teaspoons sea salt

½ teaspoon freshly ground black pepper

4 hamburger buns

### Special Sauce

120g tomato ketchup

115g mayonnaise

1½ tablespoons sweet green relish

2 teaspoons Worcestershire sauce

¼ teaspoon sea salt

¼ teaspoon freshly ground black pepper

The '80s were, like, so good to us – Lisa had like, TOTALLY excellent bangs and I had a killer perm. As for our parents, they were, like, totally mental for burgers and we were, like, um, take a chill pill. But we were, like, totally happy when they opened a wicked burger restaurant and bummed when it went the way of the DeLorean. Now, we're, like, totally walking on sunshine again with this awesome remake of the mile-high burger.

## METHOD

1) Preheat a gas barbecue or grill to medium-high. 2) Place the beef mince, barbecue sauce, breadcrumbs, mustard, oil, egg, salt and pepper in a large bowl. Mix all the ingredients together using your hands, taking care not to handle the meat too much. Form the meat into 4 patties. 3) Lightly oil the barbecue or grill rack, place the patties on the rack and cook for about 6–8 minutes on each side, depending on the desired doneness. Remove from the rack. 4) For the special sauce, in a small bowl, whisk the ketchup, mayonnaise, relish, Worcestershire sauce, salt and pepper together. Spread the sauce onto the insides of the buns and insert a burger into each.

Serves 4 very hungry carnivores

### BITE ME BIT

'I love this burger so much, I want to sew my ass shut.'

– Barney (actor Neil Patrick Harris) on the television series 'How I Met Your Mother'

# CRUSTED LAMB CHOPS with BALSAMIC REDUCTION

## INGREDIENTS

### Crusted Lamb Chops

non-stick cooking spray

3 tablespoons finely chopped flat-leaf parsley

2 tablespoons finely chopped mint

1 tablespoon finely chopped thyme

2 large garlic cloves, finely chopped

1½ teaspoons sea salt

⅛ teaspoon cayenne pepper

1 tablespoon olive oil

2 slices white bread, pulsed in a food processor until coarse crumbs

2 tablespoons mayonnaise

2 tablespoons Dijon mustard

2 racks of lamb, 675g each (7-8 chops on each), trimmed

1 teaspoon freshly ground black pepper

### Balsamic Reduction

1 tablespoon olive oil

1 shallot, finely chopped

75ml balsamic vinegar

175ml chicken stock

15g butter

LISA'S NO 1 COMMANDMENT: HONOUR THY BUTCHER.

She gets a blow dry to go see him. She defers to 'the one who wears the white apron', the gatekeeper to the most prized rack of lamb. For her, he selects the leanest, freshest pink meat. For her, he Frenches (don't be a pig…it means he trims the ribs clean of excess fat and meat) the rack, all of which enhance her meltingly tender, impressive and deceptively easy-to-make, oven-roasted lamb chops. Lisa's getting a pedicure right now – she must be going to buy some veal chops.

## METHOD

1) Preheat the oven to 230°C/450°F/Gas Mark 8. Line a baking sheet with foil and coat with non-stick cooking spray. 2) Combine the herbs, garlic, ½ teaspoon salt and the cayenne in a shallow dish. Set aside. 3) In a large frying pan, heat the oil over a medium heat. Add the breadcrumbs and cook, stirring, for 2–3 minutes to lightly toast. Remove from the pan and toss with the parsley mixture. 4) In a small bowl, stir the mayonnaise and mustard together. 5) Season both sides of the lamb racks with 1 teaspoon salt and the pepper. Over a high heat, heat the same large frying pan used for the breadcrumbs. Place one rack, meat-side down, in the pan and cook for about 2 minutes until a crust has formed. Turn the rack with tongs and sear the bottom for a further 2 minutes. Remove the lamb from the pan, wipe the pan and repeat with the remaining rack. Transfer the lamb to a plate and leave to cool slightly. 6) Coat both the top and bottom of both racks with the mayonnaise mixture, spreading it over the meaty portions but

not covering the bones. Roll the meat in the reserved breadcrumb mixture, pressing the crumbs to adhere. **7)** Place both the racks on the prepared baking sheet and roast for 20–25 minutes. Insert an instant-read thermometer into the thickest part of the lamb; medium-rare will read 60°C/140°F. Leave to rest for 5–10 minutes before carving; the temperature will rise as it stands. **8)** For the balsamic reduction, heat the oil in a medium frying pan over a medium heat. Add the shallot and cook for 1 minute until soft. Stir in the vinegar, turn the heat to high and cook for 1 minute. Add the stock and bring to the boil. Lower the heat to medium and cook for 5–6 minutes until reduced by half. Remove from the heat and stir in the butter. Spoon a little sauce over the carved chops.

Serves 4–6

# OSSO BUCO with GREMOLATA

## INGREDIENTS

6 veal shanks, 225–280g each
and 4cm thick, each tied
with kitchen string

70g plain flour

1½ teaspoons sea salt

1½ teaspoons freshly
ground black pepper

4 tablespoons vegetable oil

1 large red onion, finely chopped

3 carrots, peeled and
finely chopped

2 celery sticks, finely chopped

4 large garlic cloves,
finely chopped

6 sage leaves, chopped

1 rosemary sprig, chopped

3 tablespoons chopped
flat-leaf parsley

¼ teaspoon dried chilli flakes

2 x 400g cans chopped tomatoes

300ml dry white wine

1 litre chicken stock

Julie: Alex, I'll take 'Fired Up!'

Alex: It means 'bone with a hole'.

Julie: What is…oh dear…I don't think I can say this on television…

Alex: Sorry, Julie. Lisa?

Lisa: What is 'Osso Buco'?

Alex: Correct.

Lisa: Alex, I'll take 'On Top.'

Alex: Parsley, lemon zest, olive oil.

Julie: What is 'slather it on me'?

Alex: Sorry, Julie. Lisa?

Lisa: What is 'gremolata that garnishes succulent braised veal shanks'?

Alex: Correct. Now, for your final question. The category is 'Culinary Traditions of Northern Italy' and the clue is 'delicious to spoon'.

Julie: Who is 'Ralph Macchio'?

Alex: Unfortunately…no. Lisa?

Lisa: What is 'savoury marrow'?

Alex: Correct. You win. Julie, good luck with whatever your future holds.

## METHOD

**1)** Preheat the oven to 160°C/325°F/Gas Mark 3. Set aside a roasting tin large enough to fit the veal shanks in a single layer.
**2)** Dry the veal with kitchen paper. Place the flour, 1 teaspoon salt and 1 teaspoon pepper in a small dish. Dredge the shanks in the seasoned flour to coat, shaking off the excess. In a large heavy frying pan, heat half the vegetable oil over a medium-high

**Gremolata**

3 tablespoons finely chopped
flat-leaf parsley

1 tablespoon olive oil

1 teaspoon finely grated
lemon zest

¼ teaspoon sea salt

¼ teaspoon freshly ground
black pepper

heat. Add 3 veal shanks to the pan and sear on all sides until nicely browned, for a total of about 10 minutes. Transfer to the roasting tin and repeat with the remaining oil and veal. **3)** In a large bowl, combine the onion, carrots, celery, garlic, sage, rosemary, parsley, chilli flakes and remaining ½ teaspoon salt and ½ teaspoon pepper. Spread the mixture on top of the seared veal and around the roasting tin. Pour the chopped tomatoes and their juice, wine and stock over the veal and vegetables. Cover three-quarters of the roasting tin with foil and cook in the oven for 2¼– 2½ hours until the meat is easily pierced with a fork. Using a slotted spoon, carefully transfer the veal to a serving plate. Cut off and discard the kitchen string. With the slotted spoon, remove the vegetables and place on a serving platter along with the veal. Pour the remaining sauce into a medium saucepan and bring to the boil. Reduce the heat to medium and simmer for 10 minutes. Pour over the veal and vegetables. **4)** Just before serving the veal, combine all the ingredients for the gremolata in a small bowl. Sprinkle a small spoonful over each serving.

Serves 6

## BITE ME BIT

'Everyone has a purpose in life.
Perhaps yours is watching television.'

– David Letterman, talk show host

# Join me

**The Morning After**

# SUPERCAL...ISTIC STICKY FRENCH TOAST with CANDIED RICE KRISPIES

## INGREDIENTS

### Candied Rice Krispies

100g sugar

2 tablespoons water

105g Rice Krispies

### French Toast

non-stick cooking spray

2 egg breads (challahs), crusts left on and cubed

225g cream cheese, softened

6 large eggs

400ml milk

60ml single cream

120g maple syrup

1 teaspoon vanilla extract

### Caramel Topping

275g soft light brown sugar

115g butter

3 tablespoons golden syrup

Mary Poppins played a game with kids called 'Well Begun is Half-Done'. Ain't that the truth. Easily assembled, this decadent French toast soufflé soaks overnight and is finished by drizzling it with caramel sauce, topping it with candied Rice Krispies and baking it to a golden dome. Yes, you get a spoonful of sugar in every sticky, scrumptious bite.

## METHOD

1) For the candied Rice Krispies, in a large saucepan (deep and with a wide base), bring the sugar and water to the boil over a medium heat. Boil for 1 minute without stirring. Gently stir in the Rice Krispies and cook over a medium heat for about 5 minutes just until golden. Immediately pour onto a baking sheet to cool. Once cooled they can be stored in an airtight container for up to 2 weeks. 2) For the French toast, coat a 33 x 23cm baking dish with non-stick cooking spray. Spread the bread cubes evenly in the dish. 3) Using an electric mixer, beat the cream cheese at medium speed until smooth. Add one egg at a time, mixing well after each addition and making sure to scrape down the side of the bowl with a spatula. Whisk in the milk, cream, maple syrup and vanilla until incorporated and smooth. Pour over the bread cubes to moisten evenly, pressing lightly to submerge the bread. Cover and refrigerate for at least 8 hours and up to 24 hours. 4) Remove from the refrigerator and preheat the oven to 180°C/350°F/Gas Mark 4. 5) Combine the ingredients for the caramel topping in a small saucepan. Cook over a medium heat, stirring constantly, for about 2 minutes until well combined. Immediately pour over the French toast and cover with the candied Rice Krispies. Place the baking dish on a rimmed baking sheet and bake for 40–45 minutes until puffed and golden.

Serves 8

# BLINTZ SOUFFLÉ with STRAWBERRY SAUCE

The Eastern European cousin of the crêpe, a blintz is a thin pastry wrapped around a filling. As much as we love them, we also love not spending all our time rolling, folding and frying each individual blintz. Instead, we're doing blintzes freeform. We've transformed a 33 x 23cm baking dish into one giant, creamy, sweet-cheese-filled blintz. All of the flavour and none of the labour, this puffy and golden soufflé is served topped with sweet strawberry sauce.

## INGREDIENTS

### Sweet Cheese Filling

non-stick cooking spray

450g cream cheese, softened

750g ricotta cheese

2 large eggs

100g sugar

2 tablespoons orange juice

1 teaspoon vanilla extract

½ teaspoon finely grated orange zest

### Blintz Batter

115g butter, softened

100g sugar

6 large eggs

1 teaspoon vanilla extract

140g plain flour

2 teaspoons baking powder

350ml soured cream, plus extra to serve

125ml orange juice

### Strawberry Sauce

900g fresh strawberries

100g sugar

4 tablespoons water

1 tablespoon freshly squeezed lemon juice

1 tablespoon cornflour

## METHOD

1) Preheat the oven to 180°C/350°F/Gas Mark 4. Coat a 33 x 23cm baking dish with non-stick cooking spray. 2) For the filling, in an electric mixer, beat the cream cheese until smooth. Add the remaining filling ingredients and beat thoroughly on medium speed until a smooth, creamy consistency. Place in a medium bowl. 3) For the batter, in an electric mixer, cream the butter and sugar until light and fluffy. Add the eggs one at a time, mixing well after each addition. Add the vanilla and continue to mix. On low speed, add the flour, baking powder, soured cream and orange juice, mixing just until combined. 4) To assemble, pour half the batter in the prepared baking dish. Add the filling by placing spoonfuls on top of the batter and gently spread. Place the remaining half of the batter over the cheese filling. 5) Bake for about 65 minutes or until puffy and golden. Serve with soured cream and the strawberry sauce. 6) For the strawberry sauce, wash the strawberries and hull. Thinly slice the berries and place 300g in a medium bowl. Set the remaining strawberries aside. 7) Mash the strawberries in the bowl and pour into a medium saucepan. Add the remaining ingredients. Bring to the boil over a medium heat. Cook, stirring constantly, for 1 minute or until thickened. Remove from the heat and stir in the remaining berries.

Serves 8–10

# BERRY STUFFED-and-SAUCED FRENCH TOAST SOUFFLÉ

## INGREDIENTS

non-stick cooking spray

2 egg breads (challahs), crusts removed and cut into 1cm thick slices

225g cream cheese

340g strawberry jam

3 large eggs

4 large egg whites

350ml milk

25g butter, melted

2 tablespoons sugar

1 teaspoon vanilla extract

½ teaspoon sea salt

### Berry Sauce

200g sugar

1 tablespoon cornflour

4 tablespoons orange juice

375g frozen unsweetened berries, either mixed, blueberries or raspberries

420g hulled fresh strawberries, quartered

All you have to do with this gorgeous dish is sleep on it. This overnight French toast does the work for you as the sweet egg bread, mounded with cream cheese and strawberry jam, is left to soak up a buttery mixture. After you wake and bake, you'll have an elegant, effortless brunch.

## METHOD

**1)** For the soufflé, coat a 33 x 23cm baking dish with non-stick cooking spray. Lay a single layer of bread slices along the bottom of the dish. Spread cream cheese on each piece. Spread strawberry jam on the remaining slices and lay to face the cream cheese, creating sandwiches in the baking dish. **2)** In a medium bowl, whisk the whole eggs, egg whites, milk, melted butter, sugar, vanilla and salt together. Pour over the sandwiches and turn to coat. Cover and refrigerate for several hours or, for best results, overnight. Bring to room temperature before baking. **3)** Preheat the oven to 180°C/350°F/Gas Mark 4. Bake, uncovered, for 35–40 minutes. **4)** For the berry sauce, in a medium saucepan, combine the sugar and cornflour. Stir in the orange juice until smooth. Add the frozen mixed berries and bring to the boil over a medium heat, stirring constantly, until slightly thickened. Remove from the heat and stir in the fresh strawberries. Leave the sauce to cool and then serve spooned over individual portions.

Serves 8–10

## BITE ME BIT

'I went to a restaurant that serves "Breakfast at any time". So I ordered French Toast during the Renaissance.'

– Steven Wright, comedian

# SWEET NOODLE PUDDING – EXPOSED!

## INGREDIENTS

non-stick cooking spray

375g dried wide egg noodles

25g butter

450g cottage cheese

475ml soured cream

4 large eggs, lightly beaten

140g sugar

1 teaspoon vanilla extract

165g raisins

**Topping**

105g corn flakes,
coarsely crushed

4 tablespoons soft
light brown sugar

25g butter, melted

1 teaspoon ground cinnamon

By revealing this sweet, raisin-loaded noodle pudding we're breaking an unspoken code held by generations of Jewish women – you can kibitz about Auntie's moustache, kvetch about cousin's wet kisses, but under no circumstances should you be a yenta about your secret noodle pudding recipe. We're taking a risk, but we think the public has a right to know.

## METHOD

**1)** Preheat the oven to 180°C/350°F/Gas Mark 4. Coat a 33 x 23cm baking dish with non-stick cooking spray. **2)** Cook the noodles according to the packet instructions. Drain well and mix with the butter. Set aside. **3)** In a large bowl, combine the cottage cheese, soured cream, eggs, sugar and vanilla. Add the noodles, gently tossing to coat. Fold in the raisins and spoon the mixture into the prepared baking dish. **4)** Combine all the ingredients for the topping in a small bowl. Spread on top of the noodles and bake, covered, for 30 minutes. Remove the cover and bake for a further 10–15 minutes until the top is golden brown. Leave to cool before cutting.

Serves 8

# BAGEL and LOX STRATA

## INGREDIENTS

non-stick cooking spray

6 large eggs

350ml milk

225ml soured cream, plus extra 125ml to garnish

130g smoked salmon, cut into matchsticks

3 tablespoons chopped dill, plus extra 1 tablespoon to garnish

1 tablespoon freshly squeezed lemon juice, plus extra 1 tablespoon to garnish

2 teaspoons finely grated lemon zest

½ teaspoon freshly ground black pepper

6 plain bagels, cut into 1cm cubes

2 tablespoons capers, drained and chopped, to garnish

### A HEBRAIC HAIKU

Oy! Oy! No schmear here
Bagel, lox, sour cream and dill
In each bite. Eat! Eat!

## METHOD

**1)** Preheat the oven to 180°C/350°F/Gas Mark 4. Coat a 33 x 23cm baking dish with non-stick cooking spray. **2)** In a large bowl, whisk the eggs, milk and soured cream together. Stir in the salmon, dill, lemon juice, lemon zest and pepper. Add the bagel pieces and toss to coat. Transfer to the prepared baking dish and bake for 45–50 minutes until golden. **3)** Leave to rest for 10 minutes. To garnish, dollop the remaining soured cream on top and garnish with the capers and the extra dill and the lemon juice.

Serves 10

# NY PICKLED SALMON

## INGREDIENTS

900g salmon fillet, skinned, rinsed and patted dry

225ml water

225ml white distilled vinegar

3 tablespoons sugar

2 teaspoons mustard seeds

1 teaspoon black peppercorns

2 dried bay leaves

¼ teaspoon sea salt

2 large sweet onions, sliced 5mm thick

Here's my question – if smoked salmon is SO great, why is it always buried under a pile of cream cheese, tomato, onion, capers and lemon? To us, the true gem of the brunch world is pickled salmon. Much like what you'd find at the Upper West Side landmark, Zabar's, salmon and onions are 'cooked' in a zippy sweet and sour marinade. The resulting tender pink salmon needs no disguise – maybe just a nice slice of pumpernickel for this Broadway star.

## METHOD

1) Cut the salmon into 2.5cm x 5cm cubes, making sure to clean off any brown parts. Set aside. 2) In a large saucepan, combine the water, vinegar, sugar, mustard seeds, peppercorns, bay leaves and salt. Bring to the boil over a medium-high heat. Reduce the heat to low, add the salmon and sliced onions and cook, uncovered, for 5 minutes. Transfer the salmon, onions and marinade to a glass container. Leave to cool at room temperature, then cover and refrigerate for at least 2 days before serving. To serve, pour off the liquid and arrange the salmon with the pickled onions. Keeps in the refrigerator up to 1 week.

Serves 6–8

## BITE ME BIT

'New York is a diamond iceberg floating in river water.'

– Truman Capote, writer

# POTATO, SPINACH and GRUYÈRE FRITTATA

## INGREDIENTS

60g butter,

10 (280g) small red potatoes, sliced 3mm thick

½ teaspoon sea salt

¼ teaspoon freshly ground black pepper

120g fresh baby spinach, stems discarded

8 large eggs

½ teaspoon sea salt

¼ teaspoon freshly ground black pepper

225g Gruyère cheese, coarsely grated

When it comes to breakfast and eggs, some countries like to play the heavyweights. The French with their finicky Hollandaise and fussy soufflés. The Brits with their deep-fried Scotch eggs. So, what's the Italians' secret for La Dolce Uovo? The easy-going frittata: a thick, hearty, open-faced omelette that can be served at any temperature, eaten at any meal and, best of all, filled with whatever you like. We love this combo, but also adore peas, feta and mint...red peppers, onions and goat's cheese...

## METHOD

1) Preheat the oven to 180°C/350°F/Gas Mark 4. 2) In a deep 25cm ovenproof frying pan, melt 25g of the butter over a medium-high heat. Add the potatoes, salt and pepper and sauté for 8–10 minutes until cooked through. Remove from the pan and set aside. 3) Using the same pan, add the spinach leaves over a medium heat and cook for about 2 minutes until wilted. Remove from the pan. When cool, squeeze the spinach to drain the excess liquid. Chop and set aside. 4) In a large bowl, whisk the eggs very well. Whisk in the melted butter, salt and pepper. Spread the cooked potatoes and spinach evenly over the base of your frying pan. Sprinkle the Gruyère evenly over the potatoes and spinach. Pour the egg mixture into the pan and place in oven. Bake for 23–25 minutes until golden brown around edges and just firm to the touch. Remove from the oven and leave to stand for 5 minutes. Run a spatula around the pan edge to loosen the frittata and invert it onto a serving plate.

Serves 4–6

## BITE ME BIT

'It may be the cock that crows, but it is the hen that lays the eggs.'

– Margaret Thatcher, politician

# THE BIG CHEESE
# and MACARONI

## INGREDIENTS

non-stick cooking spray

2 large eggs

530ml evaporated milk

2 teaspoons Dijon mustard

1½ teaspoons sea salt

½ teaspoon freshly ground black pepper

⅛ teaspoon hot pepper sauce

450g dried elbow macaroni

55g butter

225g Cheddar cheese, coarsely grated

115g Monterey Jack or Gruyère cheese, coarsely grated

### Breadcrumb Topping

8 slices white bread, crusts removed

25g butter, melted

1 teaspoon sea salt

55g Cheddar cheese, coarsely grated

As lovers of movies on the W Channel, we have no problem with cheese – it's how you serve it up that counts. To get the creamiest noodles, we melt everything together on the stove, transfer the cheesy mixture to a baking dish and finish it in the oven with a tasty golden covering of crunchy breadcrumbs.

## METHOD

**1)** Preheat the oven to 190°C/375°F/Gas Mark 5. Coat a 33 x 23cm baking dish with non-stick cooking spray. **2)** In a medium bowl, whisk the eggs, evaporated milk, mustard, salt, pepper and hot sauce. Set aside. **3)** Bring a large sacuepan of water to the boil over a high heat. Add the macaroni and cook until the pasta is just tender. Drain the pasta well and return to the pan. Add the butter over a low heat to melt. Stir in the egg mixture and cheeses. Continue to cook, stirring, for about 5 minutes until creamy. Transfer the mixture to the prepared baking dish. **4)** For the breadcrumb topping, pulse the bread in a food processor until coarse crumbs. In a small bowl, toss the breadcrumbs with the melted butter and salt. Evenly top the macaroni with the Cheddar and buttered breadcrumbs. **5)** Bake in the preheated oven for 10 minutes or until the breadcrumbs are golden brown. Leave to cool for 5 minutes and then serve immediately.

Serves 6–8 as main course, 10–12 as side dish

# SPOT-ON CHOCOLATE CHIP SCONES

## INGREDIENTS

450g plain flour,
plus extra for dusting

100g sugar

2 teaspoons baking powder

1 teaspoon bicarbonate of soda

½ teaspoon sea salt

¼ teaspoon ground cinnamon

175g cold butter, cut
into small cubes

260g dark chocolate chips

225ml buttermilk

¼ teaspoon vanilla extract

**Sugar Topping**

25g butter, melted

2 tablespoons sugar

When it comes to sugary snacks Lisa and I can go either Yiddish or British. We'll gleefully indulge in a little babka or rugelach, but when 4pm rolls around, we suddenly fancy our 4pm cuppa with cucumber and cream cheese finger sandwiches, followed by a freshly baked scone. Sweet and flaky, our scones are bang-on, slathered in creamy butter, strawberry jam and, dare we say, a dollop of clotted cream.

## METHOD

**1)** Preheat the oven to 220°C/425°F/Gas Mark 7. Line a baking sheet with baking paper. **2)** In a large bowl, sift the flour, sugar, baking powder, bicarbonate of soda, salt and cinnamon together. Rub in the butter with your fingertips, or pulse in a food processor, until the mixture resembles coarse meal. Stir in the chocolate chips. Add the buttermilk and vanilla and stir just until moistened. **3)** Turn the dough onto a lightly floured surface and knead briefly, 5 or 6 times, to gather into a large ball. Do not overwork the ball or the result will be tough scones. Divide the ball of dough in half and gently pat each into 20cm flat rounds. Brush the top of each with melted butter and sprinkle with the sugar. **4)** Using a sharp knife, cut each round into 6 even triangles and place on the prepared baking sheet about 2.5cm apart. Bake for 16–18 minutes until the tops are golden.

Makes: 12 large scones

### BITE ME BIT

'It's the face powder that gets a man interested, but it's the baking powder that keeps him home.'

– Buck Barrow (actor Gene Hackman) in the 1967 movie **Bonnie and Clyde**

# WHOLESOME HONEY-BAKED GRANOLA

## INGREDIENTS

320g old-fashioned large-flake oats (not quick cooking)

115g flaked almonds

1 teaspoon sea salt

½ teaspoon ground cinnamon

115g butter, melted

100g soft light brown sugar

85g runny honey

1 teaspoon vanilla extract

160g dried cranberries

160g raisins

I'm elated. I can now join the poncho-wearing pack. For years I had granola-envy but refused to eat the highly caloric, preservative-laden boxed oats and nuts. Hemp sneakers now firmly on my feet, I'm running to get a bowl of this nourishing, crisp-baked and clustered granola overflowing with golden almonds and plump dried fruit.

## METHOD

**1)** Preheat the oven to 150°C/300°F/Gas Mark 2. Line a baking sheet with baking paper. **2)** In a large bowl, combine the oats, almonds, salt and cinnamon. **3)** In a small bowl, combine the melted butter, sugar, honey and vanilla. Whisk well and pour over the oat mixture. Toss to combine and spread the granola on the prepared baking sheet. Bake for 20 minutes, stir carefully and then continue to bake for another 15 minutes. Remove from the oven and transfer to a large bowl. Add the dried cranberries and raisins, mixing to combine. Leave to cool completely and store at room temperature in an airtight container for up to 1 week.

Makes: about 1kg

# APPLE STREUSEL MUFFINS

## INGREDIENTS

non-stick cooking spray

350g plain flour, plus extra for dusing

1 teaspoon bicarbonate of soda

½ teaspoon sea salt

½ teaspoon ground cinnamon

250g peeled, cored and diced Granny Smith apples

300g soft light brown sugar

225ml buttermilk

125ml vegetable oil

1 large egg

1 teaspoon vanilla extract

### Topping

100g soft light brown sugar

70g flour

¼ teaspoon ground cinnamon

55g butter, melted

Still obsessed with 'Seinfeld' after all these years, Lisa was sick of me 'pulling an Elaine' – I'd buy a few muffins, eat off the tops and toss the dry bottoms. Determined to put an end to my cruel decapitations, she created these super-moist apple cinnamon muffins, delectable from the golden-crusted lid to the stray crumbs on my plate.

## METHOD

**1)** Preheat the oven to 180°C/350°F/Gas Mark 4. Coat a 12-cup muffin tin with non-stick cooking spray. Lightly dust the cups with flour, shaking out the excess. **2)** For the muffins, in a large bowl, combine the flour, bicarbonate of soda, salt, cinnamon and diced apples. Gently toss to combine. **3)** In a medium bowl, whisk the sugar, buttermilk, oil, egg and vanilla together. Gently stir into the flour mixture just until blended. Spoon the mixture into the prepared tin, dividing it evenly between the muffin cups. **4)** For the topping, in a small bowl, mix the sugar, flour and cinnamon together. Add the melted butter and toss with a fork until it resembles coarse crumbs. Sprinkle the topping over the muffin cups. **5)** Bake for 23–25 minutes until the muffins spring back when gently pressed. Remove from the oven and leave to cool for 10 minutes before removing from the tin to a wire rack.

Makes: 12 muffins

## BITE ME BIT

'Some people...some people like cupcakes exclusively, while myself, I say there is naught nor ought there be nothing so exalted on the face of God's grey Earth as that prince of foods...the muffin!'

– from the 1975 Frank Zappa song 'Muffin Man'

GOLDEN-TOPPED, FULL-FLAVOURED MU-FFIN SEEKS HUNGRY DINER – Height: 6cm. Weight: 110g. I have an eye-catching golden exterior and a warm, plump blueberry interior. When I'm hot, I exude an intoxicating aroma. I'm looking for a long-term relationship and holding out hope that, one day, I'll have my own batch of mini-muffins. If you're that special someone, call me at 1-888-GR8-BITE.

# BERRY BURST MUFFINS with CRUMBLE TOPPING

## INGREDIENTS

non-stick cooking spray

280g plain flour, plus extra for dusting

150g sugar

1 teaspoon baking powder

1 teaspoon bicarbonate of soda

¼ teaspoon sea salt

290g fresh blueberries

115g butter, melted

225ml soured cream

1 large egg

1 teaspoon vanilla extract

1 teaspoon finely grated lemon zest

### Crumble Topping

70g plain flour

4 tablespoons sugar

25g butter

## METHOD

1) Preheat the oven to 190°C/375°F/Gas Mark 5. Coat a 12-cup muffin tin with non-stick cooking spray. Lightly dust the cups with flour, shaking out the excess. 2) In a large bowl, place the flour, sugar, baking powder, bicarbonate of soda, salt and blueberries. Gently toss to combine. 3) In a small bowl, whisk the melted butter, soured cream, egg, vanilla and lemon zest together. Gently stir into the flour mixture just until blended. Do not overmix – the mixture is supposed to look lumpy. Spoon the mixture into the prepared tin, dividing it evenly between the muffin cups. 4) For the crumble topping, in a small bowl, use a fork to mix the flour, sugar and butter together until it resembles coarse crumbs. Sprinkle the topping over the muffin cups. 5) Bake in the oven for 23–25 minutes until the muffins spring back when gently pressed. Leave to cool for 10 minutes in the muffin tin before removing to cool on a wire rack.

Makes: 12 muffins

# Top 10

**Crème de la Crème**

## MUSICAL ACTS THAT BELONG IN THE KITCHEN

Meatloaf

Bread

Red Hot Chili Peppers

The Cranberries

Hall & Oates

Cream

Martha and the Muffins

Peaches

T-Bone Walker

Rosemary Clooney

## MUSICAL ACTS YOU'D KICK OUT OF YOUR KITCHEN

Meat Puppets

Meat Whiplash

Smashing Pumpkins

Limp Bizkit

Hootie & the Blowfish

Poison

Dead Milkmen

Virgin Prunes

Psychotic Pineapple

Skankin' Pickle

## TOOLS WE CAN'T LIVE WITHOUT

Kitchen scissors

Microplane grater

Silicone spatula

Silicone-covered wire whisk

Silicone baking mat

Citrus press

Olive/cherry pitter

Hand-held blender

Digital timer

Meat thermometer

## MOVIES TO SATISFY YOUR APPETITE

Big Night

Moonstruck

Tampopo

Chocolat

9½ Weeks

Supersize Me

Babette's Feast

The Waitress

Willy Wonka & the Chocolate Factory

Who is Killing the Great Chefs of Europe?

## SONGS TO MAKE YOU HUNGRY

**Candy's Room,** Bruce Springsteen and the E Street Band

**Grits,** James Brown

**Honey,** Moby

**American Pie,** Don McLean

**Big Cheese,** Nirvana

**Quiche Lorraine,** The B-52's

**Tangerine,** Led Zeppelin

**Tacos, Enchiladas and Beans,** Doris Day

**Cheeseburger in Paradise,** Jimmy Buffett

**Buttered Popcorn,** The Supremes

## DUST-COLLECTORS IN THE KITCHEN

Flavour injector

Apple corer

Mini whisks

Avocado slicer

Electric knife

Egg cooker

Honey dribbling stick

Banana hanger

Prawn deveiner

Iced tea maker

# EUPHORIC LEMON LOAF

## INGREDIENTS

**Lemon Loaf**

non-stick cooking spray

210g plain flour

1 teaspoon baking powder

¼ teaspoon sea salt

115g butter, softened

200g sugar

2 large eggs

125ml buttermilk

finely grated zest of 1 lemon

**Lemon Glaze**

2 tablespoons freshly squeezed lemon juice

60g sugar

Take a big inhale. Yes, that's right. In aromatherapy, lemon lifts your mood and calms your stress. So let's take this balm of serenity out of the realm of wind chimes and Enya tunes and onto a plate – one bite of this zesty lemon loaf, drizzled with tart lemon glaze, will have you downright chilled.

## METHOD

**1)** Preheat the oven to 180°C/350°F/Gas Mark 4. Coat a 23 x 13cm loaf tin with non-stick cooking spray. **2)** In a small bowl, combine the flour, baking powder and salt. Set aside. **3)** In an electric mixer, cream the butter and sugar together on medium-high speed until light and fluffy. Beat in the eggs, one at a time, until incorporated. On low speed, gradually add the flour mixture and buttermilk alternately, ending with the flour. Stir in the lemon zest. **4)** Pour the mixture into the prepared loaf tin and bake for 45–48 minutes or until golden around the edges and just cooked through. Remove from oven and leave to cool for 5 minutes before removing from the tin. **5)** For the glaze, in a small bowl, stir the lemon juice and sugar together. Gently pierce the top of the loaf several times with a fork and pour the glaze over.

Makes: 12–14 slices

## BITE ME BIT

'We are living in a world today where lemonade is made from artificial flavors and furniture polish is made from real lemons.'

– Alfred E. Neuman, MAD Magazine

# CRANBERRY ORANGE BREAD

## INGREDIENTS

non-stick cooking spray

280g plain flour

150g sugar

1½ teaspoons baking powder

1 teaspoon finely grated lemon zest

½ teaspoon bicarbonate of soda

½ teaspoon sea salt

55g butter, softened

125ml orange juice

4 tablespoons cranberry juice

1 large egg

165g cranberries, fresh or frozen, chopped

2 tablespoons cinnamon sugar

Lisa and I speak on the phone at 8:32 every morning. If she's perky, I know she's started her day with a large slice of our citrus-flavoured, cranberry-studded loaf. If she's grunting one-word answers, I know her husband took the last piece or her jeans shrunk in the dryer.

## METHOD

**1)** Preheat the oven to 180°C/350°F/Gas Mark 4. Coat a 23 x 13cm loaf tin with non-stick cooking spray. **2)** In a large bowl, combine the flour, sugar, baking powder, lemon zest, bicarbonate of soda and salt. Rub in the butter with a fork until the mixture is crumbly. **3)** In a small bowl, whisk the orange juice, cranberry juice and egg together. Pour over the flour mixture and add the cranberries. Gently stir until the flour disappears. Pour into the prepared loaf tin and sprinkle with the cinnamon sugar. Bake for 55–60 minutes or until a skewer inserted into the centre comes out clean. Leave to cool in the tin for 10 minutes before removing from the tin and cooling on a wire rack.

Makes: 10 slices

# CINNAMON SWIRL BREAKFAST BREAD

## INGREDIENTS

non-stick cooking spray

115g butter, softened

200g sugar

2 large eggs

2 teaspoons vanilla extract

225ml soured cream

280g plain flour

1 teaspoon baking powder

½ teaspoon bicarbonate of soda

¼ teaspoon sea salt

**Cinnamon Swirl**

100g sugar

1 tablespoon ground cinnamon

25g butter, melted

Contrary to popular belief, you don't need fresh cut flowers or a coat of paint to sell your house. Heck, you don't even need a real estate agent. The homey aroma of this cake-like loaf is the ultimate welcome mat – once buyers catch the irresistible scents of spicy cinnamon and bread baking, their olfactory euphoria will blind them to any leaky tap or draughty corner.

## METHOD

**1)** Preheat the oven to 160°C/325°F/Gas Mark 3. Coat a 23 x 13cm loaf tin with non-stick cooking spray. **2)** In an electric mixer, cream the butter and sugar together on medium speed until well blended. Add the eggs, one at a time, beating well after each addition. Add the vanilla and soured cream and mix on low speed for 30 seconds. Using a wooden spoon, stir in the flour, baking powder, bicarbonate of soda and salt just until moistened and the flour has disappeared. **3)** For the cinnamon swirl, in a small bowl, stir the sugar and cinnamon together. **4)** Spoon half the loaf mixture into the prepared loaf tin and sprinkle with half the cinnamon sugar mixture. Pour the remaining loaf mixture over the top. Sprinkle with the remaining cinnamon sugar and drizzle with the melted butter. **5)** Place the loaf tin on a rimmed baking sheet to catch any drippings. Bake for 55 minutes. Leave to cool in the tin for 10 minutes before removing. Serve warm.

Serves 12

# CHOCOLATE CHUNK BANANA BREAD

## INGREDIENTS

non-stick cooking spray

200g sugar

115g butter, softened

2 large eggs

3–4 ripe bananas, mashed

125ml soured cream

1 teaspoon vanilla extract

350g plain flour

1 teaspoon bicarbonate of soda

¼ teaspoon sea salt

260g dark or milk chocolate, chopped

It's not just good things that come to those who wait. Especially where your bananas are concerned. Be patient and let them ripen to perfection – their natural sugars will take over, guaranteeing a big taste of sweetness in this moist, chocolaty loaf.

## METHOD

**1)** Preheat the oven to 180°C/350°F/Gas Mark 4. Coat a 23 x 13cm loaf tin with non-stick cooking spray. **2)** Using an electric mixer, cream the sugar and butter together on medium speed for about 1 minute until well blended. Add the eggs, one at a time, beating well after each addition. Add the mashed bananas, soured cream and vanilla. Beat on low speed for about 30 seconds until blended. With a wooden spoon, stir in the flour, bicarbonate of soda, salt and chocolate chunks just until moistened and the flour has disappeared. Spoon the mixture into the prepared tin. **3)** Bake for 70 minutes until lightly browned on top and cooked through. Leave to cool for 10 minutes in the tin before removing to cool completely on a wire rack.

Makes: 14–16 slices

## BITE ME BIT

'Intellectual property has the shelf life of a banana.'

– Bill Gates, Microsoft founder

# CHOCOLATE BAR COFFEE CAKE

## INGREDIENTS

### Chocolate Topping

350g milk chocolate, chopped

200g soft light brown sugar

2 tablespoons cocoa powder

1 tablespoon ground cinnamon

### Cake Mixture

non-stick cooking spray

200g sugar

85g butter

2 large eggs

1 teaspoon vanilla extract

225ml soured cream

1 teaspoon bicarbonate of soda

180g plain flour

1½ teaspoons baking powder

On the days we're short on sweetness and long on appetite, this is our go-to dessert. A perfectly luscious cake that's overrun with creamy chunks of chocolate, you'll be able to get it from pantry to oven in less time than it takes to brew a pot of coffee.

## METHOD

**1)** Preheat the oven to 180°C/350°F/Gas Mark 4. Coat a 23cm square baking tin with non-stick cooking spray. **2)** For the topping, in a small bowl, combine the chocolate, sugar, cocoa powder and cinnamon. Set aside. **3)** For the cake mixture, in a food processor, combine the sugar, butter, eggs and vanilla. Process for 2 minutes. **4)** Mix the soured cream with the bicarbonate of soda in a jug. Leave to stand for 30 seconds. **5)** Add the soured cream to the food processor and mix for 3 seconds. Add the flour and baking powder and pulse 4 times or until the flour disappears. **6)** Pour half the mixture into the prepared baking tin. Cover with half the topping. Repeat with the remaining cake mixture and topping. Bake for 40–45 minutes.

Serves 8–10

## BITE ME BIT

'And above all...Think Chocolate.'

– Betty Crocker

# TWINKORETTE PEACH CRUMB CAKE

## INGREDIENTS

non-stick cooking spray

225ml soured cream

1 teaspoon bicarbonate of soda

315g plain flour

200g sugar

175g butter, softened

2 large eggs

1 teaspoon vanilla extract

1 teaspoon baking powder

¼ teaspoon sea salt

625g canned sliced peaches, drained well

For years I kept my self-destructive habit a secret, burying them in shopping carts, stashing one or two in the glove box for that easy-access quick fix. I couldn't let anyone know I was addicted to Twinkies – I'm a grown woman for goodness' sake! I thought I had it under control until that fateful early morning Lisa caught me ducked down in my car, crumbs flying and a telltale smear at the corner of my mouth. Ignoring my declarations of willpower, she spent endless hours in the kitchen concocting a cure for my cravings – this golden crumb cake that tastes like my beloved 4-inch long, cream-filled ladyfingers mingled with juicy peaches. Hello, my name is Julie and it has been 6 months, 22 days since my last cello-wrapped Twinkie.

## METHOD

1) Preheat the oven to 180°C/350°F/Gas Mark 4. Coat a 20cm square baking tin with non-stick cooking spray. 2) Combine the soured cream and bicarbonate of soda in a jug. 3) In a food processor, pulse the flour, sugar and butter on and off for 10–15 seconds until blended and crumbly. Remove and reserve 150g of the flour mixture for the cake topping. 4) Add the eggs, vanilla, baking powder, salt and soured cream to the remaining mixture in the food processor. Pulse 4 times on and off, scraping down the bowl once or twice. Do not overmix. 5) Spread half the cake mixture in the prepared baking tin. Place the sliced peaches atop and cover with the remaining cake mixture. Sprinkle the reserved crumbs to cover the top of the cake. 6) Bake for 48–50 minutes or until the cake is lightly browned around the edges. Note that testing the centre of the cake with a skewer won't give an accurate result as the peaches are wet and the skewer will come out wet even when the cake is fully baked.

Serves 10

# GOOEY MONKEY BREAD with CARAMEL GLAZE

## INGREDIENTS

### Dough

4 tablespoons warm water

1 teaspoon sugar, plus 4 tablespoons

2¼ teaspoons dried active yeast

175ml milk

55g butter, plus extra for greasing the tin

1 teaspoon sea salt

2 large eggs

490g plain flour, plus extra for dusting

vegetable oil, for oiling

### Sugar Coating

100g granulated sugar

100g soft light brown sugar

½ teaspoon ground cinnamon

70g butter, melted

### Glaze

200g soft light brown sugar

55g butter

2 tablespoons double cream

### Icing

145g icing sugar

2 tablespoons milk

Yeah, monkey bread. But what do you expect when other 1950s recipes had such names as 'Cantaloupe Pickles' and 'Clever Judy Filling'? Also called bubble loaf or golden crown, monkey bread is pull-apart layers of sinfully sugared yeast dough dripping in sticky caramel glaze and topped with sweet icing. So addictive, even Nancy Reagan served it regularly at the White House.

## METHOD

1) In a small bowl, combine the warm water and 1 teaspoon sugar. Sprinkle the yeast on top, cover and set aside for 10 minutes. 2) Meanwhile, in a glass dish, heat the milk and butter in the microwave until the milk is warm and the butter is melted. Pour into the bowl of an electric mixer. Add the remaining 4 tablespoons sugar, salt and eggs. Pour in the yeast mixture and, using a dough hook attachment, mix on low speed just to combine. Add the flour 140g at a time, mixing on low speed. Once all the flour has been added, mix on medium speed for 3 minutes (or 8–10 minutes by hand on a lightly floured work surface) to knead the dough. Place the dough into a lightly oiled mixing bowl. Cover with clingfilm and set aside in a warm, draught-free spot to rise for 45 minutes. 3) While the dough rises, butter the inside of a 25cm Bundt cake tin. 4) For the sugar coating, in a small bowl, combine the sugars and cinnamon. Place the melted butter in another small bowl. Set aside. 5) When the dough has risen, turn it out of the bowl onto a lightly floured surface. Knead the dough for 1 minute. Cut off golf ball-sized pieces of dough and roll each piece into a ball. You should have about 40 balls. Lightly dip each dough ball into the melted butter and then roll them in the sugar-cinnamon mixture. As you go, stack the balls of dough in

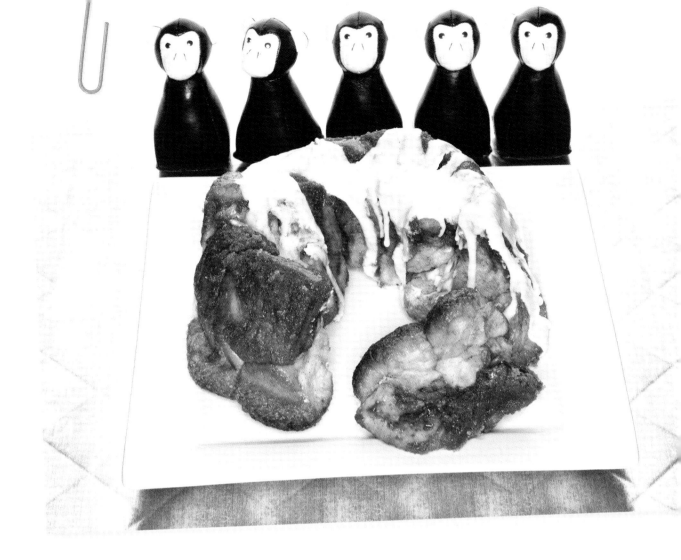

the prepared tin. Once you've covered the base of the pan, start a new layer until all the dough is used up. **6)** Put the ingredients for the glaze in a small saucepan and bring to the boil over a medium heat, stirring constantly. Once the mixture has come to the boil, immediately remove from the heat and pour over the prepared dough balls. **7)** Cover the tin with a clean cloth or clingfilm and set in a warm place to rise for 1 hour. **8)** Preheat the oven to 180°C/350°F/Gas Mark 4. Once the dough has risen and doubled in size, bake for 28 minutes or until golden brown. Remove from the oven and leave to cool in the tin for 5–10 minutes. Run a knife around the edges of the tin. Carefully flip onto a serving plate and leave to cool completely before icing. **9)** For the icing, in a medium bowl, whisk the icing sugar and milk together until smooth. Immediately drizzle over the bread.

Serves 12

# Fork me

## Desserts for a Happy Ending

# FUDGY DOUBLE CHOCOLATE LAYER CAKE

## INGREDIENTS

### Chocolate Cake

non-stick cooking spray

400g sugar

280g plain flour

75g cocoa powder, sifted

1½ teaspoons baking powder

1¼ teaspoons bicarbonate of soda

½ teaspoon sea salt

2 large eggs

225ml milk

125ml vegetable oil

175ml boiling water

### Chocolate Frosting

115g butter, softened

65g cocoa powder

6 tablespoons milk

2 tablespoons golden syrup

345g icing sugar

## METHOD

**1)** Preheat the oven to 180°C/350°F/Gas Mark 4. Coat two 23cm round cake tins with non-stick cooking spray. **2)** Add the sugar, flour, cocoa powder, baking powder, bicarbonate of soda and salt to an electric mixer. Mix on low speed for 30 seconds. Add the eggs, milk and oil and beat at medium speed for 2 minutes. With a spatula, gently fold in the boiling water (note: the mixture will be thin). Divide evenly between the tins. **3)** Bake for 23–25 minutes or until a skewer inserted into the centre comes out clean. Remove from the oven and leave to cool for 10 minutes before removing the cakes from the tins. Completely cool on wire racks. **4)** For the frosting, in an electric mixer, cream the butter and cocoa together on low speed. Add the milk and syrup and mix on low speed for 1 minute. Add the icing sugar, a third at a time, on low speed, scraping down the side of the bowl. Once all the icing sugar has been added, turn the speed to medium and beat until a smooth spreading consistency. **5)** To assemble, place one cake layer on a serving dish and top with about a third of the frosting. Spread evenly over the cake. Top with the remaining layer and spread the remainder of the frosting over the top and side of the cake.

Serves 10

# NAUGHTY-TURNED-NICE CARROT CAKE with CREAM CHEESE ICING

## INGREDIENTS

### Carrot Cake

non-stick cooking spray

280g plain flour

150g soft light brown sugar

100g granulated sugar

1½ teaspoons bicarbonate of soda

1 teaspoon ground cinnamon

½ teaspoon sea salt

125ml vegetable oil

125ml buttermilk

1 teaspoon vanilla extract

2 large eggs

2 large egg whites

6–7 carrots, coarsely grated

### Cream Cheese Icing

400g icing sugar

225g cream cheese, softened

115g butter, softened

1 teaspoon vanilla extract

As far as food folklore goes, 'carrot cake is healthy' is right up there with 'lobsters scream when boiled'. SO not true. Until now. By cutting the oil in half, lessening the number of egg yolks and upping the carrot quotient, Lisa has once again proven the impossible.

## METHOD

1) Preheat the oven to 180°C/350°F/Gas Mark 4. Coat two 23cm round cake tins with non-stick cooking spray. 2) For the cake, in a large bowl, combine the flour, sugars, bicarbonate of soda, cinnamon and salt. Stir to combine. Make a well in the centre and set aside. 3) In a medium bowl, whisk the oil, buttermilk, vanilla, whole eggs and egg whites together. Along with the grated carrots, add to the flour mixture, stirring just until the ingredients are incorporated and the flour has disappeared. Divide the mixture evenly between the prepared cake tins and bake for 22–25 minutes or until a skewer inserted in the centre comes out clean. Leave to cool in the tins for 10 minutes before removing and cooling completely on wire racks. 4) For the icing, in an electric mixer, beat the icing sugar, cream cheese, butter and vanilla together on low speed until blended. Scrape down the side of the bowl and beat on medium speed for 30 seconds until smooth and creamy. 5) To ice the cake, place one layer on a serving plate and spread with about a third of the icing. Top with the remaining cake layer and spread the remaining icing over the top and side of the cake. Store the cake in the refrigerator.

Serves 10–12

## BITE ME BIT

'She's only eating carrots to increase the size of her breasts.'

– Mike Baker (actor Justin Henry) in the 1984 movie **Sixteen Candles**

# FROSTED APPLE CAKE

## INGREDIENTS

**Apple Cake**

non-stick cooking spray

350g plain flour

1 teaspoon bicarbonate of soda

½ teaspoon ground cinnamon

½ teaspoon sea salt

375g peeled, cored and diced Granny Smith apples

175g butter, melted

200g granulated sugar

100g soft light brown sugar

120g apple butter or apple sauce

2 large eggs

1 teaspoon vanilla extract

**Cream Cheese Frosting**

225g cream cheese, softened

115g butter, softened

finely grated zest of 1 lemon

575g icing sugar

She used to pretend these mysterious disappearances were a figment of my imagination. Then she would say that she needed the fresh air and a chance to get away from it all. But I know why Lisa makes her pilgrimage to Chudleigh's apple orchard; I know why she adopted an apple tree. Because she's nuts. Every year she brings home her 42-pound box of hand-picked juicy apples and hits the kitchen. It could mean 15 quarts of apple sauce or gallons of cider. Last year's harvest yielded a chunky apple cake smothered in a smooth lemony cream cheese frosting. Now about all those secret trips to the pumpkin patch...

## METHOD

**1)** Preheat the oven to 180°C/350°F/Gas Mark 4. Coat two 23cm round cake tins with non-stick cooking spray. **2)** For the cake, in a large bowl, combine the flour, bicarbonate of soda, cinnamon and salt. Add the diced apples and set aside. **3)** In a medium bowl, whisk the melted butter, sugars, apple butter or sauce, eggs and vanilla together. Make a well in the centre of the flour mixture and add the butter-sugar mixture. Stir with a wooden spoon just until the flour disappears and all the ingredients are combined. Divide the mixture between the 2 baking tins. Bake for 15-20 minutes until golden on top and cooked through. Cool in the tins for 10 minutes before removing and leaving to cool completely on wire racks. **4)** For the frosting, in an electric mixer, mix the cream cheese, butter and lemon zest at medium speed until combined and smooth, scraping down the side of the bowl during mixing. On low speed, gradually add the icing sugar and mix until the sugar is blended and you have a smooth icing. **5)** To frost the cake, place one layer on a serving plate and spread with about a third of the frosting. Top with the remaining cake layer and spread the remaining frosting over the top and side of the cake. Refrigerate for 1 hour to set the icing.

Serves 12

# ENCHANTED COCONUT LAYER CAKE

## INGREDIENTS

### Coconut Cake

non-stick cooking spray

350g sugar

115g butter, softened

1 teaspoon vanilla extract

½ teaspoon coconut extract

4 large egg whites

280g plain flour, plus extra for dusting

1 teaspoon baking powder

½ teaspoon bicarbonate of soda

¼ teaspoon sea salt

300ml buttermilk

45g sweetened flaked coconut or desiccated coconut

### Coconut Icing

115g white vegetable fat

115g butter, softened

1 teaspoon vanilla extract

½ teaspoon coconut extract

460g icing sugar

3 tablespoons milk

90g sweetened or unsweetened flaked coconut or desiccated coconut

Once upon a time, in a land far, far away, lived a Queen. Every day she asked her magnifying mirror who was the fairest of them all? Despite her frown lines and crow's feet, the answer was always 'You, my Queen, are fairest of them all.' But, through the woods, a little distance away, lived an innocent maiden with 7 dwarfs and they all loved to bake. When the Queen next consulted her mirror she was taken aback – 'You are no longer the fairest of them all...there is a snow white cake with thick swaths of ivory icing and sweet curls of coconut.' At that, the Queen hurled her mirror in the trashcan and Heigh-Ho'ed it outta there to score a slice. THE END.

## METHOD

1) Preheat the oven to 180°C/350°F/Gas Mark 4. Coat two 23cm round cake tins with non-stick cooking spray. Dust the tins with a few pinches of flour, tapping out the excess. 2) For the cake, in an electric mixer, cream the sugar and butter together on medium speed for about 1 minute until well combined. Add the vanilla and coconut extract and continue mixing on medium speed. One at a time, add the egg whites, beating well after each addition. 3) In a separate bowl, stir the flour, baking powder, bicarbonate of soda and salt together. On low speed, add to the electric mixer in the following order: a third of the flour mixture, half the buttermilk, another third of the flour, the remaining buttermilk, finishing off with the remaining flour. Beat just until combined – do not overmix. Gently fold in the coconut. Divide the mixture evenly between the prepared tins and bake for 22–24 minutes or until the cake springs back when touched gently in the centre. Leave to cool in the tins for 10 minutes before removing. Cool completely on wire racks before icing. 4) For the icing, in

an electric mixer, cream the vegetable fat, butter, vanilla and coconut extract together on medium speed for 30 seconds. Turn down to low speed, slowly adding half the icing sugar and mixing until incorporated. Add the milk and remaining icing sugar and continue to mix until the desired spreading consistency is reached. Fold in the coconut. **5)** To assemble the cake, place one cake on a serving dish and top with about a third of the icing, spreading it evenly over the cake. Top with the remaining layer and use the rest of the icing to cover the top and side of the cake.

Serves 10–12

## BITE ME BIT

'Your good friend has just taken a piece of cake out of the garbage and eaten it. You will probably need this information when you check me into the Betty Crocker Clinic.'

– Miranda Hobbes (actress Cynthia Nixon) on the HBO series 'Sex and the City'

# *Sara Lisa's* ICED BANANA CAKE

## INGREDIENTS

### Banana Cake

non-stick cooking spray

350g plain flour

2 teaspoons bicarbonate of soda

¼ teaspoon sea salt

115g butter, softened

200g granulated sugar

150g soft light brown sugar

2 large eggs

1 teaspoon vanilla extract

150ml buttermilk

4 ripe bananas, mashed

2 teaspoon freshly squeezed lemon juice

### Banana Icing

55g butter, softened

1 banana, mashed

½ teaspoon freshly squeezed lemon juice

½ teaspoon vanilla extract

400g icing sugar

It's nice to know we're not alone. Countless others miss the irresistible 'frozen fresh' taste of Sara Lee's Iced Banana Cake. In fact, there are chat rooms dedicated to immortalising this aluminum pan sheet cake, its pronounced banana flavour and sweet rippled frosting. All you fans, you can finally log off and stop fantasising about this bygone taste of childhood. We've brought you back in time – minus the propylene glycol esters.

## METHOD

1) Preheat the oven to 180°C/350°F/Gas Mark 4. Coat a 33 x 23cm baking tin with non-stick cooking spray. 2) In a small bowl, combine the flour, bicarbonate of soda and salt. Set aside. 3) Using an electric mixer on medium speed, cream the butter and sugars together until light and fluffy. Beat in the eggs, one at a time, and then add the vanilla extract. Alternate adding the flour mixture and buttermilk until combined. Stir in the mashed bananas and lemon juice. Pour the mixture into the prepared baking tin and bake for 35–40 minutes or until a skewer inserted into the centre of the cake comes out clean. Leave to cool in the tin for 10 minutes. 4) For the icing, in an electric mixer, beat the butter, bananas and lemon juice together on medium speed until well combined. On low speed, slowly add the icing sugar until a smooth consistency is reached, scraping down the side of the bowl once or twice. Spread the icing on the cooled cake.

Serves 12

# BREAD (& banana & cranberry) PUDDING

## INGREDIENTS

non-stick cooking spray

1½ slightly hard/stale egg breads (challahs) crusts removed and cut into 1cm thick slices

55g butter

3 large eggs

150g soft light brown sugar

900ml milk

4–5 ripe bananas, mashed

2 teaspoon vanilla extract

160g dried cranberries or dried cherries

### Topping

140g plain flour

200g soft light brown sugar

55g butter, cut into small cubes

Sorry pigeons. You're outta luck. We've found a new and improved way to use our crusty loaves. This dessert is the breadwinner...stale slices are soaked in a custardy mixture of eggs, milk and mashed sweet bananas, then baked until golden and puffy.

## METHOD

**1)** Preheat the oven to 180°C/350°F/Gas Mark 4. Coat a 33 x 23cm baking dish with non-stick cooking spray. **2)** Spread the butter on the bread slices and then cut the bread into 2.5cm cubes. Set aside. **3)** In a large bowl, whisk the eggs and sugar together. Add the milk, bananas and vanilla and whisk to combine. Add the cranberries and bread and toss gently to coat. Leave to stand for 10 minutes. Pour the mixture into the prepared baking dish. **4)** For the topping, in a small bowl, combine the flour and sugar. Rub the butter into the mixture with your fingertips until crumbly. Spread the crumble mixture evenly on top of the bread pudding. Bake for 50–55 minutes or until golden.

Serves 8

## BITE ME BIT

'On a traffic light green means go and yellow means yield, but on a banana it's just the opposite. Green means hold on, yellow means go ahead, and red means where the hell did you get that banana at...'

– Mitch Hedberg, comedian

# INDOOR S'MORES

## INGREDIENTS

### Creamy Filling

non-stick cooking spray

2 (3.4oz) packets Jell-o vanilla instant pudding and pie fillng

225g cream cheese, softened

700ml milk

300g whipped dessert topping

400g digestive biscuits

### Chocolate Topping

175g milk chocolate, chopped

125ml milk

50g miniature marshmallows

55g butter

85g runny honey

230g icing sugar

Aaah. No more Birk-wearing-Neil-Young-wannabes or roll-your-own tobacco-smoking canoe trippers. The only reason I endured campfires and rambling stories was to eat S'Mores, and now, thanks to Lisa, I can enjoy them in my house. My mouth sinks into layers of digestive biscuits, creamy vanilla pudding and marshmallow-infused chocolate sauce. This is the Sugar Mountain I wanted all along.

## METHOD

**1)** Coat a 33 x 23cm baking dish with non-stick cooking spray.
**2)** For the filling, in an electric mixer using the whisk attachment, combine the vanilla pudding powder and cream cheese on the lowest speed for 1 minute. Add the milk and continue to mix on low speed for 3–5 minutes until the pudding mixture becomes firmer. Gently fold in the dessert topping to combine. Set aside.
**3)** For the chocolate topping, in a medium saucepan, combine the chocolate, milk, marshmallows, butter and honey over a low heat. Stir until melted. Remove from heat and whisk in the icing sugar. Set aside. **4)** In the prepared baking dish, arrange one layer of digestive biscuits on the bottom. Spoon half the pudding mixture evenly over the biscuits. Repeat with another layer of digestives, followed by the remaining pudding mixture. Finish the top layer with digestives and pour the chocolate mixture over the top, covering the biscuits. Refrigerate, uncovered, for at least 2 hours before serving.

Serves 10

## BITE ME BIT

**Ham Porter:** Hey, Smalls, you wanna s'more?

**Smalls:** Some more of what?

**Ham Porter:** No, do you wanna s'more?

**Smalls:** I haven't had anything yet, so how can I have some more of nothing?

– from the 1993 movie **The Sandlot**

# FROZEN CHOCOLATE-BANANA-PB PIE

## INGREDIENTS

### Biscuit Case

non-stick cooking spray

145g vanilla-flavoured or plain biscuits, crushed

55g butter, melted

2 tablespoons sugar

### Filling

175g dark or milk chocolate, melted

3 large bananas, sliced

200g soft light brown sugar

260g smooth peanut butter

115g cream cheese, softened

½ teaspoon vanilla extract

300g whipped dessert topping

150g chocolate sundae syrup or chocolate sauce for ice cream

'I'd just like to be treated like a regular customer.'
– Elvis Presley

He might have been able to swivel his hips and make women bawl, but really, Elvis was just your average Joe. I mean, look at The King's favourite food – a humble fried sandwich of peanut butter and banana. Not exactly regal. That said, this pie is our hunka-hunka-freezing-love tribute to him – a simple, velvety smooth icebox pie that would surely have elicited a 'Thank you, thank you very much' from The Pelvis.

## METHOD

**1)** Preheat the oven to 180°C/350°F/Gas Mark 4. Coat a 23cm pie plate or flan tin with non-stick cooking spray. **2)** For the case, in a medium bowl, combine the biscuit crumbs, butter and sugar. Press against the base and side of the pie plate or tin to form a case. Bake for 10 minutes. Leave to cool completely before filling. **3)** Cover the base of the biscuit case with the melted chocolate and arrange the banana slices on top of the chocolate. **4)** In an electric mixer, cream the sugar, peanut butter, cream cheese and vanilla together on medium speed until smooth. Gently fold in the topping and spread over the bananas. Drizzle the top with the chocolate sundae syrup or sauce. **5)** Cover the pie with clingfilm and place in the freezer for at least 3 hours before serving. For easier cutting, remove from the freezer 10 minutes before serving.

Serves 8

# DANGEROUSLY DELECTABLE PECAN PIE

## INGREDIENTS

### Pie Crust

210g plain flour, plus extra for dusting

½ teaspoon sea salt

2 tablespoons sugar

115g cold butter, cut into small cubes

4 tablespoons cold water

### Pecan Filling

4 large eggs

340g golden syrup

100g soft light brown sugar

35g butter, melted

1 teaspoon vanilla extract

¼ teaspoon sea salt

120g pecan nuts, coarsely chopped

### Pecan Topping

65g soft light brown sugar

3 tablespoons runny honey

35g butter

180g pecan halves

## METHOD

1) Preheat the oven to 180°/350°F/Gas Mark 4. 2) For the crust, in a medium bowl, combine the flour, salt and sugar. Rub the butter into the flour mixture, using your fingertips or by pulsing in a food processor, until it resembles coarse crumbs. Gradually drizzle the cold water over the flour mixture. Toss the mixture with a fork to moisten until the dough comes together. Gently gather the dough into a ball. On a floured work surface, roll the dough out into a round that is 2.5cm larger all round than an upside-down 23cm pie plate or flan tin. Ease the dough into the pie plate or tin to evenly line the base and go up the side. Fold the overhanging dough under itself to form a rim. Transfer to the freezer for 10 minutes while preparing the filling. 3) For the filling, in a large bowl, whisk the eggs, syrup, sugar, melted butter, vanilla and salt together. Mix in the chopped pecans and spoon into the chilled pie crust. Place the pie on a rimmed baking sheet and bake for 45 minutes. 4) While the pie is baking, prepare the topping. In a medium saucepan, combine the sugar, honey and butter over a medium heat. Cook for 3 minutes, stirring constantly, until the sugar dissolves and the mixture is smooth. Stir in the pecan halves and remove from the heat. 5) Remove the pie from the oven and gently spoon the topping over the filling. Bake for a further for 15–18 minutes until the topping is golden. Cover the edges of the pie crust with foil if they are browning too much. 6) Leave the pie to cool completely before serving, allowing at least 3 hours to set.

Serves 8–10

**⚠ WARNING**

CONTAINS VAST AMOUNTS OF PREMIUM NUTS

DO NOT USE 'PEH-KHAN' UNLESS SOUTH OF THE MASON-DIXON

NOT FOR WEAK-HEARTED – INTENSE CARAMEL-TOFFEE COVERS FLAKY CRUST

PRODUCT WILL BE HOT AFTER HEATING

NOT TO BE USED AS A PERSONAL FLOTATION DEVICE

# BONA FIDE KEY LIME PIE

On July 1, 2006, all eyes were on the State of Florida. New fashion in thongs? Winter weather? Lost ballots? None of the above. A tight race was dominating headlines — what would become the official state pie? After a real nail-biter, Key Lime beat out Pecan. Some attribute the victory to a fancy PR campaign, but when you're after some cool in the swelter of the Sunshine State no dessert can beat the tart and creamy custard and fluffy meringue cover.

## INGREDIENTS

### Biscuit Case

non-stick cooking spray

145g digestive biscuits, crushed

4 tablespoons sugar

85g butter, melted

### Lime Filling

3 large egg yolks

400ml sweetened condensed milk

125ml freshly squeezed lime juice

2 teaspoon finely grated lime zest

### Meringue Topping

4 large egg whites

¼ teaspoon table salt

150g sugar

## METHOD

1) Preheat the oven to 180°C/350°F/Gas Mark 4. Coat a 23cm pie plate or flan tin with non-stick cooking spray. 2) For the case, in a medium bowl, mix the biscuit crumbs, sugar and melted butter together. Press the mixture onto the base and side of the prepared pie plate or tin. Bake the case for 8 minutes. Set aside and lower the oven temperature to 150°C/300°F/Gas Mark 2. 3) For the filling, in an electric mixer, using the whisk attachment, beat the egg yolks on medium speed for about 3 minutes until fluffy. Gradually add the condensed milk and beat the mixture for a further 4 minutes. Add the lime juice and zest and beat for about 1 minute just until combined. Pour the mixture into the prepared case. 4) For the meringue, in the clean and dry bowl of your electric mixer, using the whisk attachment, beat the egg whites and table salt until stiff. Gradually beat in the sugar and continue to beat until stiff peaks form. Spread the meringue over the filling and bake for 25 minutes until nicely browned. Remove from oven and leave to cool completely. Place the pie in the refrigerator for at least 1 hour prior to serving.

Serves 8

# STREUSEL-TOPPED BLUEBERRY PIE

## INGREDIENTS

### Biscuit Case

non-stick cooking spray

230g digestive biscuits, crushed

2 tablespoons sugar

½ teaspoon ground cinnamon

55g butter, melted

### Creamy Blueberry Filling

580g fresh blueberries

150g sugar

45g plain flour

1 teaspoon finely grated lemon zest

¼ teaspoon sea salt

2 large eggs, gently whisked

125ml soured cream

½ teaspoon vanilla extract

### Streusel Topping

70g plain flour

100g sugar

35g butter

Fats Domino isn't the only one who found a little magic in a berry patch. Richie Cunningham, Little Richard and even Led Zeppelin also discovered ecstasy among the juicy purple orbs – and you can too. Hum along as you prepare this foolproof, sweet crisp-topped pie, so luscious it'll make the moon stand still.

## METHOD

1) Preheat the oven to 180°C/350°F/Gas Mark 4. Coat a 23cm pie plate or flan tin with non-stick cooking spray. 2) For the case, in a medium bowl, combine the biscuit crumbs, sugar and cinnamon. Add the melted butter and mix until well blended. Press the mixture onto the base and up the side of the pie plate or tin. Bake for 8 minutes and set aside to cool. 3) For the filling, in a large bowl, gently stir the blueberries, sugar, flour, lemon zest and salt together. Gently fold in the eggs, soured cream and vanilla. Spoon the mixture into the case. 4) For the topping, in a small bowl, combine the flour and sugar. Using a fork, mix in the butter until crumbly. Spread the topping over the pie filling. 5) Bake for 40–45 minutes until lightly browned on top. Leave to cool for at least 1 hour before serving.

Serves 8

### BITE ME BIT

**Mrs. Beauregarde:** I can't have a blueberry as a daughter. How is she supposed to compete?

**Veruca Salt:** You could put her in a county fair.

– from the 2005 movie **Charlie and the Chocolate Factory**

# MOM'S MILE-HIGH LEMON MERINGUE PIE

## INGREDIENTS

### Pie Crust

175g plain flour, plus extra for dusting

¼ teaspoon sea salt

115g butter, cut into 6 pieces and chilled

4 tablespoons ginger ale

1 tablespoon freshly squeezed lemon juice

### Lemon Filling

4 large egg yolks

200g sugar

45g cornflour

¼ teaspoon sea salt

350ml water

125ml freshly squeezed lemon juice

2 teaspoon finely grated lemon zest

35g butter

### Meringue Top

6 large egg whites

½ teaspoon cream of tartar

150g sugar

This pie often graced our childhood meals,
Luscious and towering, we were head over heels.
Yet the elation would last for only so long,
A few bites later, things would often turn wrong.

First we'd hoover the lemony bottom – so tart!
But here's where the bloodshed would always start,
All guarding our fluffy meringue to the end,
Upon each other's plates we'd fiercely descend.

Forks and knives flew, elbows raised high,
And with sleight of hand and blink of an eye,
Poor brother would lose his coveted prize,
As we sisters delighted in his sweet pie's demise.

## METHOD

**1)** For the crust, place the flour, salt and cold butter in a food processor bowl. Process for 2 seconds at a time, 4 times, until the mixture resembles coarse crumbs. In a cup, combine the ginger ale and lemon juice. Add to machine while it is running. Process for about 10 seconds until the dough gathers into a ball. Remove the dough and press into a circular disc about 2.5cm thick. Wrap in clingfilm and refrigerate for at least 1 hour or overnight. **2)** Preheat the oven to 200°C/400°F/Gas Mark 6. **3)** On a lightly floured surface, roll the dough into a 30cm round. Fold the round in half and transfer it to a 23cm pie plate or flan tin. Trim off the overhanging edges, leaving about a 2.5cm excess. Fold under the excess dough and decoratively flute the edges. Line the pie crust with foil, greaseproof paper or baking paper, then fill with dried beans. Bake for 14 minutes. Gently remove the beans and foil or paper. Prick the base of the pastry all over with a fork. Bake for another 12 minutes or until evenly

golden. Leave to cool for 10 minutes before adding the lemon filling. **4)** For the lemon filling, place the egg yolks in a small bowl, whisk to combine and set aside. In a medium saucepan, combine the sugar, cornflour and salt. Stir in the water and lemon juice until smooth. Bring to the boil over a medium heat and cook, stirring continuously, for 1–2 minutes or until thickened. Remove the pan from heat and add a small amount of the hot sugar mixture to the egg yolks. Stirring constantly, add the egg yolk mixture to the pan. Bring to a gentle boil over a medium heat and cook, stirring, for 2 minutes. Remove from heat and add the lemon zest and butter. Leave to cool slightly and set aside. **5)** For the meringue, in an electric mixer, use the whisk attachment and beat the egg whites and cream of tartar on medium speed until foamy. Increase the speed to high and gradually beat in the sugar until stiff, glossy peaks form. **6)** To assemble, lower the oven temperature to 190°C/375°F/Gas Mark 5. Spoon the lemon filling into the baked pastry case. Pile the meringue on top of the lemon filling, making sure that it touches the crust all around, otherwise the meringue will shrink away from the side when it is baked. Using the back of a spoon, you can create swirls and peak designs with the meringue. **7)** Bake for 10–12 minutes until the top is lightly golden. Remove from the oven and leave to cool for at least 1 hour at room temperature before serving.

Serves 8

# EASY as PIE STRAWBERRY APPLE CRISP

## INGREDIENTS

750g peeled, cored and cubed Granny Smith apples

280g hulled strawberries, halved

4 tablespoons sugar

½ teaspoon ground cinnamon

### Topping

120g old-fashioned large-flake oats (not quick cooking)

210g plain flour

300g soft light brown sugar

1 teaspoon ground cinnamon

175g butter, cut into small cubes

When we were little I was kind enough to let Lisa brush my hair and scratch my back – hey, as her big sister, it was the least I could do. Now in adulthood, she owes me a few favours. Being a professional pastry chef was a start – Lisa was going to help me conquer my fear of baking. So, my little sister started me off slowly with this foolproof, fuss-free crisp of cinnamon apples and sweet strawberries under a thick, extra-crunchy topping. Lucky for her I'm no longer intimidated by baking so she can return to massaging my shoulders.

## METHOD

1) Preheat the oven to 180°C/350°F/Gas Mark 4. Coat a 28 x 18cm baking dish with non-stick cooking spray. 2) In a large bowl, toss the apples, strawberries, sugar and cinnamon together. Place in the prepared baking dish. 3) For the topping, in a large bowl, mix the oats, flour, sugar and cinnamon together. Add the butter and mix with a fork until crumbly. Sprinkle over the fruit. 4) Bake, uncovered, for 25 minutes. Loosely cover with foil and bake for a further 10 minutes.

Serves 6–8

### BITE ME BIT

Ducking for apples – change one letter and it's the story of my life.

– Dorothy Parker, writer

# BUTTER TART SQUARES, EH?

## INGREDIENTS

### Shortbread Crust

non-stick cooking spray

115g butter, softened

4 tablespoons soft light brown sugar

140g plain flour

### Filling

240g maple syrup

135g soft light brown sugar

55g butter

2 large eggs

1 teaspoon vanilla extract

2 tablespoons plain flour

½ teaspoon baking powder

¼ teaspoon sea salt

95g currants

Y'know, there's more to Canuck cuisine than back bacon, poutine and prairie oysters. Well, hold on to your toque there because Lisa has created a wicked home and native treat. This nut-free, Northern cousin of the pecan pie has a flaky pastry crust topped with a gooey combo of brown sugar and maple syrup. Take off, pemmican – this is the new national delicacy.

## METHOD

**1)** Preheat the oven to 180°C/350°F/Gas Mark 4. Coat a 20cm square baking tin with non-stick cooking spray. Cover the base of the tin with a square of baking paper and coat again with non-stick cooking spray. **2)** For the crust, in an electric mixer, cream the butter and sugar together for about 1 minute until light and fluffy. Add the flour and beat just until the flour disappears and the dough comes together. Press the mixture evenly into the base of the prepared baking tin. Bake for 18 minutes or until the crust is golden. **3)** For the filling, in a medium saucepan, combine the maple syrup, sugar and butter over a medium heat. Simmer for 5 minutes to dissolve the sugar. Remove from the heat and leave to cool for 10–15 minutes. **4)** In a large bowl, whisk the eggs, vanilla, flour, baking powder and salt together. Add the maple syrup mixture and whisk well to combine. **5)** Scatter the currants evenly over the baked shortbread crust. Pour the filling over the currants and return to the oven to bake for 28–30 minutes or until the filling is set and slightly browned on top. Leave to cool in the tin for at least 1 hour before removing.

Makes: 16 squares

C is for: cheesy, creamy, chocolaty, caramely, calories
H ello...there are toffee chunks in the batter
E xtreme opposite of beefcake
E stelle Getty & The Golden Girls ate tons of it
S o not lactose free
E ww...grossest pick-up line: 'Show me a lil' cheesecake'
C heering at a Phish concert, yell 'cheesecake' to fit in
A erosmith claims cheesecake is 'looser than her sister'
K nown eatery (think: Factory) sells double-digit-priced-slice
E rroneous to call it a cake - technically, it's an unleavened pie

# CHOCOLATE-CRUSTED CREAMY CARAMEL CHEESECAKE

## INGREDIENTS

### Biscuit Case

175g Oreo biscuits, crushed
115g butter, melted
60ml whipping cream
175g dark chocolate

### Filling

900g cream cheese, softened
200g sugar
4 large eggs
1½ teaspoon vanilla extract
425g soft toffee, diced
4 tablespoons shop-bought caramel sauce

## METHOD

1) Preheat the oven to 180°C/350°F/Gas Mark 4. Wrap the outside of a 23cm springform tin with foil. 2) For the case, in a medium bowl, combine the biscuit crumbs with the melted butter. Press evenly and firmly over the base and halfway up the side of the springform tin. In a small saucepan, bring the whipping cream to a simmer over a low heat. Add the chocolate and stir until melted. Remove from heat and pour evenly over the biscuit case. 3) Chill in refrigerator to firm slightly while preparing the filling. 4) For the filling, using an electric mixer, beat the cream cheese on medium speed until smooth, scraping the bowl several times. Gradually add the sugar and continue to beat the mixture. One at a time, beat in the eggs, scraping the bowl as needed. Using a spatula, fold in the vanilla extract and toffee pieces. Pour the mixture into the prepared crust. Finish by spooning the caramel sauce over the top. Place the tin on a baking sheet and bake for 65–70 minutes. Remove from the oven and leave to cool to room temperature. Cover with clingfilm and refrigerate for at least 6 hours before serving.

Serves 12

# CHUNKY CHEWY BLONDIE BARS

## INGREDIENTS

non-sticking cooking spray

280g plain flour, plus extra for dusting

½ teaspoon sea salt

¼ teaspoon bicarbonate of soda

400g soft light brown sugar

175g butter, softened

2 large eggs

2 teaspoon vanilla extract

435g dark or milk chocolate chunks

We might have wanted Rod Stewart's body once upon a time – and we did think he was pretty sexy, but his contention that blondes have more fun didn't convince these two brunettes. We tried singing 'Call Me' at the top of our lungs while we ran on the beach in our 'Baywatch' bathing suits. Nope. No fun there. But just one bite of these golden-girl bars and we were reaching for the Clairol.

## METHOD

**1)** Preheat the oven to 180°C/350°F/Gas Mark 4. Coat a 33 x 23cm baking tin with non-stick cooking spray. Dust with a few pinches of flour, shaking out the excess. **2)** In a small bowl, stir the flour, salt and bicarbonate of soda together. **3)** In an electric mixer, cream the sugar and butter together until light and fluffy. Beat in the eggs and vanilla, adding the eggs one at a time until combined. Add the flour mixture and chocolate chunks to the mixer, mixing on low speed just until the flour disappears. **4)** Spread the mixture evenly in the prepared tin. Bake for 25 minutes or until lightly browned. Leave to cool for 20 minutes before removing from the tin.

Makes: 20–24 bars

### BITE ME BIT

'I'm not offended by all the dumb blonde jokes because I know I'm not dumb... and I also know that I'm not blonde.'

– Dolly Parton, singer

LIC. # ME 00001

## DR. D. LICIOUS
TEL: (416) EAT-MORE   FAX: (416) CRA-VING

**Rx**

EXTRA STRENGTH BROWNIE BAR
1-10 RICH MOIST BROWNIES
EVERY 1-2 HOURS AS NEEDED
TAKE WITH MILK OR ICECREAM

WARNING: NOT FOR THE FAINT-HEARTED.
HIGHLY ADDICTIVE

DISPENSE: 16 INTENSELY GOOEY.
BROWNIES

_____
(SIGNATURE)

REFILLS: 0 1 2 3 4 5 UNLIMITED

# R$_x$ BROWNIES with FUDGE FROSTING

## INGREDIENTS

non-stick cooking spray

4 squares dark (75% cocoa solids) chocolate, chopped

175g butter

400g sugar

3 large eggs

140g plain flour

**Fudge Frosting**

100g granulated sugar

25g cocoa powder, sifted

4 tablespoons milk

25g butter

1 tablespoon golden syrup

115g icing sugar

## METHOD

**1)** Preheat the oven to 180°C/350°F/Gas Mark 4. Coat a 33 x 23cm baking tin with non-stick cooking spray. Line with baking paper. **2)** In a microwave-safe bowl, combine the chocolate and butter. Heat in the microwave on high heat for 1 minute, stir and heat for 30 seconds more or until melted and smooth. **3)** In a large bowl, whisk the sugar and eggs together. Add the chocolate mixture and flour and stir until the flour has disappeared. Spread in the tin and bake for 25–30 minutes. Leave to cool in the tin for 15 minutes before removing. Leave to cool completely on a wire rack. **4)** For the frosting, in a large saucepan, mix the granulated sugar, cocoa powder, milk, butter and syrup together. Heat to boiling, stirring frequently, and boil for 3 minutes, stirring constantly. Leave to cool for 10 minutes. Whisk in the icing sugar until smooth.

Makes: 16 brownies

# GOOEY DOUBLE CHOCOLATY CHOCOLATE COOKIES

## INGREDIENTS

225g butter, softened

200g granulated sugar

100g soft light brown sugar

2 large eggs

280g plain flour

65g cocoa powder, sifted

¾ teaspoon bicarbonate of soda

½ teaspoon sea salt

350g milk chocolate chips

Okay. The title of this recipe alone should have you running for the baking supplies. But if I must do a little sell-job, these decadent, oozing chocolate cookies have chocolate chips in them.

## METHOD

**1)** Preheat the oven to 180°C/350°F/Gas Mark 4. **2)** In an electric mixer, cream the butter and sugars together on medium speed until light and fluffy. Add the eggs and beat well. **3)** In a small bowl, combine the flour, cocoa powder, bicarbonate of soda and salt. Using a wooden spoon, stir the flour mixture and chocolate chips into the butter mixture until blended. **4)** Drop the mixture by rounded tablespoons onto an ungreased baking sheet. Bake for 8–10 minutes. Cool slightly before transferring to a wire rack.

Makes: 35 cookies

# CHEWY CHOCOLATE CHIP COOKIES

## INGREDIENTS

350g plain flour

½ teaspoon bicarbonate of soda

¼ teaspoon sea salt

225g butter, softened

200g soft light brown sugar

100g granulated sugar

1 teaspoon vanilla extract

1 large egg

1 large egg yolk

435g milk chocolate chips

**Dear Reader:**
You're probably sick of my sister Julie by now, so I decided to try my hand at writing a recipe intro. I mean, how hard can it be? What's up with the tortured artist stuff? Dark nights of the soul? All you have to say is that these chocolate chip cookies are great. See?
Truly, Lisa

## METHOD

**1)** Preheat the oven to 160°C/325°F/Gas Mark 3. Line 2 baking sheets with baking paper. **2)** In a medium bowl, combine the flour, bicarbonate of soda and salt. **3)** In an electric mixer, cream the butter and sugars together on medium speed until well blended. Beat in the vanilla, whole egg and egg yolk until light and fluffy. On low speed, add the flour mixture and chocolate chips, mixing just until the flour disappears. **4)** Drop the dough 4 tablespoons at a time 5cm apart onto the prepared baking sheets. **5)** Bake for 15 minutes or until the edges are golden brown. Remove from oven and leave to cool for a few minutes before transferring to a wire rack.

Makes: 20–24 large cookies

## BITE ME BIT

'...I believe in the sweet spot, voting every election, soft core pornography, chocolate chip cookies, opening your presents on Christmas morning rather than Christmas Eve and I believe in long, slow, deep, soft, wet kisses that last for 7 days.'

– Crash Davis (actor Kevin Costner) in the 1988 movie **Bull Durham**

# CHUNKY WHITE CHOCOLATE CRANBERRY COOKIES

## INGREDIENTS

115g butter, softened

100g granulated sugar

100g soft light brown sugar

1 large egg

1 teaspoon vanilla extract

210g plain flour

½ teaspoon bicarbonate of soda

¼ teaspoon sea salt

260g white chocolate, cut into chunks

160g dried cranberries or dried cherries

Bite Me began with this recipe after I bought a cranberry and white chocolate cookie from a local bakery three years ago. I ate it, bought a dozen more, drove directly to Lisa's house and thrust the package at her. 'Make these,' I insisted. She sniffed them, did her little rabbit nibbles, closed her eyes, inhaled and said, 'No prob'. She made them. And then she created an irresistible cookie that far surpassed any we have ever eaten.

## METHOD

**1)** Preheat the oven to 180°C/350°F/Gas Mark 4. Line a baking sheet with baking paper. **2)** In an electric mixer, cream the butter and sugars together on medium speed. Add the egg and vanilla, beating until fluffy. **3)** On low speed, add the flour, bicarbonate of soda, salt, white chocolate and cranberries, mixing just until the flour disappears. Do not overmix. **4)** Drop heaped tablespoons of the mixture onto the prepared baking sheet. Bake for 10–12 minutes, just until the edges begin to brown. Leave the cookies to cool on a wire rack.

Makes: 16 large cookies

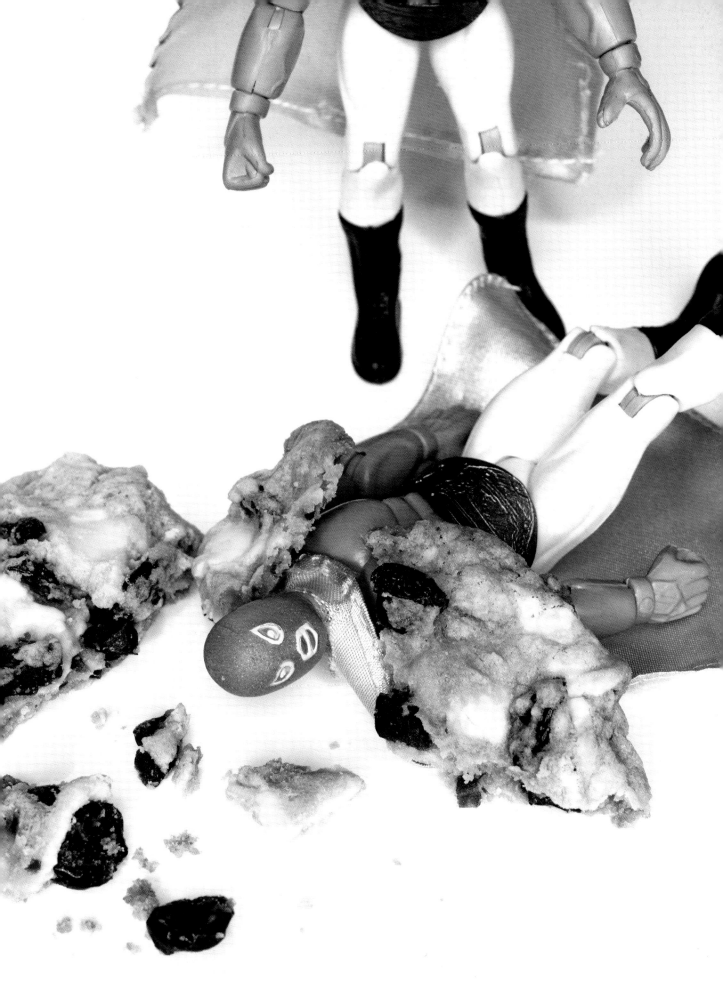

# SOFT OATMEAL RAISIN COOKIES

## INGREDIENTS

175g butter, softened

150g soft light brown sugar

100g granulated sugar

1 large egg

2 tablespoons water

105g plain flour

¾ teaspoon bicarbonate of soda

1 teaspoon ground cinnamon

240g old-fashioned large-flake oats (not quick cooking)

250g raisins or chocolate chips

Hi. We can't come to the phone right now. If you're calling to compliment our chewy, delicious cookies, press 1. If you're calling to leave a long, humble silence in homage to this great creation, press 2. If you're calling to pay tribute to one of the greatest gifts to mankind, or at least to snack time, press 3. Otherwise, hang up and try your cookies again.

## METHOD

1) Preheat the oven to 180°C/350°F/Gas Mark 4. Line a baking sheet with baking paper. 2) In an electric mixer, cream the butter and sugars together on medium speed until light and fluffy. Add the egg and water and beat at medium speed until well mixed. 3) Add the flour, bicarbonate of soda, cinnamon, oats and raisins, mixing on low speed just until the flour disappears. 4) Drop the dough 4 tablespoons at a time onto the prepared baking sheet. Bake for 12–14 minutes or until the edges are lightly golden. Leave to cool slightly on the baking sheet before transferring the cookies to a wire rack.

Makes: 15 large cookies

## BITE ME BIT

'I'm not really the heroic type. I was beat up by Quakers.'

– Miles Monroe (actor Woody Allen) in the 1973 movie **Sleeper**

# INSPIRING SUGAR COOKIES

## INGREDIENTS

175g icing sugar

225g butter, softened

½ teaspoon vanilla extract

1 large egg, lightly beaten

350g plain flour, plus extra for dusting

1 teaspoon bicarbonate of soda

1 teaspoon cream of tartar

Calling all Pollock, Rothko and Mondrian wannabes: here's your chance to unleash your subconscious. Lisa, your artistic enabler, supplies the ideal canvas – a sweet, soft-centred, sugar cookie. You can cut, shape, drizzle, dip, ice and sprinkle to your heart's content or just be very 'less is more' about it and let the buttery cookie shine au naturel.

## METHOD

1) Preheat the oven to 190°C/375°F/Gas Mark 5. 2) In a large bowl, use a wooden spoon to mix the icing sugar and butter together. Once incorporated, add the vanilla and egg, stirring well to combine. Add the flour, bicarbonate of soda and cream of tartar and stir until the flour disappears. 3) Shape the dough into a ball, cover with clingfilm and refrigerate for 30 minutes to ensure easier handling. 4) Divide the dough ball in half, keeping one half covered while working with the other. Roll out the dough on a floured surface to 5mm–1cm thickness. Cut into shapes with any cookie cutter. 5) Place the cookies 2.5cm apart on an ungreased baking sheet. Bake for 8–10 minutes until the edges are golden brown. Leave to cool completely on a wire rack.

Makes: 15 large cutout cookies or 30 small cookies

## BITE ME BIT

'Women are not in love with me but with the picture of me on the screen. I am merely the canvas on which women paint their dreams.'

– Rudolph Valentino, actor

# Celebrate Thee

## WE THANK

Our publisher Kyle Cathie for her 'bloody brilliance', Anja Schmidt at Kyle Books, Ron Longe at Media Masters, Heather Reisman, Bruce Mau Design (Bruce Mau with Joanne Bell, Tom Keogh, Erik Krim, Laura Stein), Commerce Press and Estelle Elmaleh, Craig Offman, Ian Muggridge, Michael Alberstat, Phil Alberstat, Deanna Dunn, Penny Offman, Sheila Ryles, Nadia Olenchuk, Arren Williams, Big Red, The Immunity Idol, Dale Lastman, Ken and Jen Tanenbaum, our extraordinary grandmother Alice Lieberman, and of course, our parents Larry and Judy Tanenbaum for teaching us the love of family and food.

## JULIE THANKS

Kenny A. for absolutely everything, Jamie for her kind touch, Perry for her crazy dances, Benjy for his sports updates, Dahra Granovsky, Richard Allen, Lisa Diamond, Laurence Loubieres and Sue Tanenbaum for brainstorming, Carolyn Offman for endlessly distracting me, Kevin Deonarine for my scapula, Cheryl Louvelle for babying me, Miriam, Andy, Estelle, Elise, Sacha, Wendy, Barbara, Penny and Kristi for all their sweetness.

## LISA THANKS

Jordan for late night grocery runs and sampling meatloaf at midnight, Emmy for her enthusiasm, Lauren for her sweetness, Alex for her smiles, 3 Musketeers for your support, and of course, all my friends for loving my cookies.

# Index